ELIOT, JAMES AND THE FICTIONAL SELF

ELIOT, JAMES AND THE FICTIONAL SELF

A Study in Character and Narration

Richard Freadman

MACMILLAN

First published 1986

Published by
THE MACMILLAN PRESS LTD
Houndmills, Basingstoke, Hampshire RG21 2XS
and London
Companies and representatives
throughout the world

Typeset by Wessex Typesetters
(Division of The Eastern Press Ltd)
Frome, Somerset

Printed in Hong Kong

British Library Cataloguing in Publication Data
Freadman, Richard
Eliot, James and the fictional self: a study
in character and narration
1. Eliot, George – Criticism and interpretation
I. Title
823'.8   PR4688
ISBN 0-333-38453-9

For Diane

Contents

Preface

It is a pleasure to be able to acknowledge the help and encouragement I have received from a number of people during various stages of this project. But of course the usual rider applies: the mistakes are my responsibility.

Valentine Cunningham was a patient and provocative supervisor for the doctoral thesis upon which the book is loosely based. John Bayley and Patrick Swinden made helpful suggestions about the thesis, and I wish particularly to thank John Bayley for his kindness and encouragement. Peter Corbett, Julius Kovesi, Sue Midalia, Alan Shapiro and Gail Jones have all made helpful suggestions. I am much indebted to Bruce McClintock for his detailed and expert proofing of the manuscript, to Mrs Susan Lewis for her patient and excellent work in preparing the typescript, and to the English Department of the University of Western Australia. Frances Arnold of the Macmillan Press has been extremely helpful throughout.

Much of this book was written on study leave in England and I wish to thank Sir Zelman Cowen, Provost of Oriel College, Lady Cowen and the Fellows of the College for their hospitality during that year. Kathleen Adams and Graham Handley of the George Eliot Fellowship were also most welcoming during our stay.

I have enjoyed expert assistance from the staffs of two libraries. Mrs Gwen Hampshire of the English Faculty Library, Oxford, has been particularly helpful and accommodating at every turn, and the staff of the library of the University of Western Australia have also helped in many ways.

All writers on George Eliot owe an immense debt to G. S. Haight; those writing about Henry James are similarly indebted to the work of Leon Edel. Such is the volume of work on Eliot and James that I can here only reflect a small proportion of the criticism on the novelists from which I have profited.

My greatest debt is to my wife Diane. She has been unstinting in her encouragement, help and patience. I dedicate the book to her.

R. B. F.

A Note on Texts

Unless otherwise indicated, references to George Eliot's fiction are to *The Works of George Eliot*, Cabinet Edition, 24 vols (Edinburgh and London: William Blackwood, 1878–80). References to this edition give, for the novels, volume of novel, chapter and page numbers: e.g., '*Middlemarch* i. 9, p. 121' refers to the first volume of the Cabinet Edition, chapter nine, page 121. 'The Lifted Veil', *The Impressions of Theophrastus Such*, and 'The Spanish Gypsy', being in single volumes, are referred to solely by page numbers.

In the case of *The Mill on the Floss*, *Felix Holt* and *Daniel Deronda* references are to the more recent, but as yet incomplete, Clarendon Edition of the novels of George Eliot (Oxford: Clarendon Press, 1963–). References to those novels give book (except in *Felix Holt*), chapter and page numbers: e.g., '*Daniel Deronda* vi, 45, p. 521' refers to the sixth book of the novel, chapter 45, on p. 521 of the Clarendon edition.

Unless otherwise indicated, references to Henry James's fiction are to *The Novels and Tales of Henry James*, New York Edition, 24 vols (New York: Charles Scribner's Sons, 1907–9, repr. 1961–5; reissued New York: Augustus M. Kelley, 1971). References to this edition give volume of series, book (where necessary), chapter and page numbers: e.g., '*The Golden Bowl* xxiii, i. 1, p. 12' refers to volume 23 of the New York Edition, chapter one of the first book, on page twelve of that volume.

Editions cited of novels not included in the New York Edition are:

Roderick Hudson (1876; London: Macmillan, 1921);
The Bostonians (1886; London: Rupert Hart-Davis, 1959);
The Secret Fount (1908), vol. iii of *The Bodley Head Henry James*, 11 vols (London: Rupert Hart-Davis, 1967–74).

A Note on 'George Eliot'

For the sake of simplicity I have used George Eliot's authorial name, even when referring to times or contexts in which she was known by one of her several other names. A tendency on my part to shorten George Eliot to 'Eliot' less often than I shorten Henry James to 'James' is merely a matter of habit. It implies nothing about the relative status of the two writers. My tendency to designate readers and people in general as masculine is likewise merely a matter of habit.

Introduction

On Sunday, 9 May 1869, a young American man of letters gained
an introduction to a great novelist and intellectual whom he had
revered since childhood. The following day the twenty-six year
old Henry James penned this description of George Eliot for his
father:

> I was immensely impressed, interested and pleased. To begin
> with she is magnificently ugly – deliciously hideous. She has a
> low forehead, a dull grey eye, a vast pendulous nose, a huge
> mouth, full of uneven teeth and a chin and jawbone *qui n'en
> finissent pas*. ... Now in this vast ugliness resides a most
> powerful beauty which, in a very few minutes steals forth and
> charms the mind, so that you end as I ended, in falling in love
> with her. Yes behold me literally in love with this great
> horse-faced blue-stocking. I don't know in what the charm lies,
> but it is thoroughly potent. An admirable physiognomy – a
> delightful expression, a voice soft and rich as that of a
> counselling angel – a mingled sagacity and sweetness – a broad
> hint of a great underlying world of reserve, knowledge, pride
> and power – a great feminine dignity and character in these
> massively plain features – a hundred conflicting shades of
> consciousness and simpleness – shyness and frankness –
> graciousness and remote indifference – these are some of the
> more definite elements of her personality. Her manner is
> extremely good tho' rather too intense and her speech, in the
> way of accent and syntax peculiarly agreeable. Altogether, she
> has a larger circumference than any woman I have ever seen.[1]

George Eliot was at this time forty-nine years of age and the
writers were to meet again on perhaps no more than three
occasions. As we shall see, James's recollection of one of these
occasions is anguished and appalled, but his account of another is
almost unreservedly enthusiastic:

1

The Leweses were very urbane and friendly, and I think that I shall have the right *dorénavant* to consider myself a Sunday *habitué*. The great G. E. herself is both sweet and superior, and has a delightful expression in her large, long, pale equine face. I had my turn at sitting beside her and being conversed with in a low, but most harmonious tone; and bating a tendency to *aborder* only the highest themes I have no fault to find with her.[2]

In fact, James managed in a highly complex and admiring way to 'find fault' with his mentor. Over a period of five decades he was to appraise and reappraise her personal qualities, her philosophical outlook, her aesthetic attitudes and, most importantly, her art. In so doing he was clearly trying to define himself as a writer and as a man. A central subject of this study is this prolonged, at times painful, but always extraordinarily perceptive, process by which James sought psychic and artistic individuality through comparison with his great precursor and peer. Needless to say, a vital part of this process was the creative reworkings of George Eliot's magnificent – but, James thought, imperfect – aesthetic enterprise.

In so reviewing and revising George Eliot's achievement James was to join her in using the novel to explore a set of momentous psychological, philosophical and aesthetic problems. This connection could be charted in many ways, but the present study centres upon fictional character: upon what Eliot and James believed about the individual self and its depiction in narrative prose. For both writers, persons constituted the most compelling, complex and characteristic feature of novelistic art; yet here, as in other matters, their careers present an intriguing pattern of kinship and difference. James was to retain much of importance in George Eliot's conception of character and narrative technique, but he was also pointedly to amend her example. In so doing he not only established himself as a major novelist in his own right; he also joined Eliot in powerfully shaping the novel's evolution from nineteenth-century modes into modernism.

1 Character, Narration and the Novel

ELIOT, JAMES AND THE NOVEL

'Character . . . is a process and an unfolding': thus wrote George Eliot in *Middlemarch* (i.15, p. 226) in 1873. 'What is character but the determination of incident? What is incident but the illustration of character?'[1] Henry James had read, sifted and reviewed all of George Eliot's fiction when he penned this famous rhetorical question in 1884. Though James was to take issue with important aspects of George Eliot's art, his fascination with novelistic character was no less intense than hers; indeed it is this which motivates many of their common qualities as novelists. Neither, however, believed character to be a simple matter. It is, they knew, all very well to speak of characters in novels as if they are 'real people', but in what sense, and to what extent, can this in fact be so? Eliot and James pose this question in their aesthetic writings, their letters and in their private musings. They also, of course, pose it in their novels, either openly or by implication.

Both thought of the novel as a provisional and highly complex form of experimentation. George Eliot describes her fiction as 'a set of experiments in life';[2] James thinks of his as a series of 'experiments of form'.[3] Though there are significant differences in the notion of 'experiment' at work here, both writers see fiction as heuristic: novels are in their view a proper place to open out momentous questions without the constraints of restrictively rational discourse. This is not of course to say that novels cannot achieve impressive philosophical precision; rather that they can also simulate the sorts of situations in which complex ethical and conceptual problems actually arise. As they see it, fiction can be at once questioning and concrete: it creatively reconstructs individuals in context.

The individual is, then, central to both conceptions of the novel.

3

Eliot and James are fictional humanists who ask a set of questions fundamental to any humanist account. What constitutes a self? What degrees of freedom do individuals possess? How far do their choices shape their destinies? What is the status of the inner world we impute to others? How much can we know of it? How is it implicated in the moral lives we lead? What value ought we ultimately to assign to the individual? But these writers were also aestheticians and the problems of novelistic form were a constant concern for them. It was one thing to conceive of individuals in certain ways, another to find fictional structures that could confer upon characters the illusion of human depth and complexity necessary for Eliot's and James's ethical, social and psychological 'experiments'. Character could not, they believed, be dissociated from questions about narrative technique. Character and narration were mutually implicating and entailing.

This comparative reading of George Eliot and Henry James centres on their concepts of character and narration and on the interplay between character and narrative structure in their novels. In this limited sense the readings that follow are formal, but they are also more than merely formal; and here it is important to distinguish them from a current version of critical formalism that reads novels and other genres in the light of an analogy between linguistic signification and literary texts.

THE LINGUISTIC ANALOGY: THE DOCTRINE OF ARBITRARY SIGNIFICATION

The linguistic analogy has informed the tradition of structural, semiotic and post-structural literary theory that descends from Ferdinand de Saussure. At the heart of this movement lies the assumption that linguistic signs are arbitrary. Reality does not as it were inhere in signs; rather, our language system produces – or structures – our sense of reality. This process takes place through patterns of conventional association: we learn to associate certain concepts (signifieds) with particular linguistic signals (signifiers), and these together comprise the sign. Crucially, these associations are conceived as arbitrary, both with respect to the connection between signifier and signified, and the sign and any ostensible 'referent' (here a problematic notion) in the 'real world'. Thus there is no necessary or natural connection between the notation 'cat' and the concept with which it is associated; nor between the sign 'cat' and some 'real' creature existing beyond our linguistically constituted sense of things. The connection (or relation) Saussure does however insist upon is that between 'cat' and other signs within the language system in which it figures. In this view, meaning derives not from a referential function, but from the differential relations between signs within the language system: 'cat' only makes sense because it differs from other signs ('cab', 'mat' and so on), and then only to English language users, since the language system is culture specific. The implications of this language model for literary criticism have been various. One is the inference, common in post-Saussurean theory (at least in its formalist varieties), that a text, too, is part of a larger system of structures whose relation to any extra-textual 'reality' either is not an issue or is arbitrary. Indeed some theorists claim exemption from questions about referentiality as a virtue of this outlook. Thus Anne Jefferson argues that 'the chief advantage of the linguistic analogy in any narrative theory is that it allows literature in general and narrative in particular to be read as a self-contained system independent of any realist function'.[4] It must, I think, be conceded that we can learn much of importance about the internal systematics of literary texts by at least temporarily suspending questions about the nature of their relationship to an extra-textual reality. However, such procedures are surely limited and may even be fundamentally misleading. I shall presently suggest that the epistemology upon which referential views of language rest is far from the naïve thing often supposed by theorists after Saussure; but let us for the moment consider the implications of the linguistic analogy for a theory of character in fiction.

Put simply, the linguistic analogy tends to privilege systems over selves when it is applied to characters. As Fredric Jameson notes, structuralism (and related movements) is an attempt 'to rethink everything through once again in terms of linguistics',[5] including our descriptions of individuals. This attempt involves the 'valorization of the Symbolic Order' and an 'accompanying humiliation of the old-fashioned subject or personal and individual consciousness'.[6] Thus the system of codes by which a society constructs its sense of the world is seen as constituting rather than reflecting or expressing individual selves. An impressive example of this approach is Roger Fowler's *Linguistics*

and the Novel. Fowler advances a theory of 'characterological
semes'[7] which he believes may explain how selves are
systematically constituted in novels, which in turn encode larger
cultural processes of signification.

Fowler's account is admirably undogmatic, but more extreme
versions are often calculated affronts to the very notion of human
individuality. As Jameson notes, 'the most scandalous aspect of
structuralism as a movement [is] its militant anti-humanism'.[8] I
wish in this study of character in Eliot and James to query this
anti-humanism and its capacity to formulate an adequate theory
of the human subject, either for literary or for social analysis. After
structuralism the individual needs to be rethought in relation to
our notions of social and psychological structure. In recent years
structuralism has of course provided its own critique from within:
post-structuralism serves to explode the myth of the
determinately coded individual as it reconceives the linguistic
analogy. According to Lacan and Derrida, consciousness is
indeed constituted through language; in fact it *is* a language. For
these theorists, however, the self is in a sense decentred (Lacan
refers to its 'radical ex-centricity'): since signs defer, decentre and
displace meaning, subjectivity, which is linguistically constituted,
must be a precarious and shifting fiction.[9] Many critics – liberal
humanists especially – will agree that selves are to a marked
degree heterogeneous, undecidable and inconsistent; what is at
issue is post-structuralism's way of accounting for this fact.
Though Derrida's notion of the 'trace' purports to account for
manifest forms of psychological and social consistency,[10] a
concern is that in positing the self as decentred, as produced and
problematicised by language so conceived, such theories will tend
(and this of course is their intention) to neutralise a discourse of
the self which begins by locating (however metaphorically) a
capacity for rational discrimination, choice and action within the
individual and offers its descriptions of social (and textual)
behaviour accordingly. Without denying the power of the
post-structural alternative, it may therefore be worth asking again
certain fundamental questions about the self, questions that bear
directly upon the way we perceive and describe characters in
novels. What *are* we to say about the relationship between words,
the world and individuals? How far is the individual
consciousness in fact constituted by culture? Can we argue
persuasively for our received and intuitive belief that individuals

are aptly described in terms of 'centredness' and rational agency? Before turning to Eliot and James let us review some of these pivotal problems in critical theory.

WORDS AND THE WORLD: THE CASE AGAINST ARBITRARINESS

Though highly influential, the doctrine that linguistic signs are arbitrary has met with persuasive resistance from several quarters. These objections are important for literary criticism. One is that, in using arbitrariness to deny a 'realistic function' in literature, formalist structural theory has tended to isolate narrative art from aspects of our experience about which it can tell us most: the ethical, the intersubjective, the private. As post-structuralism's preoccupation with the production of subjectivity seems so explicitly to concede,[11] such experiences, which are in any case a perennial problem for philosophical analysis, present particular difficulties to theories whose orientation is essentially public – that is, predicated on a transpersonal linguistic systematics. Moreover, it is notoriously difficult to distinguish between 'referential' and 'non-referential' descriptions of what we are here terming private phenomena.

To say this is to raise a further objection: namely, that to elevate arbitrariness to the status of a metaphysical principle is to understate the extent to which language users in fact creatively and continually employ language to *produce* certain states of affairs. Thus does a Marxist theorist such as Raymond Williams argue that the doctrine of arbitrariness cannot account for the many levels at which cultural production actually takes place.[12] Clearly, linguistic conventions are highly and historically variable and we must beware of generalising too sweepingly about them.

Such indeed is the contention of the century's other seminal language theorist, Ludwig Wittgenstein. According to Wittgenstein's later works, we cannot get sufficiently beyond particular contexts of language use in order so to generalise. It is in his view more important to reconstruct the social–linguistic contexts within which language actually functions and facilitates action than to equivocate about some transcendental or referential foundation. In this sense Wittgenstein's later work, especially the *Philosophical Investigations*,[13] offers an important corrective to the theories of Saussure and followers. It displaces attention from general linguistic systematics to localised language use; and from the arbitrariness of linguistic signs to their conventionality. What is important to Wittgenstein is that linguistic conventions do facilitate various forms of situated communications and behaviour. Thus, 'the *speaking* of a language' is likened to a convention-governed 'game'; it is, moreover, and as Martin Price has emphasised in a recent book on character, 'part of an activity, or of a form of life'.[14]

What implications might such a view have for the reading of literature when contrasted with the structural and post-structural models? It is becoming apparent that the implications are various and far-reaching, but we may summarise thus. The Saussurean model tends to impugn what we take to be the 'naturalness' of selves, both in life and in works of fiction, and to direct attention at our self and reality-constituting systematics. Thus Roland Barthes argues of the sort of novels Eliot and James write that 'The writing of Realism is far from being neutral, it is on the contrary loaded with the most spectacular signs of fabrication'.[15] Fictional realism does not picture the world; it deceptively gives the impression of so doing. The Wittgensteinian view might be that the representational power of a novel is a more complex matter than this; that a novel is better thought of as being continuous with certain forms of life than as either an image or a subversion of them. Thus in his recent study *Act and Quality* Charles Altieri in effect sets Wittgenstein against the excesses of post-Saussurean theory, especially against post-structuralism. Altieri argues that the doctrine of arbitrariness has been so fetishised that it now constitutes a threat to 'humanistic understanding',[16] not only in literary criticism but in the social sciences as well. If you picture the individual as linguistically displaced and radically unstable you cannot, according to Altieri, make sense of the sense we do in fact make of the world. In particular, you cannot make sense of the moral agent who, day in and day out, interprets and responds to his experience with a significant degree of confidence and rational self-determination. In Altieri's view post-structuralism, and especially deconstruction, decimates the moral agent so conceived.

Altieri's invocation of Wittgenstein is not without its own dangers in this respect, since Wittgenstein demurs at notions of privacy in relation to language and language usage. On this point, indeed, Altieri is characteristically candid in his uncertainty:

I cannot imagine an approach to practical social life which . . .
tries consistently to do without an idea of agency. We must have
a conceptual basis for distinguishing degrees of responsibility,
adapting ourselves to expressive implicature, and analyzing
incongruities between statements and deeds. Thus, while I am
by no means sure what psychological or ontological foundation
to give such attributes, I assume that one can rely on such
compelling phenomenological evidence.[17]

We must, that is, have a substantive concept of the moral agent if
we are to make sense of others,[18] and this must entail making
assumptions about the inner worlds – the thoughts and intentions
– of others. Though he is uncertain what 'ontological foundation'
to impute to this dimension in others, Altieri appears to believe
that society equips us to make complex and accurate inferences
about it by habituating us to multiple contexts of expectation and
interpretation. These he terms, after Wittgenstein, a cultural
'grammar'.[19] Altieri appears, moreover, to believe that, since
selves are linguistically constituted, various terms of linguistic
competence and analysis can give us access to the inner man as
our cultural grammar has trained us to conceive of him. One such
form is literature, since it projects images of interiority, and Altieri
urges that we read literature with an emphasis upon images of the
moral agent: upon how literature simulates the process whereby
we predict, reconstruct and test the motivation behind certain
acts. Altieri's concept of intention proves in fact to be immensely
complex and possibly even circular: 'I propose as the most general
idea of intentional agency a description of an act that interprets its
intentional features to some specific predicates typically used to
characterize human motives';[20] however, he uses the example of
James's fiction to argue for something more than a simple concept
of rational causality.[21] Psychological novels, he believes, make us
aware of just how complex a thing moral agency is. This indeed is
one of their most important functions. Thus does Altieri's
complex (and, by his own admission, at times opaque) account
seek to reassert the concept of an ethically active and inward
individual that crude structural and post-structural theories have
seemed to deny. The language of literary texts, he suggests, is
somehow continuous with this person and his context. Yet Altieri
follows the later Wittgenstein in demurring at the suggestion that
language is in any simple sense referential. Language may in some

instances function referentially: it refers to certain widely held
assumptions about the world. But it is so deeply implicated in
those assumptions that Altieri in many instances prefers what he
calls a 'procedural approach to meaning': that is, one which
emphasises the ways in which our linguistic–cultural grammar
equips us to interpret and negotiate particular situations which
are themselves deeply shaped by habits of linguistic usage.[22]
Language, then, bears a complex and multiple set of relations to
the world and its analysis must rest upon a recognition of its
specificity and its variability.

   Altieri's theory has the immense virtue of returning the moral
agent to philosophical and literary centrality; however it is
arguably at its most uncertain on the nature of this individual,
both for social and literary analysis, and it is to this problem that
we must now turn.

THE SELF: ESSENCE AND CULTURE

Altieri's image of the self is in part complicated by the transition
Act and Quality makes from a Wittgensteinian model of the self to a
dialectical Hegelian one (Ch. 9). But the most obvious form of
uncertainty in the book concerns the kind of inwardness the moral
agent possesses. Altieri apparently sees the 'private' world as a
complex continuation of a social grammar. He does not on the
whole (though he acknowledges uncertainty here) believe that
this privacy can be characterised as radically private; in other
words, that we might talk of individuals as possessing inner
worlds that are anything other than a socially constructed sense of
subjectivity.

   This kind of assumption is often disparagingly dismissed as
naïvely essentialist. Its critics argue that we cannot know
anything about a core or essence of self which is by definition
pre-social. We can only know the self as it arises from the process
of culturation. There are, however, significant philosophic and
social scientific theories which wish to retain a concept of essence
for the self, and it is, I believe, a concept to which literary criticism
might again pay attention. What does it imply about individual
persons?

   One implication can be that individuals possess a margin of self
which is not socially constituted, which is extraordinarily difficult

to characterise, but which nevertheless enters significantly into our social and moral lives. We might wish to argue such a claim from intuition and introspection, from some conception of genetic determination of the self (though there are clear dangers here), from a concept like Freud's much-debated notion of an instinctual unconscious, or we might rest the claim upon the familiar empiricist belief that much of our experience is in fact not linguistic or linguistically constructed in any recognisable sense. Crudely, we are encased in bodies and much of our experience is sensory rather than cognitive. Structuration, it may be argued, does not articulate our lives at this level.

A second implication of such a view might be that it makes sense to talk of a biologically given 'human nature' which enters into any conceivable form of social life. Thus does G. J. Warnock argue in *The Object of Morality* for something like a 'human predicament' which results from certain species limits, drives and tendencies that all people possess.[23] The political scientist C. B. Macpherson rests his theory of socialist liberal democracy upon a similar assumption. He asserts that

> any ethical theory, and therefore any justificatory political theory – whether idealist or materialist, and whether liberal or not and democratic or not – must start from the assumption that there are specifical or uniquely human capacities different from, or over and above, animal ones.[24]

This assumption Macpherson describes as an 'empirical postulate':[25] that is, it seems verifiable from observation even if it cannot be ascribed any transcendental foundation. According to this view, it makes sense to talk of a dimension of self that exists prior to culturation and which can be more or less comprehensively, or more or less satisfactorily, articulated through various forms of social and political organisation.

Precisely how this postulate relates to the problem of the inner person is not clear, but many liberal humanists seem to assume that our possession of a sensory and biological essence is somehow implicated in our possession of privacy, moral agency and a certain capacity for distance from particular or coercive forms of cultural conditioning. Let us delay for the moment further discussion of this alleged connection and note two things about the kind of essentialist theory of the self here outlined. The first concerns its literary implications. Those who read character from this point of view will tend to impute some referential function to the depictions of the inner person offered in psychological novels. Eliot and James, they will assume, linguistically simulate a private world that does in fact exist in people but which transcends the linguistic medium in which they as novelists are compelled to describe it. Such readers may also see character in a larger metaphysical context which corresponds to some generalised notion of 'human capacities' or a human 'predicament'. Thus, while the structuralist will look in *Middlemarch* for the key to the social constitution of selves as George Eliot's society practised it, a liberal-humanist critic may look beyond the codes for larger and quite possibly valid comment about human affairs. Eliot's 'tragic outlook' may seem to reflect certain general realities about human drives, limitations and suffering. Secondly, it is important to note that the essentialist model runs counter not only to structuralist theories but also to the Wittgensteinian one proposed by Altieri, and that, further, many varieties of Marxism also oppose it.

Among the movements to influence literary criticism, Marxism has provided the most searching critique of the liberal-humanist position on the self. It is difficult to generalise here (not least because of disputes about Marx's early essentialist premises), but Marxists will generally deny ostensibly 'natural' categories like 'self', 'privacy', 'moral' and 'human nature'. These they argue are deeply embedded features of a certain ideologically constructed model of the self – that of bourgeois or liberal humanism – and it is its constructedness that must be demonstrated, or even 'ruthlessly historicized'.[26] The implication for literary theorists and critics here is that their readings of literature ought to expose the ideological constructedness of 'character' in literature and to unravel the historical and political discourses that comprise it. Thus in various ways the Marxist literary theories of Adorno, Althusser, Macherey, Benjamin, Bakhtin, Eagleton, Jameson[27] and others tie reading to ideological elucidation. Terry Eagleton's call to 'refuse' the ' "naturalness" ' of the text is here characteristic.[28] The Marxists are clearly right that the reading and production of literature are powerfully shaped by socio-economic factors; clearly right to argue that novels (for example) both encode and subvert the ideological matrices within which they are embedded; and, again, right in emphasising not only the historical specificity of certain concepts of self, but the extent to which a sense of differentness between individual selves is actually culturally produced. However, in querying more general aspects of Marxist theory – historically specific theories of class, its difficulties in formulating a theory of the individual subject – one is inevitably expressing reservations that have literary implications, and the most compelling alternative is perhaps a model which, whilst recognising the historically embedded liabilities of a 'bourgeois humanist' account of the self, wishes to retrieve and elaborate some of its central values – freedom, justice, equality and so on – and indeed to insist upon these as the proper objectives of any theory. Such an appeal to embedded values might merely reinforce critical conservatism (though it is familiar enough among Marxist humanists); but it might also inform a kind of reading that centres upon fictional explorations of concepts of self – their adequacy, their generalisability and so on.[29]

Some liberal humanists have of course attempted to formulate a theory of this kind, though often from a position fundamentally antagonistic to Marxism. One of the most important figures here is the novelist and philosopher Iris Murdoch.[30] In her polemical article 'Against Dryness' Murdoch calls upon philosophical and literary liberalism to discharge its obligations in formulating more complex images of the self and its linguistic-social entanglements. There is, according to Murdoch, a 'transcendence of reality'[31] – a human predicament – to which we as 'benighted creatures'[32] habitually react in facile panic and destructiveness. Like Simone Weil, Murdoch believes that we need a 'new vocabulary of attention'[33] to persons that will strike a balance between collectivity and individuality, and will reflect a sense of 'moral difficulty'[34] in our ethical and social lives. For Murdoch this entails conceding a marked degree of contingency and heterogeneity in human affairs. She does not believe that Marxist or other systematics can explain all social and psychological phenomena, and she insists that individual persons must necessarily remain somewhat opaque to our understanding.

What does such a position entail as regards culture, language and the self? It apparently does not involve a crude correspondence theory of language. It does not entail claiming, for example, that signs bear necessary logical relationships to the features of the world they designate, nor that such features are somehow mystically immanent in signs. But it does suggest that it makes sense to talk about orders of reality that precede and exceed specific sign systems. Aspects of the physical world seem simply to register in sense experience; regions of the 'individual consciousness' seem to elude symbolic ordering. It further suggests that, where sign systems do mediate our experience, they can do so with a marked degree of stability: key terms in social, moral and legal vocabulary do in practice prevail on the basis of a rough general consensus. Certain things *do* mean with something like a determinate force. The claim that language is internally coherent need not, at least at a general level, conflict with this account; what it does not, however, accept is the methodological premise (in fact far from consistent in Saussure, Eco, Peirce and other semiologists/semioticians) that analysis can properly stop at the codes, the internal relations posited. Murdoch wants somehow to characterise the inner world of the moral agent, but without resorting to a structural systematics that must elucidate it in essentially discursive or public terms. Clearly, there is a tension here between wishing to theorise and wishing to valorise the essentialist individual self; between the desire to respect the individuality of other persons and the philosophical undertaking to explain them. The same tension will be apparent in the readings of George Eliot and Henry James that follow here. Iris Murdoch's contention appears to be that the literature of personality, and especially novels, can at least partially resolve the tension because in them the self is presented both as a challenge to philosophical elucidation and as a kind of ethical example reminding the reader of the necessary and proper limits of our understanding of others. Novels do not, then, simply depict human beings; they simulate certain familiar forms of contextual moral difficulty through a dialectic of knowing and not knowing. But what relation does knowledge gained in reading bear to that involved in non-literary contexts?

SOCIAL FICTIONS: THE SELF AND NARRATIVE INTELLIGIBILITY

Many answers have been proposed to the question just posed. One, which has achieved wide currency among structuralists and post-structuralists, is that since our experience is mediated by narrative codes there is a radical similarity between literary and non-literary narratives, texts and contexts. In this view society itself can be seen as a kind of 'worldtext',[35] or reality as 'textual'. Extreme formulations may carry the familiar idealist implication that 'reality' is merely a social fiction without ontological foundation.

There are notorious dangers in collapsing distinctions between the actual and the textual, not least that unexplained, highly generalised or even threatening aspects of experience tend to be omitted from our descriptions of human affairs. Nevertheless, literary texts clearly do share certain narrative structures and assumptions with other forms of social understanding and it is necessary to inquire what kinds of authority various narrative modes possess. Here the work of the contemporary moral and social theorist Alasdair MacIntyre may be of value to literary criticism. In his recent study of moral theory, *After Virtue*, MacIntyre attempts to link the idea of social narrative to a belief that certain societal values – of 'virtues' – are ideally more compelling or more authoritative than others. All is not in any simple, undifferentiated sense textual; some narrative truth claims are more powerful than others. MacIntyre's account appears to be neo-Aristotelian: he does not argue that the virtues have any universal or transcendental foundation; rather he argues that they are constituted as hierarchically meaningful by particular societies. According to MacIntyre, modern societies of the West are in fact beset by a plurality of ethical and social norms and this makes for incoherence, both philosophical and political. MacIntyre attempts to reconstruct historically the sources of our present confusions by examining linguistic and moral 'survivals'[36] that remain current. He also asks how in a better rationalised society a coherent hierarchy of values might function. Whilst emphasising the incompleteness of *After Virtue*,[37] MacIntyre argues that social narratives predicate values which make claims on individuals, but do not entirely subsume those individuals. He draws an important, though not an absolute, distinction between 'roles', 'characters' and 'individuals'. Roles involve individuals in stereotypical social functions; characters assimilate individuals to patterns of behaviour and expectation that render them intelligible and exemplary as ethical beings; individuals typically enter into both categories. However, while

individuals coincide with social characters, they may to a
significant degree elude roles.[38] Here MacIntyre's discussion is
difficult and the status of individuals in relation to characters may
require further elucidation. MacIntyre's position appears to be
guardedly anti-essentialist. He repudiates the concept of 'human
nature':

> Our biological nature certainly places constraints on all
> cultural possibility; but man who has nothing but a biological
> nature is a creature of whom we know nothing. It is only man
> with practical intelligence – and that, as we have seen, is
> intelligence informed by virtues – whom we actively meet in
> history.[39]

Nevertheless, *After Virtue* strenuously opposes what it terms the
philosophical 'liquidation'[40] of the 'substantial self' into 'roles'.[41]
The individual, he believes, must be conceived as ethically
constituted and active within his given social context. In this
MacIntyre makes a claim familiar to critics of literary
structuralism. Thus it is that in his review of the movement Terry
Eagleton objects that structuralism has 'liquidated' the individual
'subject'.[42]

MacIntyre's theory (which, as it happens, refers frequently to
Henry James) may be valuable to literary critics for a number of
reasons. First, it concedes the importance of social narratives but
without capitulating to crude versions of textuality. Narratives
are seen as possessing determinate descriptive and prescriptive
power by virtue of the social conventions in which they are
embedded. Second, the theory is (however complexly) historical
in its orientation. It charts changing and jostling philosophical
assumptions and uses imaginative literature extensively in so
doing. Finally, MacIntyre insists that the self must be accorded a
certain narrative coherence, for without this persons would be
unintelligible, both to themselves and to others. This he terms the
'concepts of narrative, intelligibility and accountability'.[43] As we
shall see, Eliot and James both test precisely these concepts in
their novels. What might they imply for a theory of character in
fiction?

CHARACTER AND SELF: CONTEXTUAL PRIVACY

Though MacIntyre is generally unsympathetic to philosophical accounts of private language, the unconscious and what we have loosely termed the inner world,[44] his emphasis upon the 'substantial self' may invite further speculation as to the nature of the individual moral agent. If, as MacIntyre claims, we can make narrative sense of the acts and intentions of others, perhaps we can – and do – effectively characterise the inner world. Perhaps, indeed, this is one of the important functions of imaginative literature. This is precisely Iris Murdoch's contention in her study in moral theory, *The Sovereignty of Good.*[45] Here, and especially in the essay 'The Idea of Perfection', she develops the position outlined in 'Against Dryness'. She posits certain relatively stable features of human experience ('human nature',[46] 'reality'[47]) but without undue recourse to obscurantist notions ('ineffable experience'[48]) such as bedevil Moore and the intuitionalists. Murdoch here proposes an 'inconclusive undogmatic naturalism'[49] that concedes the key fact that 'public concepts are in [an] obvious sense sovereign over private objects'[50] and individuals, but *not* that such concepts exhaust the self. Unlike Wittgenstein and the structuralists, she insists not only that a margin of self eludes the categories, but that this margin must be acknowledged. The great novels do just that; so must moral philosophy. To this end Murdoch proposes the notion of 'contextual privacy':[51] the individual is to a high degree structured and directed by public concepts, but the self so conceived possesses an ontological essence which may be said to elude total structuration. Here the Marxists and the structuralists are likely to take issue. The Marxists may say that self is constituted through and in a particular ideological matrix and that it cannot be known beyond this. Claims for a pre-social essence are unverifiable, irrelevant and ultimately mystical. Similarly, the structuralist will tend to assume that selves are socially constituted and cannot be known in a pristine state prior to culture.

The force of these objections must be conceded. We cannot extricate ourselves comprehensively from received descriptive and conceptual perspectives. Nevertheless, I believe Iris Murdoch's position to be less naïve than is often supposed by critics of liberal humanism. Several points may be made in its favour. One is that the implausibility of an unconditioned and objective view of human phenomena besets proponents of all theories, including those theories most calculated to unmask ideological and social bias. Again, it is not clear that the assumption of pre- or extra-social margins of the self is entirely foreign to structural theories. As Fredric Jameson observes,

> In any case, in practice, all the Structuralists: Lévi-Strauss with his idea of nature, Barthes with his feeling for social and ideological materials, Althusser with his sense of history, *do* tend to presuppose, beyond the sign-system itself, some kind of ultimate reality which, unknowable or not, serves as its most distant object of reference.[52]

Put crudely, sign systems go to work on or process *something*. Thus does Lacan's (post-)structural psychoanalytic theory rest on an assumption of a pre-linguistic phase in individual development. This is the 'mirror stage' in which 'consciousness' is inchoate and unmediated by language structures.[53] Typically, Lacan's theory is directed at the subsequent phases when language has produced subjectivity in a recognisable or accessible form, yet the status of the extra-linguistic in the theory arguably remains problematic, especially in Lacan's pronouncements about the 'real' and the familiar and stubborn question of the referent. Lacan acknowledges a something beyond the codes but believes it – perhaps with prophetic circularity – to be inaccessible to analysis. The liberal humanist, by contrast, insists that we calculate the something into our descriptions, however opaque and resistant to elucidation it may be.

Does this mean, as is often urged, that liberal humanism pictures the self as radically and anarchically private, a sort of Cartesian cell in a social world? Some versions no doubt do, but I do not believe this assumption to be intrinsic to the position. Iris Murdoch's belief seems on the contrary to be in a relationship of mutual entailment between selves and systems: systems (social and textual) constitute selves but are also dialectically constituted by them. You cannot have systems without selves, nor the reverse. Here Alasdair MacIntyre, in many respects an opponent of liberalism, is in agreement. According to MacIntyre, the relationship between the concept of personal identity and the larger cultural narratives through which we make sense of persons is one of 'mutual presupposition'.[54] Descriptions of the self presuppose the existence of selves; conversely, individuals require social narratives in order to conceptualise their own existences.

A great virtue of Iris Murdoch's account is that it extends questions about private and public narratives to complex forms of language use. This is particularly valuable for readings of literature that ostensibly centre upon character. Unlike crude forms of structural and semiotic theory, Murdoch's theory tries to account for the way in which we in effect privatise language as we use it. The signs are, she concedes, socially derived, but they get refracted through individual subjectivities. This has two important implications: one, that language use is creative, a kind of individual rule-governed creativity; the other, that we actually *explore* the meaning of words as we absorb and use them. What is more, these meanings are bound in complex cases to differ from one individual to another. How is this process to be conceived?

Murdoch suggests that the subjectivity into which one individual absorbs words is significantly dissimilar from that of other individuals, since it is the upshot of an individual – that is, both sensory and social – narrative history. We internalise and interpret words in the light of this history. Language, then, does not stop at fixed interpersonal meanings.

> We do not simply, through being rational and knowing ordinary language, 'know' the meaning of all necessary moral words. We may have to learn the meaning; and since we are human historical individuals the movement of understanding is onward into increasing privacy, in the direction of the ideal limit, and not back towards a genesis in the rulings of an impersonal public language.[55]

Many critics will feel that literary language works in just this personalising–communicative way. The writer infuses his or her public medium with an individual sensibility that extends and subtilises it. But the most important implication for our purposes concerns literary character. Iris Murdoch has here proposed a model of language use which enables us to impute a significant margin of individuality to persons – and, by extension, characters – without denying the self's inevitable linguistic entanglements. Individuals live at once through and beyond language, and any linguistic analogies we propose must acknowledge this cardinal fact. One valuable consequence of so qualifying the hypothesis that selves are linguistically constituted might be to maintain, among other and competing modes, a discourse of moral intention and complexity for literary criticism.

SUMMING UP: READING CHARACTER IN ELIOT AND JAMES

The broad features of the approach proposed here will now be apparent. In the absence of a more precise term, the regrettably variable and tendentious one of 'humanist' will perhaps have to suffice. I read character in Eliot and James in the light of four key assumptions. First, selves are neither analogically nor practically to be conceived as subordinate to sign systems. They possess a contextual privacy, and so an effective individuality, within such systems. Second, it is politically and critically dangerous to so reorder priorities as to marginalise the intending moral agent. The image of this agent may loosely be characterised as Kantian: it assumes that individuals possess a capacity to make considered ethical decisions predicated upon the assumption that other peoples' ethical entitlements are roughly – perhaps somehow radically – continuous with one's own. In one of liberalism's classic texts, *Groundwork of the Metaphysic of Morals*, Kant envisions a society comprised of such moral beings as the 'Kingdom of Ends', for persons will there be treated as ends and not means.[56] Third, I impute to such beings an interiority that can ultimately be neither demonstrated nor disproved, either by Kant's strategies or by any that I can formulate. I do however claim that we know this inner world by intuition, introspection and inferences from recurrent social experience and that one of the fundamental functions of imaginative literature is to give us public access to verbal simulations of it. Indeed, important literature is important often precisely because it makes available for contemplation and use complex images of this inner world. This is surely true of the novels of Eliot and James. Finally, and consequently, I impute particular value here to novels which seem to me to open out creatively, and often conflictingly, images of the moral agent. Indeed, this study is an attempt to chart the moral agent from George Eliot to late James. I shall argue that in creatively rethinking this individual each novelist experiments with variations upon a humanist image of self, and that in either case, though more far-reachingly in James's, this leads them to test what we should now think of as phenomenological assumptions about central philosophical problems: the nature of perception, choice, intersubjective knowledge and morality. The readings that follow thus attempt to connect formal questions about character and narration with larger epistemological and ethical ones. I therefore relate character and narration in *Daniel Deronda* and *The Portrait of a Lady* to those novels' explorations of choice (Ch. 3); the comparative reading of *Middlemarch* and *The Golden Bowl* (Ch. 4) links character and narration to these works' assumptions about intersubjective knowledge, the kinds and degrees of knowledge we can in fact have of the inner worlds of others; and Chapter 5's discussion of character and narration centres on the problem of morality and moral judgements on fiction. Throughout I assume that 'formal' and 'thematic' issues cannot in fact be separated in reading complex narrative; also that the heuristic energies of such narratives – their preparedness to 'experiment' with multiple, complex and even contradictory images of human situations – are a virtue that must be respected by the critic.

In saying this I am, of course, proffering value judgements about literature. Here again I am to some extent writing against the current. Thus in his recent and impressive study of character in post-modern fiction, *Reading (Absent) Character*, Thomas Docherty suggests that liberal humanism can do little with the hollowed-out character of the post-modern novel.[57] Perhaps he is right; but perhaps liberal humanists can have something of importance to say about the fictional attack on the substantial self that Docherty so brilliantly documents. Perhaps this attack ought, with proper political and aesthetic qualification, to be called into question. The problem is of course to know how – and how far – to reference one's politics to one's reading. There are, it seems, no easy equivalences here. In so far as the readings of Eliot and James that follow are informed by political assumptions, they are very broadly of the kind outlined in C. B. Macpherson's socialist–democratic model.[58] Like Macpherson, I place an image of the substantial, essentialist individual and his fulfilments at the centre of my account. In so doing I no doubt draw on an problematic plurality of theory and assumption, and also privilege the category 'individual' in a fashion unacceptable to critics of liberal humanism.[59] I can offer no simple solution here, but this study assumes that, as humanists, George Eliot and James saw both the perils and the powers of this view and that we can learn much about these from a sympathetic reading of their novels.

In so far as Eliot and James are central figures in the English novel's evolution from Victorian modes to modernism, this essay, which begins with Eliot's and James's theories of fiction, and with James's responses to Eliot's work, may also be read as a kind of history in microcosm of the form since the Victorians. Here as elsewhere, however, readers will make their own judgements as to the larger import of the things I think I see.

2 Two Views of the Novel: Eliot and James on the Novel, James on George Eliot

GEORGE ELIOT'S THEORY OF THE NOVEL

James in a sense formalised and finalised his 'theory' of the novel in the first decade of this century. The extent of our debt to him in the increasingly analytic critical ambience of the 1980s is extraordinary. His hope that the New York Prefaces (1907–9) would constitute 'a sort of comprehensive manual or *vade-mecum* for aspirants in our arduous profession'[1] is well known; but in the five decades prior to the Prefaces he had already given English novel criticism its first comprehensive poetics of the form. This he was ideally qualified to do. Being equally conversant with his native American tradition of symbolic realism and allegory, with French naturalism and with his beloved (if, he felt, in some respects blighted) English tradition, he was able to range freely through many of the formal, representational, 'expressive' and 'receptive' questions that now preoccupy novel theory. (The exception here, of course, is anything like a material analysis of literary forms.) But, needless to say, James himself had much to draw upon. His central tenets have a long history and much of his work was a gathering and formalisation of the more scattered insights of others.[2] One such was George Eliot.

There is no need here for a duplication of the detailed expositions of George Eliot's novel theory elsewhere available.[3] But a selective review will be germane to our purposes. Certain important qualifications need to be made at the outset. The first of these is that, formidable synthesising intellect though Eliot had, her aesthetic is markedly inconsistent. It is essentially romantic in outlook and is riven by many of the contradictions documented in Abrams' study of romantic theory, *The Mirror and the Lamp*:[4] the writer is here conceived as visionary, there as a patient quasi-scientific viewer; imagination is here reckoned a faculty for transcendence and what Coleridge termed 'esemplastic'[5] reconstitution, there as a passive mirror; the novel is sometimes urged as the ideal vehicle for Comtean sociological report, at others as a sort of Cartesian theatre of ethical subjectivity. Again, George Eliot invests the novel with varying degrees of formal autonomy and internal coherence. The reader, likewise, is at once held to be in moral and emotional need of great novels, and already in a condition to appreciate them. Many of these inconsistencies are of course received, and (a second qualification), unlike James, George Eliot did not set herself a comprehensive rationalising task as a theorist. Third, her 'theory' is much more fragmented than his and, unlike his, did not keep pace with her creative output. Many of her famous and representative formulations date from her years on the *Westminster Review* and, latterly, the *Leader*, between 1851 and 1857. Thus an aesthetic of sorts was well in place before *Adam Bede* (1859). Finally, however, it is clear from subsequent letters, essays and novels that her position did evolve to some extent and that this evolution can usefully be charted, as it is in Sally Shuttleworth's admirable *George Eliot and Nineteenth Century Science*,[6] in terms of a fundamental commitment to organicism.[7]

The tensions within George Eliot's aesthetic can best be understood with reference to a divided inheritance she shares with James. This is none other than the narrative grammar they took over in the third-person, omniscient novel form. No teacher gets far in introducing this form to an inquiring class without being asked to talk his or her way through the many first-person passages in *Middlemarch* and kindred works. This question is often cited as a telling pedagogic point in favour of narratology, but its more general philosophical implications need to be recognised. The questioner has, after all, hit upon an aesthetic contradiction that runs deep in Eliot's and James's fiction. Both wrote predominantly in a divided narrative form in which a transcendent consciousness constitutes the narrative situation in the third person whilst also attempting to present itself as an empirical being, an authenticating presence to whom the reader can relate. This split between omniscience and limitation

generates many of the characteristic formal effects of an Eliot or
James novel and it is at root a problem familiar in Kantian and
post-Kantian epistemology.[8] How can the constructive faculty of
the narrative consciousness be reconciled with what the novelist
takes to be the undeniable reality of the other lives it narrates?
Does this narrative grammar not embed within the novel an
asymmetry between self-knowledge (the narrator's consciousness
of his own status in the fiction) and the knowledge of others? What
implication does this have for character in an Eliot or James
novel?[9]

One is clear. A problematic of character is as it were encoded in
the narrative structure they use,[10] and both are quite open about
this with the reader. The reader is often urged not to 'naturalize'[11]
characters too readily, to see that fictional selves cannot simply be
reduced to the status of the 'life-like'. Indeed, as we shall see, Eliot
and James often use the novel to query just such an assumption.
This entails a second point. As aestheticians (and, of course,
writers), both address themselves centrally to the problem of the
discontinuous narrator: should the narrator intrude in the first
person or retreat into omniscient anonymity? It will become
apparent that James's reading of George Eliot (and others)
convinced him that she had as it were edged the empirical ego too
much out into the open. Increasingly, as he approached the late
phase, he preferred a relative impersonality. Here is the problem
of 'narration' given in the sub-title to this book, and it is clear that
the problem of 'character' is closely implicated. As Dorrit Cohn's
apt title for his book on characterisation, *Transparent Minds*,[12]
implies, the great paradox of novelistic realism has been to claim
an account of life that is unprecedentedly 'life-like', but which at
the same time rests upon a vast and presumptive claim of direct
access to other minds. This dualism haunts just about everything
George Eliot wrote; it is also a source of great – though rather less
panicked – creative impetus to James. What then were the
alternatives? Again, you could edge the artificiality out from the
margins and own up, often guiltily and self-consciously, to the
liberties you were taking with your characters. On this point
James derived from his extended reading of Eliot a conviction that
it was better unfussily and opaquely to exhibit characters than
to expatiate upon them.[13] This of course testifies to the
interdependence of the problems of character and narration: the
subliminal third-person technique, like its reverse, constitutes

character as a textual and extra-textual entity of a particular kind. A choice of discretion and exhibition over intrusion and exposition is a choice of a certain mode of *knowing*,[14] and this choice has implications for author, characters and reader alike. Such implications may appear in the first instance to be epistemological, but they are also – indeed consequently – *ethical*. In novels at least, formal choices express assumptions about the kinds of attention to which the human subject is ideally entitled. In this sense the question 'how write?' also entails 'how right?'

George Eliot's formal preferences, both in theory and practice, are an uneasy attempt to keep novels 'true to life' whilst insisting that they are in any case radically, indeed necessarily, continuous with it; that, just as problematically, novels have at once to 'mirror' 'life' and to improve upon it. The histories of critical theory will indicate the roots of such a position and the nature of the contradictions inherent in it. Let us see what it entails for realism, character and narration in George Eliot.

It seems to entail seeing 'reality' in at least three competing ways. On one view it is an intractable entity that is descriptively, and it would seem ontologically, prior to mind; on another it is the creative precipitate of a set of innate categories in the mind; a third pictures it as a kind of spiritualised process not properly understood in terms of subject and object since it is precisely such categories that it transcends. Eliot offers, then, a kind of unstable romantic mimeticism. The last view described is also the rarest. It is most prominent late on, in the selfless mysticism of *Daniel Deronda*, but it is also present elsewhere, notably in that Gothic nightmare of category collapse, 'The Lifted Veil'. Reality as ontologically prior is given in this famous neoclassical statement of intention in *Adam Bede*: 'My strongest effort is . . . to give a faithful account of man and things as they have mirrored themselves in my mind' (I.17, p. 265). But, immediately, a suggestion of innate and creative mental faculty surfaces guiltily in: 'The mirror is doubtless defective; the outlines will sometimes be disturbed, the reflection faint or confused . . .' (pp. 265–6). In its most developed form this issues in the idealist conviction of an authoritative authorial 'inner state': 'sincerity' is ultimately indistinguishable from realism because these 'states' constitute what there is to be seen. The truthful and genuine writer earns our trust and esteem because he 'never breaks loose from his criterion

– the truth of his own mental state.'[15] The states, however, can have no finally situated authority – let alone some transcendental foundation – because the writer expresses an 'unfolding self'.[16] This does not prevent his having, if he is good enough, the 'power'[17] to influence the 'inner states' of others – indeed that, the 'extension of our sympathies', is art's sublime function[18] – but it does seem sometimes to imply that in passionately importuning the reader the novelist–narrator is necessarily gesturing at an unstable sign. What, after all, is this 'reality' that confronts 'perennial human nature'?[19] What, further, is its status when given in narrative fictions?

George Eliot's answers to these questions vary. One of the most interesting is given in the essay 'Leaves from a Note-Book', which was written in the 1870s but not published until 1884. Here she hints at the position recently developed in Barbara Hardy's highly suggestive study of the narrative imagination, *Tellers and Listeners*. That 'we get interested in the stories life presents to us through divers orders and modes of presentation '[20] may suggest, first, that a novel is just one narrative mode among a system of narratives and is therefore continuous with our 'extra-literary' experience; second, that we so experience things because the mind is as it were keyed to narrative structures. This view does not reflect the characteristic emphasis of George Eliot's aesthetic but it does hint at perhaps the most plausible theory of representation she advances. Roughly: reality is at once essential and relational. That is, it is antecedent to consciousness, but largely as a kind of 'raw material'.[21] Man has access to this 'material' in two modes. The first (understated, in my views, in K. M. Newton's admirable recent discussion[22]) is intuitive. Through a 'generous leap of impulse'[23] mind can gain a kind of unmediated access to phenomena (including other minds). The second mode would now perhaps be thought of as proto-structuralist. George Eliot (with Lewes and contemporaries) had heard of the Language Animal and often argues that the 'raw material' is mediated by constitutive codes which are biologically and incorrigibly grounded in the mind. These codes mediate both 'perception' (training a light on a 'particular' part of a larger relational 'web': *Middlemarch*, I.15, p. 214) and 'feeling'. Thus, the 'great artist' can as it were simulate, and so activate, a structure of feeling that is already mentally encoded. She argues that 'a picture of human life such as a great artist can give, surprises even the trivial and the selfish into that attention to what is apart from themselves, which may be called the raw material of moral sentiment'.[24]

More of art presently. Here it may be noted that George Eliot clearly thought deeply about the range and status of the codes: about how innate they were; about the nature of their systematics; and about their expressive and representational capacities. 'The Natural History of German Life' (1856) suggests that she saw these capacities as strictly limited: one might picture a hypothetically rationalised synchronic language system; such a 'language may be a perfect medium of expression to science', but it 'will never express *life*, which is a great deal more than science.'[25] As her organicist position evolved, however, she seems to have thought the system both (metaphorically) more inclusive and more expressive. The extraordinary unpublished 'Notes on Form in Art' (1868) postulates a vast system of binary relations which constitutes various cultural and perceptual phenomena. The foreshadowings of Saussure are striking in

> And as knowledge continues to grow by its alternating processes of distinction & combination, seeing smaller & smaller unlikenesses & grouping or associating these under a common likeness, it arrives at the conception of wholes composed of parts more & more multiplied & highly differenced, yet more & more absolutely bound together by various conditions of common likeness or mutual dependence. And the fullest example of such a whole is the highest example of Form: in other words, the relation of multiplex interdependent parts to a whole which is itself in the most varied & therefore the fullest relation to other wholes.[26]

One such 'whole' is art, where the 'mental states of the constructor' constitute the object as a thing coded in the same manner (put another way, in the same system) as other things. She asks, 'what is a structure but a set of relations selected & combined in accordance with the sequence of mental states in the constructor, or with the preconception of a whole which he has inwardly evolved?'[27] The implication is that such structures, both in art and in life, are innate; that art is therefore radically continuous with life; and that the greatest art is, as it was for Ruskin, that which is the most relationally rich, both internally and in respect of other phenomena: 'The highest Form, then, is the highest organism, that is to say, the most varied group of relations bound together in a wholeness which again has the most varied relations with all other phenomena.'[28] This generally idealist account seeks to resolve the correspondence–coherence duality elsewhere apparent, but without denying either the biological foundation of 'perennial human nature', or the necessity for art to potentiate man's counter-egoistic propensity for a self–other structure of 'attention'.[29] This notion of 'attention' of course recalls Iris Murdoch's; the self–other dynamic owes much to Feuerbach and is, as we shall see, central to the fiction. On this view a narrator such as the one in *The Mill on the Floss* is indeed doing what a natural scientist does: assimilating the 'observation of human life' to 'a large vision of relations'. Moreover, as a famous passage in 'The Natural History of German Life' insists, this an urgent moral obligation:

> If any man of sufficient moral and intellectual breadth, whose observations would not be vitiated by a foregone conclusion, or by a professional point of view, would devote himself to studying the natural history of our social classes, especially of the small shopkeepers, artisans, and peasantry, – the degree in which they are influenced by local conditions, their maxims and habits, the points of view from which they regard their religious teachers, and the degree in which they are influenced by religious doctrines, the interaction of the various classes on each other, and what are the tendencies in their position towards disintegration or towards development, – and if, after all this study, he would give us the result of his observations in a book well nourished with specific facts, his work would be a valuable aid to the social and political reformer.[30]

What is sought, then, are those 'vital' or constitutive 'elements' that are to be contrasted with life's 'more transient forms'[31] or manifestations. One such element is human character, and Eliot, like Iris Murdoch, believes this properly to be the subject of a 'fond minuteness of attention that belongs to love'.[32] Yet here she believes even the genius sometimes falters: Dickens is gifted with the 'utmost power of rendering the external traits of our town population', but he fails to give us their 'psychological character'.[33] This is of course what George Eliot's psychological realism seeks to do and it is here that she so creatively and anxiously submits herself to the inherited divisions[34] in her form. What she desires is a structure that will reconcile the narrator as the anonymous and transcendental foundation of character, and the empirical 'I', enmeshed in a reader-like, life-like drama in which the opaque other is knowable only through the progressive solicitude of 'love'. George Eliot's spectrum of narrative tones,[35] ranging from an Olympian impersonality to the anguished voice of love by exemplification ('But why always Dorothea?'), reflects a tension she seems unable to resolve. 'Unless I am condemned by my own principles, my books are not properly separable into "direct" and "indirect" teaching'.[36] Her narrator, that is, may ideally be obtrusively present in some places and remote in others without invalidating the mimetic illusion. Such organicist principles might conceivably hold for the presentation of character; but it is everywhere apparent that she fears that they might not. This, however, is to anticipate. Though narrative intrusion is less prominent in *Daniel Deronda* than in *Adam Bede*, Eliot seeks generally to combine exposition and exhibition; to surround character in a loving but ostensibly limited analytic expertise. It is revealing and typical that she should think Sterne's (first-person) technique open to objections that 'lie more solidly in the quality of the interrupting matter than in the fact of interruption'.[37] George Eliot's intrusive narrator is then metonymic[38] in her presentation of character: she[39] aspires to the fullest contingent account that will not compromise the solicitude that is the essence of love or the incompletion that is the soul of narrative art. She was keenly conscious of the pitfalls of a metonymic method ('curiosity becomes the more eager from the incompleteness of the first information'[40]) but less inclined to surrender descriptive detail on this account than a writer like James. Such detail could and should project images of 'real complex human being[s]', not *'types'*[41]; it entails an account of self that is at once genetic ('inherited internal conditions'), historical (inherited 'external conditions'[42]), sociological ('the medium in which a character moves'[43]) and psychological. The subject so pictured is of extraordinary and insoluble 'complexity'[44]: 'character too is a process and an unfolding' (*Middlemarch*, 1.15, p. 226) that exceeds the artificiality alike of beginnings and endings;[45] but it is also, and very centrally, an *ethical* subject. George Eliot's fiction is marked by a high degree of movement and indeterminacy, but there are limits: in her novels self hardens into a thing with clear social referents and obligations. These are often tragic in outcome: sometimes in the general sense that growth and individual accommodation come only through suffering;[46] at others by virtue of character being conceived in the generic terms of Greek tragedy; most often, though, in an Hegelian sense: suffering, and so literary tragedy, are often perceived as the outcome of competing goods. One of her favourite tragedies, the *Antigone*, seemed in fact to gather in all these strands with extraordinary power and moral lucidity.[47]

As we shall see in coming chapters, the self conceived in terms of fundamental categories – 'character', 'choice', 'knowledge', 'morality' – is in George Eliot's fiction a strikingly various and speculative thing. Though she subscribes to a form of humanism predicated upon a loving reverence for the individual, her anxious fictional 'experiments in life'[48] are majestically and multifariously framed in order to ask what a person really is.

ANXIETY AND APPRECIATION: JAMES ON GEORGE ELIOT

In one of his superlatively circular late sentences James recalls in *The Middle Years* his life-long immersion in George Eliot's fiction. The first of his many appraisals of her may have been evaluative, but obligation is now, he reflects, mercifully behind him: 'Reflective appreciation may have originally been concerned, whether at its most or at its least, but it is well over, to our infinite relief – yes, to our immortal comfort. . .'.[49] 'Appreciation' is one of James's favourite terms for the subtleties of aesthetic response. He uses it to describe the ways in which we experience, assimilate and evaluate works of art. Since this process was for him an essentially mystical thing, he is reluctant wholly to rationalise it; however, he does repeatedly recall his experience of it and reconstruct his own 'appropriations' of imaginative literature. George Eliot's works are but one example among many. Yet, as the striking intensity of 'infinite relief' and 'immortal comfort' suggest, there was something special about her creative importance for James. In the 1870s he in fact places her in an august category of novelistic mentors: 'George Eliot belongs to that class of pre-eminent writers in relation to whom the imagination comes to self-consciousness only to find itself in subjection'.[50]

No one who is familiar with Harold Bloom's psychoanalytic theories of literary indebtedness and influence can read this pairing of 'self-consciousness' and 'subjection' without suspecting a connection here that far exceeds what can be demonstrated through a simple critical enumeration of Eliotean materials in James's novels. It is of course Bloom's contention that writers must wrest creative 'self-consciousness' from a potentially crippling psychological and creative 'subjection' to decisive – or 'strong' – literary predecessors. This they must do by strategically deforming and reworking received materials, and Bloom follows Freud in terming the emotion that so impels them 'anxiety'.[51] The extraordinary intensity of the recollections of George Eliot that James pens in old age in *The Middle Years* clearly indicate a relationship reminiscent of the desperate and defensive struggle for artistic and psychic individuation envisaged by Bloom. Indeed, James's comment about 'appreciation' is preceded by an admission of relief that he has at last 'shaken off the anxieties of circumspection and comparison' in relation to his mighty mentor.[52] Having liberated his own talent, he need no longer struggle to disentangle it from hers. Appreciation need no longer entail anxiety.

Yet even *The Middle Years* bears anguished testimony to the ambivalence of James's attitude to George Eliot. She had clearly been a powerful and problematic presence throughout his adult literary life. Thus James recalls with mingled pleasure and humiliation his meetings with the great lady. We know of at least four: one (its date apparently misrecollected in *The Middle Years*) on Sunday, 9 May 1869; and three others in 1878, two in April (the 10th and 21st) and the last on 1 November.[53] The first of these was for James immensely exhilarating, despite the poignancy of his finding George Eliot in attendance upon Lewes's son, Thornie, who, unbeknown to James, was dying from tuberculosis of the spine. James recalls himself as 'a young spirit almost abjectly grateful' and remembers his euphoric pleasure in being able to render service by seeking medical attention for Thornie: 'I again feel myself borne very much as if suddenly acting as a messenger of the gods'. The account of the visit in *The Middle Years* also contains an intriguing physical description of George Eliot:

It infinitely moved me to see so great a celebrity quite humanly and familiarly agitated – even with something clear and noble in it too, to which, as well as to the extraordinarily interesting dignity of her whole odd personal conformation, I remember thinking her black silk dress and the lace mantilla attached to her head and keeping company on either side with the low-falling thickness of her dark hair effectively contributed.

His reaction to her 'personal conformation' in a letter to his father on the following day was this: 'she is magnificently ugly – deliciously hideous'. Nevertheless: 'behold me literally in love with this great horse-faced blue-stocking'.[54] The character of this 'love', either on this occasion or subsequently, is impossible to determine, but a reading of James on George Eliot suggests that his sexual ambiguity was deeply implicated in the fight for psychic and artistic definition that drew him to her fiction and to that of other favoured writers. He was clearly fascinated by her manliness, yet, as we shall see, he expresses constant disapproval at the androgynous range of her narrative medium and is by turns fulsome and begrudging about her conflicted heroines.

The most momentous of James's visits was, alas, less euphoric. In *The Middle Years* he describes an encounter with the Leweses that clearly left a life-long scar. He remembers that he approached this visit with 'no great flush of assurance' that they would want to see him, and that he found his insecurities confirmed: 'I catch once more the impression of no occurrence of anything at all appreciable but their liking us to have come, with our terribly trivial contribution, mainly from a prevision of how they should more devoutly like it when we departed.' The uncharacteristic acerbity of this owes much to what followed. Lewes apparently bade James and his companion Mrs Greville wait in their brougham while he retrieved something of importance. This proved to be a 'pair of blue-bound volumes' for return to Mrs Greville, and James recalls Lewes's exhortation: 'Ah those books – take them away, please, away, away!' 'Those books' were James's novel *The Europeans*, and James remained (probably incorrectly) convinced of 'the horrid truth' that Lewes had not even been aware of the connection. 'The bruise inflicted', 'the taste of barrenness', 'the vivid demonstration of one's failure to penetrate' as an artist the 'pitch of intellectual life' that George Eliot and Lewes represented – in such phrases James reflects on his humiliating sense of failure with the great writer he had reverenced.

What he apparently did not know was that Lewes was at this stage fatally ill. So the sense of rejection must have gone unqualified. The enormity of his embarrassment is clear from his descriptions of the scale of his psychological and artistic dependence upon George Eliot. In *The Middle Years* he thinks of her not as a finished fact of novelistic history, but rather as a 'living and recorded *relation*' whose significance he recognised by its sentimental 'excess'. And he remembers his deep need for her novels both to succeed and to leave room for the completion of their task by a successor. Of reading *Felix Holt* he says, 'I had been conscious of absolutely needing it, to work'. He alludes also to the 'impetus proceeding from this work', and to the way in which his 'relation' with George Eliot enabled him both to exhaust and to refine upon *Middlemarch* and *Daniel Deronda*. Of the 'process of appropriation' of these great novels he notes,

> The process of appropriation of the two fictions was experience, in great intensity, and roundabout the field was drawn the distinguishable ring of something that belonged equally to this condition and that embraced and further vivified the imaged mass, playing in upon it lights of surpassing fineness. So it was, at any rate, that my 'relation' – for I didn't go so far as to call it 'ours' – helped me to squeeze further values from the intrinsic substance of the copious final productions I have named, a weight of variety, dignity and beauty of which I have never allowed my measure to shrink.

James here confirms his earlier belief that his 'relation' with his mentor would 'simply never be able not somehow to act'. Knowing her and reading her were deeply and mutually implicated in both his fiction and his literary criticism.

The importance and chronology of this 'relation' must be borne in mind when assessing James's critical appraisals of George Eliot's art and life. In 1868, when he first met her, he was eight years off his first important novel but had 'appropriated' and reviewed all her fiction up to and including *Romola*. Indeed, the first critical article to bear his name was 'The Novels of George Eliot', published in 1868. Lewes's 'valedictory hurl' of *The*

Europeans in 1878 occurred shortly before the great novels James was to produce in the 1880s, but after he had reviewed all of George Eliot's fiction. Moreover, it is quite possible that some of her revisions for the Cabinet Edition (1878–80) reflected James's admiring but often qualified appraisals of her work, and that the feelings of defensive and creative ambivalence between the two great writers were in some degree mutual.

There is clearly a detailed psychoanalytic study to be written about this extraordinary literary 'relation'. James, after all, recalls it as a part of what he terms his 'rage for connections'. 'Rage' – he could hardly have chosen a stronger word to express the depths of need and defensiveness the writer experiences in respect of peers and predecessors, not least when such predecessors' very words fall like messages from 'the gods'. Here, as elsewhere, Bloom's theory seems to find ample, indeed lavish, licence.

This essay owes something in a very general sense to Bloom's intertextual model of indebtedness and influence, but its central concerns lie elsewhere: with demonstrable textual influences between Eliot and James and with a set of philosophical problems to which they addressed themselves as novelists. To my knowledge, the detailed psychoanalytic account has yet to be written. When it is, it will surely have to contend with two deficiencies in the theory Bloom advances. It will have to reinterpret a poet-centred theory in order that it obtain for relations between novelists; and it will have to correct the Oedipal emphasis in Bloom's Freudian account if it is to accommodate connections between male and female writers (just as in other instances it requires revision in order to chart the history of influence between women authors).[55] Such a study will help us understand what James meant in old age by terming himself 'a very Derondist of Derondists'. As we shall see, he was never quite this uncritically devoted to George Eliot.

James in fact devoted at least ten critical pieces to George Eliot and there are countless incidental references in letters, reviews, essays and his biographical writings. The sustained written appreciations span the period 1866 (four years before his first novel, *Watch and Ward*) to 1885. Though he writes less about George Eliot prior to and during the late phase, James had, as we have seen, read and reviewed *Scenes of Clerical Life*, *Adam Bede*, *The Mill on the Floss*, 'The Lifted Veil', *Silas Marner*, *Romola* and *Felix Holt* before his first novel was published. The example that he was to think heroic but imperfect was, then, already powerfully established.

That sense of imperfection has many sources, but one perhaps underlies them all. James esteemed George Eliot's acknowledgement of 'the essential crookedness of our fate'.[56] Both sensibilities were essentially tragic in outlook. However, he did not entirely condone her artistic response to this 'crookedness'. It seemed to drive her as an artist into the inartistic, into a defensive and divisive polarisation of 'life' and the 'art' that sought to rationalise it. This is not the doctrine of 'Notes on Form in Art' but it is a substantially fair – if somewhat sweeping – appraisal of George Eliot's romantic mimeticism. What James puts in its place is the sort of thoroughgoing idealism that she rarely countenanced. Paul B. Armstrong's *The Phenomenology of Henry James*[57] identifies this idealism, rightly in my view, as a form of phenomenology, and without for the moment broaching the varieties of this tradition of thought[58] it will suffice to say that James's version of it tended to dissolve dualisms: between 'mind' and 'world' and between 'art' and 'life'. The world as we have it arises from the 'illimitable power'[59] of 'consciousness', of creative perception in which the perceiver and the perceived cannot properly be separated. Seen in this light George Eliot's anxious undertaking to 'mirror' 'life' as best she can appears to James at once misguided and gratuitously sober. James is struck by her not conceiving of the 'novelist's task' as the 'game of art',[60] not because he denied art's importance (who ever insisted more upon that?), but because such a view implied that the serious artist might conceivably be involved with anything *other* than life. A novel, he believes, is an act of consciousness; it is of a piece with our meaning-creation elsewhere in other modes, including that of 'everyday life'.

In James's view George Eliot's ethos of anxious imitation travestied the organicist aesthetic they ostensibly shared. *Middlemarch* is a 'treasure-house of detail but it is an indifferent whole'[61] because here, as elsewhere, she has been divided between picture and proposition, abstraction and artistry. This is not always the case – '*brain*' and 'imagination' do sometimes cohere[62] – but in general she works, in the legendary formulation, from the 'abstract' to the 'concrete'. Conception, that is, takes undue priority.

We feel in her, always, that she proceeds from the abstract to the concrete; that her figures and situations are evolved, as the phrase is, from her moral consciousness, and are only indirectly the products of observation. They are deeply studied and massively supported, but they are not *seen*, in the irresponsible plastic way.[63]

This in turn leads her to conceive of the novel in just the spirit she wished to avoid: not 'primarily' as a 'picture of life', capable of deriving a high value from its form, but as 'a moralised fable, the last word of a philosophy endeavouring to teach by example.'[64] Here is the shift to 'form' earlier cited in the two authorial notions of 'experiment'. On the whole James regrets that a more rigorous conception of organic form did not shape George Eliot's practice of narration. Those narrative intrusions can be sublime – he refers unforgettably to her 'luminous brooding',[65] to 'messages from mysterious regions'[66] – but she is too often either portentously Olympian[67] or plain indelicate. Here narration again implicates character. The intrusive narrator 'thinks for' characters 'more than they think for themselves';[68] moreover, narration so conceived as it were overwrites the reader. James's phenomenology is evident in an image of the literary text as a form of co-creation between writer and reader. Again, memorably:

> In every novel the work is divided between the writer and the reader; but the writer makes the reader very much as he makes his characters. When he makes him ill, that is, makes him indifferent, he does no work; the writer does all. When he makes him well, that is, makes him interested, then the reader does quite half the labor. In making such a deduction as I have just indicated, the reader would be doing but his share of the task; the grand point is to get him to make it. I hold that there is a way. It is perhaps a secret; but until it is found out, I think that the art of story-telling cannot be said to have approached perfection.[69]

As this passage about *Adam Bede* in an essay on George Eliot's novels indicates, James's phenomenology envisages 'character' not as a thing captured or pictured in all its 'life-like' contingency, but as a set of signs and textual signals offered for creative completion by the reader. His method, then, is primarily and increasingly metaphoric, symbolic and synecdochic. This does not mean that character is thereby abrogated: the late novels indeed seem to be about almost nothing else. But it does suggest that its 'presence' is sufficiently contingent to threaten commonplace 'moral realist' images of individual entitlement – epistemological, aesthetic and ethical. To anticipate: this is what gives the late novels their extraordinary aura of transfixed, apocalyptic humanism.

James is by no means uniformly critical of George Eliot's characterisation. Some of her creations indeed seem Shakespearean;[70] he esteems her sympathetic psychological realism;[71] he acknowledges the extraordinary sense of vastness-within-form achieved in *Middlemarch*;[72] and, as we shall see, he is lavish in acknowledgement of his great debt to George Eliot's conception of her heroines.[73] However, he avers that she seldom achieves 'free aesthetic life',[74] 'irresponsible' plasticity; that she is prone to philosophical typification;[75] and, most significantly, that she fails to reconcile the claims of 'character' with those of 'form'. Her plots and conclusions are weak and she lacks an instinct for design.[76]

James was not primarily an aesthetician and his fiction reveals inevitable discrepancies between theory and practice. Moreover, his critical appreciations and formulations were penned over a long-enough period to render unavoidable certain changes in emphasis. Yet for all this he is impressively consistent: what he is saying and what he is doing at any given time are generally in close accord, and the Prefaces, though more insistent than earlier writings upon delegated narrative points of view, are on the whole continuous with many of his earlier celebrated statements. Finally: his assessments of other people's novels – George Eliot's certainly – are clearly reflected in his own art. The art follows in Chapter 3. Let us here briefly recall the theory.

JAMES'S THEORY OF THE NOVEL

'Notes on Form in Art' suggests that, really, in fact, relations stop nowhere. But it was of course James who made this contention legendary: 'Really, universally, relations stop nowhere, and the exquisite problem of the artist is eternally but to draw, by a geometry of his own, the circle within which they shall happily *appear* to do so.'[77] One of the most fundamental contrasts between the two writers lies in George Eliot's not finding the 'problem' quite so 'exquisite'. Indeed, much of her anguished creative energy went into an attempt to read origin, agency and essence back into the unnerving spectre of mere systematics. To this extent 'Notes on Form in Art' takes a firmer line on these matters than her novelistic heurism and is therefore somewhat unrepresentative. As we shall see, *Daniel Deronda*, which was written eight years after her private meditation on form, is pervasively concerned with the problem of system and substance. We may anticipate thus: would the discovery of Jewish origins and 'genes' render a young man essentially – that is, radically – something, or would it merely locate him in a system of social categories?

A comparison of *The Portrait of a Lady* and *Daniel Deronda* (Ch. 3) indicates that the same sort of questions exercised James: for 'Jew' read 'American'. Why then does he apparently welcome ('exquisite') what so worries her? One answer no doubt lies in his personal history. James lived most of his adult life in England but was naturalised only in his final year, and then in response to the shock of the Great War. He might thus be said to have suspended or 'bracketed' any gross ethnic account of himself in order to consult a far more creative and authoritative one: the report of his own consciousness. James is here engaging in an activity fundamental to phenomenologists from Husserl onwards – a sort of existential 'reduction' – which actually sets its sights higher than the answer consciousness gives on any particular issue. What it in fact seeks to discover is the nature of consciousness itself. For Kierkegaard, Heidegger, Sartre and others, such a search has its inception in 'anguish', 'dread' or 'anxiety'[78] and seldom emerges from torment. For James it seems, despite isolated emotional crises, to have met the requirements of an imagination to which the creative energies and subtleties of typology were more real than type, or indeed than 'reality' itself. Put another way, the reality in brackets was largely notional – a sort of descriptive convenience. James had relocated the 'real reality' in the mind itself. George Eliot's – the 'artist's' – 'problem' was 'exquisite' because art, being *par excellence* the act of self-conscious creative perception, could reveal more about consciousness than any other activity.

But, if 'reality' was as it were a seamless mental fiction, it could not properly be reduced to its constituent parts. This conviction meant embracing organicism with a degree of commitment George Eliot could never find. To James she seemed, in a phrase he coined for Flaubert, one of 'the most conspicuous of the faithless':[79] she might image life as seamless – a web – but that availed little if one had then to know how it was 'woven and interwoven'. Better, as a famous tale of his suggests, to leave the figure in the carpet.

James's aesthetic formulations are almost gratuitous in their enchanted luxuriance. At every turn the theory is memorable, familiar, classical. A brief account will recall main features, though only a less compacted one than space allows here could do the meditative splendour of James on aesthetics anything like justice.[80]

Despite what some see as its dogmatism and its self-indulgence, James's theory is nothing if not provisional. He insists that 'The rule misleads',[81] and as a critic generally avoids 'the possible picturesqueness . . . of a high moral tone'.[82] Aesthetic problems are immensely complex. He writes in 1884,

> I am perfectly aware that to say the object of a novel is to represent life does not bring the question to a point so fine as to be uncomfortable for any one. It is of the greatest importance that there should be a very free appreciation of such a question. . . . For, after all, may not people differ infinitely as to what constitutes life – what constitutes representation?[83]

George Eliot might have read this and wished for a similarly chastened spirit of conciliation in James's appreciations of her aesthetic; certainly, as we have seen, she would have recognised the uncertainties involved; and these in fact run surprisingly deep in James's own thought. It is again a question of the neoclassical mirror. She would wish hers to be 'faithful' in reflecting the world, but finds it 'defective'. Perception is not simply passive. Just so, Balzac, James's favourite novelist, in his view gives us an imaginative gigantism that 'proceeds from . . . the very complexion of the mirror in which the [subject] material is reflected'.[84] 'Complexion', like 'defective', implies construction. But how far? Novels depend upon an 'air of reality' which is somehow tied to 'truth', the 'solidity of specification'.[85] However, take that 'air' too far and you get Zola's 'magnificent treadmill of the pigeonholed and documented'.[86] While this is impressive it is somehow uncreative and unreflective of creative consciousness itself. By contrast, the greater writers – Turgenev, Balzac – project a sort of precipitate of reality, a thing constituted as meaningful and interesting by mind. This is the 'transmuted real'[87] of James's phenomenology and it explains some of his most audacious and opaque pronouncements. If it is conceded that art is a heightened form of a general perceptual dynamism, it makes eminent sense to claim, as James did to the exasperated Wells, that art '*makes* life, makes interest, makes importance'.[88] Again: art resists the '*constant* force that makes for muddlement'.[89] 'Life' is, after all, 'all inclusion and confusion'; 'art' is 'all discrimination and selection'.[90] More of 'selection' presently. Here, and in consequence of the above: art is 'the great extension, great beyond all others, of experience and of consciousness'.[91] Literary art gives us reading which is 'experience concentrated'.[92] This image of art is profoundly idealist and it contributes to an aspect of the theory for which there is little space here: James's typology of literary kinds. Briefly, James believes that all writing may as it were issue from the mind, but that some (realism, for example) holds closer to the 'natural attitude' – social fictions about what the world is like – than others. In the other, more fanciful, direction lie 'romance', allegory and so on.[93]

The radical subjectivity of 'reality' means that 'the deepest quality of a work of art will always be the quality of the mind of the producer'.[94] George Eliot of course agrees. But James's phenomenology is again apparent in his conception of that 'quality'. It is in one sense an 'atmosphere'[95] (a favourite word), but in a deeper one what Sartre or Heidegger, for instance, would call a 'project': that is, a sort of prior choice of a mode of 'Being-in-the-World', of one's orientation and approach in life, that must inevitably be reflected in what a writer writes.[96] But James will also concede that such a project is expressed endlessly in the way we live, in the forms we choose, and that such choices – to write a novel, a drama or a biography, for instance – have powerful, if not prescriptive, moral implications. The *locus classicus* here is the famous metaphor of the 'house of fiction'. It is known to most students of the novel but nevertheless deserves to be recalled at some length:

The house of fiction has in short not one window, but a million –

a number of possible windows not to be reckoned, rather; every one of which has been pierced, or is still pierceable, in its vast front, by the need of the individual vision and by the pressure of the individual will. These apertures, of dissimilar shape and size, hang so, all together, over the human scene that we might have expected of them a greater sameness of report than we find. They are but windows at the best, mere holes in a dead wall, disconnected, perched aloft; they are not hinged doors opening straight upon life. But they have this mark of their own that at each of them stands a figure with a pair of eyes, or at least with a field-glass, which forms, again and again, for observation, a unique instrument, insuring to the person making use of it an impression distinct from every other . . . there is fortunately no saying on what, for the particular pair of eyes, the window may *not* open; 'fortunately' by reason, precisely, of this incalculability of range. The spreading field, the human scene is the 'choice of subject'; the pierced aperture . . . is the 'literary form'; but they are, singly or together, as nothing without the posted presence of the watcher – without, in other words, the consciousness of the artist. Tell me what the artist is, and I will tell you of what he has *been* conscious. Thereby I shall express to you at once his boundless freedom and his 'moral' reference.[97]

The difficulty lies in the imaginative passivity implied in the image of the watcher at the window. It is not only implausible but arguably inconsistent with the existential notion of choice that the passage elsewhere endorses. Yet here, as Paul Armstrong's excellent discussion suggests, James is in fact exploring a tenet fundamental to much phenomenology: the asserted 'positionality' of individual consciousness; that is, the subject's foredoomed but potentially freeing uniqueness of perceptual viewpoint.[98] The formal correlative of this is James's famous doctrine of the 'point of view' in fiction, of which more presently. Thus does the writer at the situated window know his 'freedom'. But some, even some of the greatest, cannot seize it. Flaubert, prophet of a non-positional impersonality, inhibits himself and his work through the 'long spasm of his too-fixed attention'.[99] This is not Eliot's 'attention'. The great leisurely, genial counter-example for James is Turgenev: a natural writer; the writer's writer.[100] And James himself? The task of bridging the impassioned prolixity of Balzac and Eliot on one hand, and the 'still-born'[101] Flaubertian art novel on the other, appealed to a temperament not unlike the one described in James's early biography of Hawthorne: one divided 'between his shyness and his desire to know something of life'; between 'his evasive and his inquisitive tendencies.'[102]

How then do temperament, vision and creativity find expression in a literary text? It has to be conceded that on this matter James is less satisfactory than George Eliot. He will contemplate 'style'[103] at inordinate length, but very rarely, so far as I can see, language in its undifferentiated communicative aspect. There is nothing like Eliot's prefigurings of Saussure's binary linguistic systematic in James. But in general his view resembles that of the one in 'Notes on Form in Art': a literary text is a particular generic emanation of a larger constitutive system. As such it is, as we have seen, structurally continuous with life, indeed a typification of the process of life-creation. This is organicist. So too is the conviction that the text's internal relations ought to be integrated: 'A novel is a living thing, all one and continuous, like any other organism, and in proportion as it lives will it be found, I think, that in each of the parts there is something of each of the other parts.'[104] Malcolm Bradbury has a character aver that he would rather lose a hand than a head – an apt reflection on what can be a lazy commonplace. In fact there are revealing moments, especially in relation to character, in which James concedes the point: 'It is a familiar truth to the novelist, at the strenuous hour, that as certain elements in any work are of the essence, so others are only of the form.'[105] The 'light *ficelle*' Henrietta Stackpole in *The Portrait of a Lady* is on his own admission a character of the 'form', not the 'essence'.[106] No doubt George Eliot knew the 'strenuous hour' in all its 'exquisite' difficulty too; and some of his concessions might have prompted James not to lay the charge of inorganicism quite so unceremoniously at her door. But the 'synthetic "whole"'[107] is no doubt a laudable ideal, if – see James on Tolstoy and Dostoevsky[108] – a seriously limiting one. John Bayley is surely right to suggest that James's notion of form, his belief in a precious 'deep-breathing economy',[109] ultimately circumscribed his achievement because it set such limits upon artistic range and suggestiveness.[110] Tolstoy is a power of another order.

A familiar Jamesian metaphor for the organicist text is the picture. The 'analogy between the art of the painter and the art of the novelist' seems in the famous essay 'The Art of Fiction' (1888) to be 'complete'.[111] This assertion will presently resurface in discussion of *The Portrait of a Lady*. Here one of its central difficulties may be noted. It implies a further analogy between words and (roughly) colours. This he will at times deny – a 'dictionary' is not 'a palette of colors' and 'a goose-quill' not 'a brush'[112] – but on the whole his incurious, or uncomprehending, attitude to words as such issues in evasive analogy with other arts. Another instance concerns Stevenson, who (according to James) 'regards literary form not simply as a code of signals, but as the key-board of a piano, and as so much plastic material'.[113] The implication seems to be that, after all, 'relations' won't entirely avail: in a novel, as in a piano, a certain expressive emotional scale or syntax is latent. The musician sets it singing; the novelist infuses it on, through and beyond the page. How? James's answer here is again visual rather than verbal, but it is fundamental to his aesthetic: the novelist, being 'a sort of phenomenologist',[114] encodes certain incomplete 'impressions' in the text which the reader, doing 'half the work', then completes out of his own experience, 'literary' and other. 'Experience', after all, 'consists of impressions'.[115] The impression, then, appears to be James's inclusive term for the sign, and it posits reading as something like the activity envisaged by Ingarden, Iser and other hermeneutic phenomenologists in which 'spots of indeterminacy'[116] present themselves for readerly co-completion. James, that is, had a 'reception theory' that, like contemporary versions, conceived of the text as a kind of quasi-potentiality. Armstrong aptly terms this James's 'teleology of the impression'.[117]

Three implications of this theory for character will be apparent, and indeed two have already been mentioned. First, it is conducive to metaphor and synecdoche as modes of characterisation rather than to metonymic inclusiveness: the writer provides a limited set of impressions and lets the reader complete them. Second, it tends to 'decentre' character: essence is as it were displaced from actor to reader. This is a tendency that James's novels both admit and resist. The third implication is ethical and just as central: if the reader is creatively completing what he reads through his own subjectivity, he is necessarily infusing it with his unique ethical sensibility. A definitive authorial or narrating perspective thereby dwindles. Character is no longer offered, as it is in Eliot, as already-ethical; ethics no longer emanate self-evidently from a stable source. The burden of judgement is upon the reader. The 'impression' is the icon of novelistic relativism. It is perhaps ironic that James should have memorably associated George Eliot's kind of narrative structure with the 'mere muffled majesty of irresponsible "authorship" '.[118] The description fits *The Golden Bowl* or *The Wings of the Dove* better than it does *Middlemarch* or *Romola*.

This, however, is consistent with a belief that 'there have been no great didactic novelists'[119] (Fielding appears to be one of few exceptions); also with the view that suppressing narrative intrusion best allows the 'appeal to incalculability'[120] that is so much a part of the phenomenology in question. But – importantly – James is not talking about the suppression of the author; *that* sort of impersonality is implausible (and indeed undesirable): 'we take for granted by the general law of fiction a primary author.'[121] Again, this is taken as read. What is in question, then, is the *management* of the omniscient third-person convention. George Eliot is not alone in attracting criticism from James in this respect. The most memorable example of all concerns Trollope's suicidal 'slaps at the credulity'[122] of the reader, the problem being that the convivial commentator fails to engage the creativity of the said meaning-constructor. Indeed, it 'takes account but of a tenth of his attributes'.[123] The problem, however, is *not* that Trollope and Eliot possess moralised imaginations. James insists that 'every out-and-out realist who provokes serious meditation may claim that he is a moralist for that, after all, is the most that the moralists can do for us'.[124] James did not approve of 'art for art'.[125] The problem is one of technique: James believes that intrusions, however wise or humane, diffuse the fictional illusion and so, paradoxically, the moral status of the very characters to whom the reader is intended to impute a life-like sense of ethical entitlement. Again, 'character' and 'narration' are profoundly and mutually implicated.

James will concede that here it is difficult 'to draw a hard and fast line on the borderland of explanation and illustration'.[126] Indeed, it would make no sense to try in a truly organic novel. Thus: 'Character, in any sense in which we can get at it, is action, and action is plot'.[127] This sublime circularity even extends to the presentation of consciousness in fiction. The partially linguisticised inner life proposed by Eliot is inverted and transformed into an externalised 'picture' or 'portrait' for exhibition: 'A psychological reason' can thus be 'an object adorably pictorial'.[128] In order to make it so the novelist needs to objectify the fiction, though within humane limits. James's predilection for dramatic form in novels is notorious (and often unfortunate). His call for narrative indirection which exhibits a response through an enmeshed or observing consciousness is equally famous and, as we shall see, artistically more rewarding. The slogans about 'lucid reflector[s]', *'ficelles'*[129] and the like need no further elaboration. It is understood that James wishes ever 'to make the presented occasion tell all its story itself'.[130]

Cutting through the terms in the novelist's 'manual' will bring the reader out at a place not so remote from George Eliot's position on character. Like her, he is against 'types',[131] for creations both 'particular' and 'general',[132] for characters of 'invention' rather than chilly 'observation'.[133] He further shares with her a predilection for seeing the 'whole person' spring 'into being',[134] but on the understanding that the reader contributes. Characters are not unlike persons, and the greatest creators of them are in the least need of the 'manual'. One of his most moving statements here concerns Trollope. If Trollope 'was a knowing psychologist he was so by grace; he was just and true without apparatus and without effort'.[135] Even more so, Balzac's creations: 'It was by loving them . . . that he knew them; it was not by knowing them that he loved.'[136] Thus does the knowledge of others proceed, for James as for Eliot, through a loving solicitude. James's catalogue of characterological terms ought not to conceal his humanism.

But occasionally the theory does, and here the politically conscious critic is needed to read back in what James leaves out. Novels are for James best focused through situated minds; those minds must therefore be privileged, gifted, interesting in order not to bore the reader.

> We care, our curiosity and our sympathy care, comparatively little for what happens to the stupid, the coarse and the blind; care for it, and for the effects of it, at the most as helping to precipitate what happens to the more deeply wondering, to the really sentient.[137]

Flaubert ought, according to James, to have borne this in mind in fashioning the trite Emma Bovary. George Eliot, as we shall see, is reckoned to have a far superior conception of her heroines. The

Flaubert judgement reflects an undeniably elitist notion of culture: if you make novels about interesting people in order to interest those who are interested in such things, you can bypass the teeming populace altogether. Here 'The Natural History of Germany Life' is a welcome corrective.

James's conception of culture resembles that of another American expatriate, T. S. Eliot. James saw in the subtle and ritualistic usages of the Old World a cultural ideal of sublime and superlative richness. As *The Portrait of a Lady* shows, James did not deny 'human nature'; nor was he blind to the existential perils of expatriation. But, as the following revealing excerpt from *Hawthorne* confirms, the process of culturation, the typology of Being Human, was an endless fascination:

> The individual counts for more, as it were, and, thanks to the absence of a variety of social types and of settled heads under which he may be easily and conveniently pigeon-holed, he is to a certain extent a wonder and a mystery. An Englishman, a Frenchman – a Frenchman above all – judges quickly, easily, from his own social standpoint, and makes an end of it. He has not that rather chilly and isolated sense of moral responsibility which is apt to visit a New Englander in such processes; and he has the advantage that his standards are fixed by the general consent of the society in which he lives.[138]

James, who thought the traditional English novel a 'veritable paradise of loose ends', opted of course for England. Was he echoing Kant's Kingdom of Ends? The thought is intriguing, for it is Isabel Archer, the 'isolated' New Englander abroad, enchantedly adrift in the sublime systematics of the Old World, who occasions one of the most chilling admissions in any humanist novel: 'I don't pretend to know what people are meant for. . . . I only know what I can do with them' (*The Portrait of a Lady*, III.22, p. 345).

3 Choice: *Daniel Deronda* and *The Portrait of a Lady*

DANIEL DERONDA

I

The concluding words of the last chapter are of course uttered by an expatriate. Like so many of James's 'Europeans', Madame Merle is in fact American. It is true that his early international novel *The American* tends to polarise Americans and Europeans, innocence and Old-Worldliness; but thereafter the famous 'international theme' blurs many such distinctions. James is clearly fascinated by the expatriate's attraction to an antecedent culture: by the way he makes it a mode for his own life, but, also, very centrally, by the *choice* involved in adopting it.

Madame Merle is one such chooser, and her chilling and ultimately tragic career in Europe epitomises the case of many a Jamesian expatriate: having sought in the Old World an implausible richness of culture and consciousness, she has arrived merely at what, after Kant, may be called the Kingdom of Means. This is the form of human community in which the value of the individual is appropriated as transactional, expedient and manipulative. Knowing what can be done with people is its ethos. In James's fiction this kingdom can and does occur virtually anywhere; indeed, its tendency to cross cultural boundaries suggests that behind its perennial patterns of occurrence, its familiar tragic plots, resides a set of generalised human tendencies that can neither safely be named nor safely be ignored. Such indeed is the finding of the second of this chapter's texts, *The Portrait of a Lady*.

Like James's novel, *Daniel Deronda* wishes to ask how far human nature is constant and given under widely divergent cultural circumstances and how far individual choices may be said to shape or give expression to human possibilities. The centrality of choice in the work is apparent at every turn. Few novels, indeed, have submitted this great *Bildungsroman* theme to more comprehensive or urgent inquiry. It is there in the novel's ubiquitous concern with election: is a man chosen, a chooser or a combination of the two? Book titles repeat it: 'Maidens Choosing', 'Gwendolen Gets Her Choice'. The word surfaces constantly in meditation and discussion. Gwendolen, pondering Grandcourt's approaches, resolves privately that 'If she chose to take this husband she would have him know that she was not going to renounce her freedom' (ii.13, p. 117). Reflecting upon Mirah and his crisis of origin Deronda asks himself, 'What did he really know about his origin?' The passage continues, 'Strangely in these latter months when it seemed right that he should exert his will in the choice of a destination, the passion of his nature had got more and more locked by this uncertainty' (v.37, p. 437). Mordecai, expatiating upon the question at a level of visionary cultural destination, argues that Jews 'have to choose that God may again choose them'; that, indeed, 'the strongest principle of growth lies in human choice' (vi.42, p. 499). No less dramatic is the extraordinary figure of Deronda's mother, Leonora. As passionately averse to Judaism as Mordecai is committed to it, she insists to Deronda that, after her long rebellion, 'I am still the same Leonora'. Pointing to her own breast she continues, 'here within me is the same desire, the same will, the same choice' (vi.51, p. 588). Other choosers are legion. Catherine Arrowpoint chooses Klesmer against parental wishes; Lapidoth, in a ghastly inversion of Mordecai's visionary faith, chooses a slow and ignominious spiritual suicide; Mirah, Hans, even the demonic Grandcourt – all choose not just circumstantial paths in life, but modes within which their lives may be lived. Then of course there is the ubiquitous motif of gambling. A later discussion may be anticipated thus: gambling is deeply and paradoxically implicated in choice: one chooses to gamble but in so doing forfeits the power of self-determination. For Gwendolen, Lapidoth or whoever, fate is then in the fall of the dice.

Choice, then, implicates almost every character in *Daniel Deronda*, but not, it would seem, coincidentally. On the contrary, George Eliot has apparently ranged before the reader a spectrum of choices and choosers in an effort to unravel the mysteries of volition and consequence. Thus Gwendolen is in the first instance

the egoistic instrumental chooser of many a *Bildungsroman*.
Deronda is rather the reverse: a selfless supplicator before a
destiny he cannot choose until his chosenness is disclosed. Like
Mordecai's, his mode of choosing is intuitive, visionary,
discontinuous with Gwendolen's 'sphere of goal-directed verbs'.[1]
Leonora, the self-proclaimed summation of a set of self-
authenticating choices, is different again. Little though she
sympathised with her, George Eliot has here fashioned a female
forerunner of Existential Man. Indeed existentialism reveals
much about George Eliot's last and great heuristic fiction, for it
has traditionally asserted the centrality of choice in the self-
shaping drama of individual growth and change.

One further chooser is sufficiently central to be easily
overlooked. If 'how write?' does in some sense entail 'how right?',
the narrator in *Deronda* comes sharply into focus: it is she who
determines what we shall know, how we shall know it, whom in
this gallery of choosers we shall know most of. This much George
Eliot concedes in declaring her purpose in writing a novel about a
minority group. She hoped to 'widen the English vision a little'.[2]
It is an undertaking also apparent in 'The Spanish Gypsy', 'The
Lifted Veil' and an important late essay, 'The Modern Hep! Hep!
Hep!' (1879),[3] other works in which Judaism figures prominently.
(Judaism and the fate of Jews is also of course an important
concern in *Romola*.)

Widening vision is another term for the 'extension of our
sympathies'. As always the question is not just what attitudes to
exemplify, but how to embed them in a narrative structure. Here
the narrator in *Deronda* shares a dilemma with its protagonist.
Having discovered his 'origins', Deronda feels that

> It was as if he had found an added soul in finding his ancestry –
> his judgment no longer wandering in the mazes of impartial
> sympathy, but choosing, with that noble partiality which is
> man's best strength, the closer fellowship that makes sympathy
> practical – exchanging that bird's-eye reasonableness which
> soars to avoid preference and loses all sense of quality, for the
> generous reasonableness of drawing shoulder to shoulder with
> men of like inheritance.   (viii.63, p. 693)

He has chosen, in other words, a mode of perception and response;
a mode of knowing. Indeed, Deronda here in a sense transcends

the dilemma that forever traps the omniscient narrator: how far ought 'impartial sympathy', a 'bird's-eye reasonableness', to figure in the 'generous reasonableness' of an avowed novelistic humanism? In strictly formal terms *Daniel Deronda*'s answer lies in a modified structure for character and narration. Narrative commentary in *Daniel Deronda* is on the whole less extended than in many of the previous works; and, correspondingly, the inner lives of characters, though in some instances given in remarkable detail, seem at times to evince an unprecedented illusion of unmediated report. Tone too can at times reflect a tougher, less accommodating narrative ambience. Indeed, here more than in any other novel George Eliot sees her doctrine of sympathy through to its unwelcome but undeniable conclusion. Sympathy, she sees, must entail a preparedness to condemn. In *Daniel Deronda*, as in no other work, George Eliot admits disapproval, denunciation, outrage as proper strategic recourses of narrative report. Nowhere else does she vilify a character through nuance and psychological notation as she vilifies Grandcourt; in no other novel does she let silence – the withdrawal of an assumed trusting narrative solicitude – so conclusively signal the limits of ethical acceptability. In all respects *Deronda* looks forward to *The Portrait of a Lady*.

Yet James's novel can seem listlessly aloof by comparison, its eerie enchantment with style, freedom and fate an 'exquisite' simulation of care. This is not an Eliotean atmosphere. At one of its many levels *Daniel Deronda* is of course a sort of epic of disenchantment with George Eliot's beloved 'Englishness', or at least with late Victorian travesties of it.[4] She does not spare the villains. But neither does she generally implicate the victims. The familiar tendency to exempt well-intentioned frailty from all but an analytic altruism is marked – indeed, almost Dickensian – in this her final novel; and this late Manicheism of course raises the much-debated question of the 'Jewish' element. It is easy to take sides here, but perhaps more helpful to ask why George Eliot should have wished to write a Jewish novel and what bearing this might have on her conception of character and choice therein.

The answers here are various and in some respects no doubt beyond reconstruction. However, certain features of George Eliot's spiritual and intellectual development are clearly decisive. Many of these are documented in William Baker's valuable *George Eliot and Judaism*.[5] A brief résumé will have to suffice here.

George Eliot's evangelical childhood gave her a deep and abiding interest in biblical Jewish history. By the age of twenty she was familiar with many images of Judaism, scriptural, historical and popular. In the early 1840s she encountered the new biblical criticism through the circle which included the Hennells and the Brays. Unlike Casaubon in *Middlemarch*, she read German and knew German scholarship. Indeed, the process that began with her learning the language in 1840 culminated in her trip to Germany with Lewes in 1854. Here she'gained, either in person or through more general cultural exposure (Lewes claimed in a letter of 1875 that 'her *direct* knowledge' of Jewish life 'has been very slight'[6]), a rare appreciation of the multifarious and troubled thing that is Judaism. They witnessed performances of Lessing; they learned of Jews who had sought to qualify or even repudiate their inheritance: Rahel Levin, apparently the model for Leonora; Heinrich Heine, a favourite writer of George Eliot and one tormented by his ethnic status; Spinoza, whose *Ethics* she translated and whose stoical defiance of institutionalised Judaism so impressed her; Strauss, the early proponent of comparative religious mythology, and the subject of another Eliot translation. Then there were exemplary models of ethnic tolerance: Mendelssohn, Goethe, Lewes himself. More generally, she absorbed the philosophical and social ambience of mid-nineteenth-century Germany: its creative greatness, but also the seeds of what it was to issue in a century later. She saw the dangers of the celebration of the *Volk* in Schlegel and drew attention to just such a danger in the great review of Riehl, 'The Natural History of German Life'. Crucially, in Hegel, Comte, Strauss and various post-Hegelians she found a historical account of religion often predicated upon the obsolescence of Judaism. Finally, there was, elsewhere and in rather a different mode, the increasing presence of genetic theory, most notably in Spencer and Darwin – a force that, as Gillian Beer suggests, profoundly shaped George Eliot's fictional explorations of racial and religious categorisation.[7]

Amongst it all there was also Feuerbach. Of the German philosopher she wrote, 'With the ideas of Feuerbach I everywhere agree'.[8] Yet he clearly caused her misgivings and it is hard to imagine her translating the violent post-Hegelian anti-Jewish polemic of *The Essence of Christianity* with complete comfort. Thus Feuerbach on Judaism: 'The principle which lies at its foundation is, however, not so much the principle of subjectivity as of egoism.'[9] An understandably hostile epistolary reaction to the jingoism of Disraeli's *Coningsby* and *Tancred* suggests a youthful ambivalence on George Eliot's part,[10] yet nothing to match Feuerbach. The truth no doubt is that she found too much of value in Feuerbach to dwell upon what were after all familiar failures of accommodation;[11] also that, amidst the dizzying diversity of her exposure to German Judaism in the 1850s, she encountered more plausible and compassionate explanations elsewhere. Nevertheless, it is clear that the unequivocal artistic commitment to Judaism that culminates in *Daniel Deronda* really only began to crystallise in the mid 1850s and early 1860s, and it may surely be the case that, however subliminally, *Deronda*, like 'The Spanish Gypsy' and 'The Modern Hep! Hep! Hep!', reflects George Eliot's struggle with a 'strong' imaginative predecessor of her own. This strand in her spiritual biography must remain largely a matter for speculation; but it would seem to have been one task of her fictional heurism to separate out the humanism from hectoring secular hell fire in Feuerbach; perhaps even in part to exorcise complicity in the offending chapters in *The Essence*. Herein may lie one source of the Manichean over-compensation so apparent to generations of readers of *Daniel Deronda*.

This, then, was the intellectual background. The historical one was just as complex. In England Jewish settlement in Palestine was under discussion. Enactments in 1858, 1866 and 1878 had removed many professional and academic restrictions on high offices, but, as George Eliot knew, especially from her friendship with the scholar Emanuel Deutsch,[12] the period leading up to *Daniel Deronda* saw an increase in anti-Semitic social and economic tensions in England. Yet, as the influx of Russian and Polish Jews during the same period indicates, things were, typically, less comfortable elsewhere.[13] Systematic oppression in Eastern Europe was commonplace; from 1873 German nationalism was on the rise under Bismarck. Age-old patterns of dispersion continued. The Western European, and especially the German, scene was, however, mixed. By 1830 Jews were in many areas enjoying unprecedented emancipation. The integrationist Reform Movement was gathering support in Germany and George Eliot would have seen a German Jewish community in a relatively emancipated form of Jewry's perennial state:[14]

integrated yet not entirely, at once culturally peripheral and creatively participant. This clearly engaged her highly spiritual socio-historical sense.

And of course her humanitarian one. The Jews in *Deronda* reflect the protean uncertainty of their condition, nineteenth-century and earlier. The narrator, in this novel a questing and devoted reconstructor of personal narratives, takes immense care over the tragic and triumphant details of dispersion. The patterns are central to an understanding of the novel. Deronda is from a long line of Sephardic Jews (parents Italian, an English grandmother of Portuguese descent, an Italian grandfather). Raised as an English gentleman, he turns to 'Zionism' under Mordecai's influence. As Gwendolen painfully discovers, assimilation thus ceases to be a serious possibility for him. Mordecai and Mirah are born in England as Cohens (a priestly class) into a paternal line of Ashkenazic Jews. Their mother is religious and has a brother who is a rabbi in Holland; their father, a Jew of Polish descent, is the quintessence of the diasporic 'phantom personality' described by Sartre: the 'over-determined' individual haunted by a psychic doubling: 'himself' and 'himself as others see him'.[15] This *Doppelgänger* status drives him into psychological dependence upon non-Jews and a kind of suicidal self-erasure. He changes the family name, wastes a good formal education and takes no interest in his religion. His personal relationships are grotesquely distorted: he exploits his children and he lives in perpetual spiritual and metaphysical exile. The most destitute of all the novel's gamblers, he has all the insecurity of Joyce's Leopold Bloom but none of the innate humanity. Mirah is very much her mother's child: a true (if idealised) daughter of Israel with an invincible loyalty to a largely undisclosed spiritual inheritance. Mordecai is more intense still. He is a visionary Jew educated in Holland and Germany and is a self-proclaimed medieval man. His tradition is 'the soul fully born within me. . . . It brought its own world – a mediaeval world' (v.40, p. 464). He rejects assimilation (a subject of close discussion), writes in Hebrew not German, and is a passionate 'Zionist'. For him Israel constitutes both a metaphysical and a physical return from exile. Daniel's mother, the Princess, is perhaps the most disturbing, certainly one of the most fascinating, Jewish portraits in the book. Born an Italian Jewess, she repudiates her religion, undergoes baptism and achieves worldly success in the larger non-Jewish community. More pointedly still, she forgoes her son and witholds knowledge of his origins from him.

Other Jewish characters – Klesmer, Charisi – are plotted with equal care, and in general the picture is one of displacement, disorientation, cultural indeterminacy and a longing for spiritual completion. *Daniel Deronda* is one of the great spiritual-quest novels: almost every central character is in some form of exile, almost all are implicated somehow in Judaism. Again, why should Judaism be so central? The answer lies partly in George Eliot's life-long exposure to Judaism; partly in the Jewish 'condition' as she found it; but also in a larger implication of the Jewish predicament. In *Daniel Deronda* George Eliot seized upon the incorrigible continuity of a spiritual tradition in dispersion. This entailed seeing the phenomenon not, of course, as exclusively Jewish, but rather as impressively central to Judaism. Moreover, it enabled her to work, as she so wished to do, at the margins of society; to inquire after the nature of self beyond the reach of cultural hegemony. What does it mean to be a Jewish individual in Christendom? (Sartre, writing in 1944, is again tragically memorable: 'Have we ever stopped to consider the intolerable situation of men condemned to live in a society that adores the God they have killed?'[16]) Which sort of cultural or religious designations, if any, reach deepest to an individual 'essence'? And so to the question Deronda must ask himself: what difference would it make to find that you were 'genetically' something other than your peers, or than your understanding hitherto?

The question goes to the heart of the novel, for it is a question about personal origin and agency and choice. What meaning can individual origin or a religious identification have in a world without a god? Is faith anything other than a designation in a system of socially given fictions? Such questions had of course haunted George Eliot since her adolescent crisis of faith. They are central to all her novels. In *Daniel Deronda*, however, the high sobriety of the earlier novels' sociological moralism yields to a sense at once more dynamic, intuitive and uncertain. This one reaches for a 'lovelier order than the actual'.[17] George Eliot had explored an extra-rational or visionary 'order' of experience in *Felix Holt*, *Romola* and 'The Lifted Veil', but in *Deronda* it is given a new freedom and confidence of expression. Similarly, the possibility of a truly momentous heroism is also here conceded for the first time in her fiction. The 'Zionistic' Daniel is exempt from the constraints that so limit other Eliot protagonists. Her understanding of human potentiality opens out remarkably in her final novel, though it is precisely here, especially in the resultant aesthetic and epistemological contradictions, that critics most often find fault with the work.

At the heart of the novel's heroic uncertainty, and of its Jewish 'element', lies the problem of teleology. It seems that in her final novel George Eliot entertains four notions of teleology (that is, of the end towards which things are presumed to be proceeding) and that their compatibility or incompatibility concerns her quite as much as the intrinsic merit of each. She begins with a now-legendary concession:

> Men can do nothing without the make-believe of a beginning. Even Science, the strict measurer, is obliged to start with a make-believe unit, and must fix on a point in the stars' unceasing journey when his sidereal clock shall pretend that time is at Nought.   (i.1, p. 3)

Thus does *Deronda* raise, even before its first paragraph, the cognate problems of narrative authority, unity and movement. If human kind is, as it appears to be, a creature in movement, towards what end is it in fact to be proceeding? One answer is that of religious supernaturalism: his life is, at least ideally, the realisation of a divine intention. In many forms this entails what may be called a teleology of ascent, the myth of a return to a divine origin. A second answer is closer to Iris Murdoch's or Alasdair MacIntyre's and, depending upon its form, it may accord with the first: the individual proceeds inward and/or outward towards an abstract, socially given 'idea of perfection'. Kant's 'ontological concept of *perfection*'[18] is here characteristic in its ethical emphasis. A third answer, which is essentially determinist and Darwinian, threatens the first two: according to this, man partakes of an open-ended adaptive typology. He has no 'origin'; he has no end; he is the incarnation of a universal process. His purpose cannot be named; the system precedes, needs and finally discharges him into anonymous genetic absolescence as the species descends through further mutations. This view Gillian Beer calls the 'teleology of descent'.[19] Finally, there is a position that more than any of the others embraces the 'make-believe of a beginning'. Let us for the moment loosely call it existential. Kant had rejected an ethical principle based on feelings, impulses and inclinations.[20] He wants a rational social teleology, a sense of ethical and communal obligation, to stand firm against sentiment. Sartre, and other existentialists in revolt against Kant, want just the reverse: a personal teleology in which movement resides in a 'self-surpassing'[21] towards some form of individual actualisation. Indeed it is here, as it were transitively, that Being for the existentialist is lodged. Taking its cue, ironically enough from Kant's individual legislator, existentialism's provisional and changeable self fashions its own subjective reality: 'Freedom . . . forces human-reality to *make itself* instead of *to be*'.[22]

We may seem to have come a long way from a simple thematic account of character and choice in *Daniel Deronda*, yet it is important to see that each of the teleological concepts just described entails, among other things, an account of choice. A teleology of ascent will often imply that individuals have been chosen for a particular destiny by a god; an ethical teleology tends to focus the onus of choice upon the individual who must make decisions in the light of social obligations. Existential choices are by contrast more individual. The self chooses in the direction of personal transformation and change. For an increasing number of George Eliot's generation, the Darwinian model superseded the supernatural Christian account. But choice was not thereby clarified. How could individuality be other than marginal or notional if persons were subject to a remorseless universal determinism? Deronda himself meets this challenge, as Darwin was at times tempted to do, by arguing in Kantian fashion that the individual will is distinct from the world of natural causality: ' "I really can't see how you arrive at that sort of certitude about changes by calling them development," said Deronda. "There will still remain the degrees of inevitableness in relation to our own will and acts . . ." ' (vi.42, p. 488). Deronda insists that people can choose, that they are not wholly determined from without. Yet George Eliot is reluctant to concede too much to the individual's power of choosing. In that direction, she fears, lies asocial existential self-assertion, a posture against which her novels repeatedly warn, though necessarily by other names. In *Daniel Deronda* the gambler is the icon of existential recklessness and self-indulgence. His is the mode of risk and ethical negligence. For Lapidoth there is no return from this state; for Gwendolen Harleth only a slow and painful one.

The Jew, then, apparently meets the requirements of George Eliot's imagination in part because he focuses problems of authority, typology and choice. More generally, he confronts the novelist, historian or social scientist with one of the most fundamental problems involved in human social report: are communities to be conceived of as genetic (or racial) continua, as collective fictional (or hermeneutic) projects, or as both? This is the nature/culture problem in another form. If biblical genealogies characteristically envisage the Jew as descended from a common genetic pool, the extraordinary plurality of Jewish precept and practice suggests something more akin to a habitual *Praxis* or an act of cultural construction, the reconstitution of culture under particular and varying historical conditions. As we shall see, George Eliot's conception of Judaism was both genetic and hermeneutic. Moreover, she saw its hermeneutic daring and energy as at once rich and reckless. The Jews had after *all* – or so she thought – chosen for themselves the ultimate plot, the definitive cultural narrative: the role of the Chosen People. But in so doing – and this further explains their appeal – they had tied risk, self-dramatisation, prophecy and a power of social transformation to a tradition of ethical severity. The narrator in *Daniel Deronda* is thus not just choosing to plot in certain ways; nor merely exhibiting certain kinds of choice and choosers; she is exploring the act of plotting itself; the sense of plottedness, moreover, in which Christianity took root. Such an undertaking may seem to render the familiar critical quarrel about the aesthetic success and integration of the 'Jewish' and 'English' elements secondary,[23] and so in some respects it is.

Typically, such questions concerned George Eliot only in so far as they had a bearing upon her larger purposes in the novel.[24] These she describes in a letter to Harriet Beecher Stowe. She wishes 'to rouse the imagination of men and women to a vision of human claims in those races of their fellow-men who most differ from them in customs and beliefs'.[25] In order so to enlist and enlarge the sympathies of the reader, however, the 'aesthetic teacher' needed the communicative refinements of art, and in *Daniel Deronda* this involves a perilous balance between an anxiously attentive narrative commentary and an often awkward typicality in the conception of character. The Jews in the novel are in this sense examples of what John Bayley calls the 'pastoral of intellect'[26] in Eliot's fiction: they are laboriously researched, carefully framed and lovingly explained, but they lack the relaxed inwardness of some of her less deliberate examples of characterisation. This much can be conceded to traditional criticisms of the novel.

Gillian Beer, however, rightly cautions against letting judgements rest there. As she argues, such assessments can tend to reinforce the assumption that *Daniel Deronda* proposes a dichotomy between 'English' and 'Jewish' elements. But this was not George Eliot's intention. The novel is in fact more about 'common sources: the common culture, story, and genetic inheritance of which the Jews and the English are two particularly strongly interconnected expressions'.[27] (Thus does George Eliot assert in 'The Modern Hep! Hep! Hep!' that 'There is more likeness than contrast between the way we English got our island and the way the Israelites got Canaan.'[28]) *Daniel Deronda* explores this commonality, asking what features and practices are internal to particular 'ethnic' groups and how far human experience may be said to traverse cultural boundaries. Hence its concern with acts of cultural transmission, with the ways in which tradition is maintained, retrieved or transformed despite the fragmenting and benighting pressures of history. Judaism is more than merely symbolic in *Daniel Deronda*, but it does symbolise a common origin, a protean survival, an appeal to sympathy that is not merely sectarian.

Daniel Deronda's concern with commonality does not however mean that George Eliot endorses naïve organicist assumptions about human societies. She writes with no expectation of a perfectly integrated community. On the contrary, she suggests that a modern society will be by historical necessity a miscellaneous thing comprising groups whose common sources may be obscured by more recent cultural disparities. Pure or radical 'Englishness' is thus a chimera, a dangerous fiction which will tend to aggravate and rationalise intolerance. George Eliot's wish, then, for 'everything in the book to be related to everything else there'[29] refers to *Daniel Deronda* as an aesthetic and thematic structure, not to its implicit sociological model. Yet these two aspects of the novel are not so easily separable and it may be that in *Daniel Deronda* George Eliot's belief in organic integration in art creates complications that she is unable to resolve. One concerns character.

In general she assumes that character – or human personality more generally – is also a miscellaneous thing; yet in *Daniel Deronda* it is at times seen as monolithic, determined by a single trait or legacy. Jewishness is the obvious example. The Jews in *Daniel Deronda* are genetically Jewish, and they seem destined to find themselves only when they align their genetic inheritance with their cultural one. Such a view, of course, has many sources and many proponents, but, as Sartre has argued in *Anti-Semite and Jew*, it also entails tremendous dangers. Sartre terms this monolithic view of self 'the spirit of synthesis':[30] it assumes that all aspects of the self cohere, that (for example) a Jew is essentially and in all respects a Jew. It is organicist. But Sartre's point in his chilling analysis of typological sadism (the book was written in the wake of Hitler) is that such an assumption is entirely congenial to the bigot. Once a Jew, always and in every respect a Jew – so the sickness runs. Sartre prefers the metaphor of the mosaic:[31] the Jew, like any other person, eludes 'universal' abstraction;[32] he is as it were assembled out of a terminal heterogeneity.[33] Substitute certain physical features and the stereotype vanishes; yet you are still left with a 'man' or a 'woman'. Precisely what this person entails in Sartre's account is not entirely clear, but it is clear that he denies a metaphysical Jewish essence; that, moreover, he sees the social typologies that so categorise selves as unacceptable fictions.[34]

Such a view would not have surprised George Eliot; indeed, despite its apparently programmatic insistence upon genetics, at another level *Daniel Deronda* profoundly questions this model of human individuality. Thus the novel contains a vein of rich semiotic inquiry which seems calculated to explore what we would not think of as the signifying practices of its ethnic and religious groups: the structures of communication and definition internal to these groups and the contradistinctions they draw between themselves and others.[35] *Deronda* concedes that religion and religious observance thus depend heavily upon codes; but it does not reconcile this understanding with its essentialist image of genetic identity.

William Baker describes the sources of George Eliot's historically specific notion of genetic Judaism in some detail. Two points are particularly pertinent here. One is that even her vast familiarity with nineteenth-century Jewish history, historiography and theological exposition (Zunz, Geiger, Jost, Sachs, Delitzsch, Munk, Graetz, Ginsburg) permitted only a limited acquaintance with her impossibly various subject. She knew most about the Judaism of medieval Spain, Renaissance Italy, and nineteenth-century Britain and Germany, and the mysticism of Eastern European communities. The second point follows. This selective exposure renders partial any account she could give. An authoritative non-fundamentalist introduction such as Louis Jacobs's *A Jewish Theology*[36] reveals the extraordinary variability of what are often taken to be cardinal 'precepts' of Judaism, and one such, which is central to *Daniel Deronda*, is the notion of choice and the 'Chosen People'.[37]

For better or for worse, George Eliot's notions of these things owe much to remote or trenchantly sectarian sources. Depending upon time, place, text and temperament the idea of the Chosen People in Judaism can entail (among other things) martyrdom, a special task, separateness, superiority. Mordecai – and so, it would seem, George Eliot – is influenced by the medieval Spanish poet and philosopher Jehuda Halevi.[38] The notion of personal choice dramatised in the relationship between Mordecai and Deronda derives initially from the medieval Kabbalistic doctrine of the transmigration of souls, according to which a soul may enter another body in its journey of reunification with its divine origin. But these are of course only two sources among many, a great number – the *Bildungsroman* choice narrative, for instance – not 'Jewish' at all, and a critical assessment of the novel needs to recognise the provisional and exploratory nature of its depiction of choice and related themes. George Eliot, after all, likened her novels to an experiment. In writing them she undertook 'a set of experiments in life – an endeavour to see what our thought and emotion may be capable of.'[39] This 'endeavour to see' is to be the novel's example to the reticent and conventionalised social 'imagination' of the reader. It forces us to ask how our categories for selves and characters function. In a sense this effort entails one so far unacknowledged displaced person in *Daniel Deronda*: the narrator herself. She too is a speculative and equivocal creation: her narrative authority is continually questioned, qualified, even undermined, as her immense effort of creative reconstruction unfolds. Narration in *Deronda* is not all-knowing. Explanations do not exhaust the complexities imaginatively offered. This is especially true of characters in the novel, and it is significant that *Daniel Deronda*'s greatest character – Gwendolen Harleth – is not Jewish.

II

The portrait of Gwendolen constitutes an extraordinary convergence of social, historical, feminist, epistemological and psychological speculation. If it owes more than any other Eliot creation to Jane Austen, it is also characteristic of George Eliot in its range of inquiry, not least its interest in the powers and limitations of language. This semiotic concern surfaces revealingly towards the end of *Daniel Deronda*. When Daniel tells Gwendolen that he is Jewish he falters: 'he could not go on easily – the distance between her ideas and his acted like a difference of native language, making him uncertain what force his words would carry' (viii.69, p. 746). Yet, typically, the 'distance' is less vast than they know. Though non-Jewish, she is metaphorically diasporic, a 'princess in exile' (i.4, p. 35). Indeed, as Gillian Beer notes, the name 'Gwendolen' includes amongst its fields of allusion a Judaic resonance. Beer also aptly describes the imaginative ambience in which Gwendolen moves: 'Anxiety is the generative emotion'.[40] Anxiety is of course a byword of existentialism from Kierkegaard to Sartre, and Gwendolen is one of fiction's great studies in existential precariousness. In a world of portent, risk and intimation she is a kind of inverted visionary: her 'dread' (i.6, p. 57), 'terror' (p. 54), 'anxiety' (v.35, p. 386) and 'world-nausea' (iii.24, p. 253) – all existential designations – are the antithesis of Mordecai's, and later Deronda's, visionary sense of destiny. Deronda urges her to make of her 'sensibility' a 'faculty' (v.36, p. 422), to give her anguish a trajectory; but it is not the trajectory of existential self-authentication. On the contrary, it involves a universalising Kantian sense of community, and is as stiflingly social as her insecurities are portentously and clearly metaphysical. Gwendolen is one of the Eliotean 'frail vessel[s]' celebrated in James's (occasionally inaccurate[41]) Preface to *The Portrait of a Lady*, and is clearly a prefiguring of Isabel Archer. In a more general sense she also anticipates the existential image of Heidegger's *Dasein*. The images of existential isolation and cosmological immensity that surround Gwendolen suggest a character 'thrown-into' 'Being'.[42] She is homeless on the 'face of earth':

> Pity that Offendene was not the home of Miss Harleth's childhood, or endeared to her by family memories! A human

life, I think, should be well rooted in some spot of a native land,
where it may get the love of tender kinship for the face of earth
. . . a spot where the definiteness of early memories may be
inwrought with affection. . . . (i.3, p. 18)

Panicked by the vast wastes of the not-self,

> Solitude in any wide sense impressed her with an undefined
> feeling of immeasurable existence aloof from her, in the midst of
> which she was helplessly incapable of asserting herself. The
> little astronomy taught her at school used sometimes to set her
> imagination at work in a way that made her tremble; but always
> when some one joined her she recovered her indifference to the
> vastness in which she seemed an exile; she found again her
> usual world in which her will was of some avail. (i.6, p. 57)

As such passages indicate, George Eliot's theme here is one
customarily associated with the modernism of Conrad, Woolf,
Ford and others: it is the terrible tenuousness of the ego, and it is
opened out with an intricacy and insight unsurpassed in this
century. Moreover, among its various implications are a number
formalised only in and beyond Freud.

George Eliot's modernity is strikingly evident in a phrase used
to intimate the range and nature of Gwendolen's insecurities. The
girl suffers from 'a large discourse of imaginative fears' (v.35,
p. 394). Theorists of narrative, especially structuralists and
post-structuralists, will note with interest the term 'discourse'.
Does it confirm their belief that the structures of consciousness are
radically social, that they encode the structures of language? It is
difficult to be certain (the usage is uncommon, both in Eliot and in
the period), but in general such an emphasis is foreign to her.
Whilst her code-rich organicism concedes a high degree of primary
linguistic ordering in the self, her general assumption is usually
that something of great importance eludes such ordering. Like Iris
Murdoch, George Eliot is a votary of 'contextual privacy', and
critics have often felt that she writes best when most under the
sway of just this assumption. Her most memorable characters –
Hetty Sorrel, Mrs Transome, Casaubon, Gwendolen herself – are
creatures of metaphor:[43] they are most powerfully suggestive
because most suggestively selective. Thus, even Gwendolen's
inner life, profuse in detail though it is, is said ultimately to be a

thing of nature (climate) which cannot be entirely charted or mapped: 'There is a great deal of unmapped country within us which would have to be taken into account in an explanation of our gusts and storms' (iii.24, p. 257).

Like the Book of Daniel, which so much impressed the young George Eliot,[44] *Daniel Deronda* is everywhere concerned with 'explanation', 'interpretation' and prophetic intuition. It is very much a novel wishing to transcend type, to reconceive the self as dynamic and mystical. Yet, as we have seen, the work is at another level stubbornly – indeed disconcertingly – typological in outlook. Thus the 'Jew' is a genetic type who is only available – mystically, intuitively – to other Jews. Can these assumptions be reconciled? The answer is surely that they cannot, but also that it is entirely characteristic of George Eliot's fictional 'experiments' that such contradictions be there. She uses fiction to revolve images of the self through various epistemological frameworks and to test their adequacy, not in order to impose a monolithic point of view. Aesthetic disunity and philosophical inconsistency are, then, aspects rather than defects of her method. Nevertheless, general tendencies in her thought can be discerned, and this is true even of her varying assumptions about the self. Let us, before considering Gwendolen in more detail, review some of these assumptions.

What in fact did George Eliot assume about the self? Very generally, she pictures it as possessing a genetic essence which interacts intricately, instinctively and integratively with culturally specific conditions. There are any number of sources for this view, but two strands appear especially germane to such a novel as *Deronda*. One goes back to Feuerbach's essentially special account in *The Essence of Christianity*, where the self is conceived of as a kind of inchoate universal potential, encoded to actualise itself through interaction with others. George Eliot seems never to have entirely abandoned her 'agreement' with Feuerbach in this:

In another I first have the consciousness of humanity; through him I first learn, I first feel, that I am a man: in my love for him it is first clear to me that he belongs to me and I to him, that we two cannot be without each other, that only community constitutes humanity. But morally, also, there is a qualitative, critical distinction between the *I* and *thou*. My fellow-man is my objective conscience . . .[45]

Three important points emerge here. First, the image of self involved is essentially dialectical: according to it, an anonymous pre-social substance finds, defines and refines itself through social interaction. A second follows. Social relationships subsume experiences formerly associated with supernatural revelation. There is no transcendental being; 'God' is in other people and the divine 'essence' of Christianity is the 'thou' of one's fellow beings. Finally, and in consequence, human teleological structures are conceived as intrinsically *social*, other-directed. So too are ethical ones, for 'conscience' is only produced through interaction with others. Though immensely influential for George Eliot's fiction, this account raises problems that such a novel as *Daniel Deronda* seems intent upon probing. One is descriptive or methodological. Ought that pre-social and nameless substance be named (human nature?) and, as it were, calculated into accounts of the human subject? Another is experiential. Does Feuerbach's humanist denial of a transcendental being leave open a sufficient relational range and richness to the individual? Her answers vary. *Adam Bede* urges that relationships with others are an adequate, and indeed the ultimate, form of spiritual experience. *Daniel Deronda* agrees in seeing the self as substantial and knowable through loving intersubjectivity, but it also asserts the possibility, at times even the necessity, of relationship with a transcendent being. Other people are deeply implicated in achieving such a relationship, but they do not constitute an experiential limit.

Feuerbach's I–Thou structure looks forward to such a writer as Martin Buber. (Indeed, we shall see that this is no mere coincidence.) A second strand in George Eliot's theorising about the self owes much to contemporary organicist psychological speculation, not least to the work of George Henry Lewes. As Sally Shuttleworth suggests, Lewes denies both the logical priority and the Cartesian separation of consciousness: 'In any positive meaning of the term, that [Thinking] Principle is not an antecedent but a resultant, not an entity but a convergence of manifold activities'.[46] This thoroughgoing organicism apparently implies the lack of a conscious co-ordinating psychic principle such as that proposed in Freud's work prior to 1919. Consciousness 'is not an agent but a symptom';[47] mind constitutes 'the activities of the whole organism in correspondence with a physical and social medium'.[48] Something like the unconscious is, then, being proposed: we live, according to Lewes,

Dallis and perhaps George Eliot herself, in an unacknowledging assimilative dynamism. This in turn suggests – and here the anticipations of Freud recede – an innate and unchartable heterogeneity in the mind. The organism in movement ultimately eludes the methodological structures we propose for it. Neither Freud's understanding of the unconscious as language-like, nor Lacan's as linguisticised, will suffice for the 'gusts and storms' of such a mind as Gwendolen's. This must remain, finally, an 'unmapped country'.

But how typical is Gwendolen's mind? It would seem that it coincides only in part with the self as pictured by Lewes; also, and importantly, that it diverges still more markedly from some of the alternative images of the self that are dramatised through other characters. Even here, however, it is difficult to generalise, for Gwendolen is not a philosophically consistent creation and her personal narrative seems to urge deeply incompatible conclusions about choice and its existential consequences.

Again, one reason for this lies in the extraordinary convergence of assumption and modes of appraisal that make up the portrait. The *Bildungsroman* pattern is clear enough; indeed, it is managed with remarkable power and precision. At the outset Gwendolen is the classic manipulative solipsist. She has an 'inborn energy of egoistic desire' (i.4, p. 36) and a 'decision of will' (p. 35) that tends to command respect: 'her usual world' is one 'in which her will was of some avail' (i.6, p. 57). Moreover, like many of James's heroines, she has a naïve and cerebral concept of freedom: 'her horizon was that of the genteel romance' (p. 47). This 'horizon' does not permit her to see the paradox of her youthful condition. Gwendolen is a study in the presumptive energies of individualising choice. She is unable to see soon enough that such energies entail a psychological dependence upon precisely those whom she would wish to master. That determination that, 'if she chose to take this husband [Grandcourt], she would have him know that she was not going to renounce her freedom' (ii.13, p. 117), identifies her as the master in something like Hegel's master–slave relationship. She is bound precisely because she thinks herself unconditionally free and dominant; also, of course, because she is young and ignorant. In a marginal addition to the manuscript of the novel George Eliot writes with reference to Grandcourt and Lush that Gwendolen 'had no sense that these men were dark enigmas to her' (ii.11, p. 109). Thus do the familiar Eliot–James abstractions of 'freedom', 'will', 'choice' and 'knowledge' converge.

Gwendolen of course has a choice of a kind that often arises in Eliot's fiction. Lydia Glasher's revelation confronts her with a choice between acting 'with a force of impulse against which all questioning was no more than a voice against a torrent' or from a 'dread of wrong-doing' that combines an unformulated sympathy for the fate of another ('another woman's calamity thrust close on her vision') and an equally unformulated sense of universal moral propriety:

> Whatever was accepted as consistent with being a lady she had no scruple about; but from the dim region of what was called disgraceful, wrong, guilty, she shrank with mingled pride and terror; and even apart from shame, her feeling would have made her place any deliberate injury of another in the region of guilt.   (iii.27, p. 275)

These 'regions' are a sort of primitive ethical demarcation in the immature soul, but Gwendolen chooses to interpret the choice she faces in a way that subtly (and somewhat ambiguously) blurs the moral issue. She concludes that choosing to refuse Grandcourt would be a capitulation to passion, to the elemental, natural, torrential romantic individualist within her. Yet accepting him is equally problematic, since it involves a capitulation to conventional restraint, to 'the region of guilt'. What is at issue is the nature of moral convention and of Gwendolen's adherence to it. Doing what is 'consistent with being a lady' is inauthentic, yet so in another way is a denial of Lydia's claims upon her.

An existential reading of *Daniel Deronda* would suggest that the marital choice here presented is in a sense secondary. The more important one is a sort of prior choice in which Gwendolen has elected to live in a mode of manipulative conventionality. Sartre's existential psychoanalysis addresses itself to a 'fundamental' 'choice of being'[49] which informs particular (and often self-defeating) choices that the individual makes. For Sartre, it is 'not possible not to choose':[50] each life has a mode. But fundamental choices can be amended; inauthenticity can be overturned; the self can seize its freedom through a daring and decisive determination to choose. According to Sartre, however, this means repudiating Kant's categorical imperative: 'So every man ought to say, "Am I really a man who has a right to act in such a manner that humanity regulates itself by what I do." If a man does not say that, he is dissembling his anguish.'[51] Significantly, Sartre sees Maggie Tulliver's passionate choice of Stephen Guest in *The Mill on the Floss* as an expression of just this kind of rebellious intensity.[52]

Gwendolen, however, is described as dissembling her anguish, and she does so in this instance by persuading herself that a rational moral response to Grandcourt's proposal – rejecting him in favour of what we should think of as a Kantian view of Lydia's entitlements – is in fact irrational. She is here in what the existentialists call bad faith: she is rationalising her motives in order to support the utterly conventional choice she eventually makes. She accepts him, though the choice lacks both passion and propriety, and it requires all the ingenuity of her 'constructive imagination' (iii.27, p. 275) to do it. Here is the moment during which she emotionally capitulates to Grandcourt:

> The little pauses and refined drawlings with which this speech was uttered, gave time for Gwendolen to go through the dream of a life. As the words penetrated her, they had the effect of a draught of wine, which suddenly makes all things easier, desirable things not so wrong, and people in general less disagreeable. She had a momentary phantasmal love for this man who chose his words so well, and who was a mere incarnation of delicate homage. Repugnance, dread, scruples – these were dim as remembered pains, while she was already tasting relief under the immediate pain of hope-lessness. (p. 279)

This, one of the great evocations of bad faith in George Eliot, bristles with implication. The 'words' which Grandcourt 'chose so well' have 'penetrated' her childish consciousness. The passage describes the first phase of a psychic rape. Grandcourt's choice is a species of typological sadism, indeed the most common form of all – man mastering woman – but it is skilfully concealed. The 'absence of all eagerness in his attentions to her' (ii.11, p. 106), the 'refined drawlings' of his bogus diffidence, suggest that she retains mastery. But of course she is being mastered and the choice is Grandcourt's, his deadly conventionality enabling him to exploit both her derivative desires and the social embarrassments that have befallen her family. In this 'dream state' her potentially salving faculty for 'dread' deserts her.

It is Deronda who revives it. His view is that we should 'use of our choice' (v.35, p. 388); that few decisions are spiritually irreversible (though the famous Eliotean Nemesis theme suggests they may be circumstantially so); that Gwendolen ought to press her dread into ethical service. 'We are not always in a state of strong emotion', he tells her:

> 'Take your fear as a safeguard. It is like quickness of hearing. It may make consequences passionately present to you. Try to take hold of your sensibility, and use it as if it were a faculty, like vision.' Deronda uttered each sentence more urgently; he felt as if he were seizing a faint chance of rescuing her from some indefinite danger. (v.36, p. 423)

That vision of 'consequences' is essentially (though again, only roughly) Kantian, even if 'passionately' is not. Deronda is taking George Eliot's line. And so ultimately, of course, does Gwendolen, though, of all George Eliot's pedagogical[53] relationships, hers with Deronda is the most charged with tension, ambivalence and unacknowledged sexual intensity. Daniel becomes a super-ego figure for Gwendolen and she begins increasingly 'to see all her acts through the impression they would make on Deronda' (vii.54, p. 627). While Freud believed the super-ego's action to be increasingly gratuitous as the individual develops, Deronda's influence over Gwendolen becomes progressively more rational and it combines with Grandcourt's providential drowning to present her with the chance for a second choice. Bereft of her now consciously Jewish mentor, she passionately assures her mother that 'I shall live. I shall be better' (viii.69, p. 751).

Sartre insists that 'Life is nothing until it is lived',[54] but most readings of the latter stages of *Daniel Deronda* will concede that this is not quite what George Eliot has in mind. Precisely what she does have in mind, however, is arguably – indeed, it may be deliberately – unclear. Deronda's exemplary selflessness, his capacity for the 'transmutation of self' (v.37, p. 435), is supposed to have elicited in the erring heroine a will to change, to exercise particular choices within a mode of revealed and chosen altruism. Does this square with George Eliot's general assumptions about choice? Her position here is well known[55] and would suggest that

Gwendolen now possesses a circumstantially circumscribed, but still ethically significant, margin of choice. The position is summed up in *Middlemarch*: 'We are on a perilous margin when we begin to look passively at our future selves, and see our own figures led with dull consent into insipid misdoing and shabby achievement' (III.69, p. 384); it is there in the earnest refutations of 'necessitarianism' penned for George Eliot's anxious correspondent Mrs Ponsonby: she urges 'willing to will strongly',[56] denies 'a hideous fatalism',[57] and insists that life perceived as a structure of 'necessary combinations' need not, *must* not, 'petrify your volition'.[58] In a rather different key, she writes in an important letter to Charles Bray that,

> In the fundamental doctrine of your book [*The Philosophy of Necessity*] – that mind presents itself under the same condition of invariableness of antecedent and consequent as all other phenomena (the only difference being that the true antecedent and consequent are proportionately difficult to discover as the phenomena are more complex) – I think you know that I agree.[59]

Such early statements gradually modulate into a Kantian belief in the autonomy of the will. She believes that will supervenes in a vast causal system (natural, social, genetic, historical) and constitutes itself as a limited rational cause. It is of obvious significance for the evolution of the English novel that this position was designated 'soft determinism' by William James,[60] brother of Henry. What are the implications of this view for the 'frail vessel' that is Gwendolen Harleth?

The most glaring and disturbing one is that she appears to be constrained by precisely the kind of earlier formulation that *Daniel Deronda* seeks to transcend. Daniel finds a mystical path to plenitude; Gwendolen must, like so many Eliotean questers before her, accept the 'middle-way' ('middlingness' – v.35, p. 383). Yet the novel does not embrace this solution without a good deal of creative contradiction, and S. L. Goldberg is surely right to find in its commentary clashing orders of valuation. Goldberg argues that Gwendolen is assessed by and in terms both of a 'conduct-morality'[61] and 'the morality of "life" '.[62] The first might roughly be termed Kantian; the second (again roughly) existential. Though a highly conscious thematic exploration of choice is apparent in many of the personal plots so far discussed, Goldberg has surely hit upon important unconscious conflicts that are embedded in George Eliot's narrative structure and assumptions. Some of these correspond to the 'moral judgments' Alasdair MacIntyre believes to be 'linguistic survivals' from earlier periods,[63] and they further confirm his belief that modernity has enmeshed the self in a hopeless plurality of evaluative norms. Certainly, the portrait of Gwendolen is characterised by contradiction and jostling orders of appraisal. The resultant narrative tensions present character as almost insolubly complex.

The fields of allusion surrounding Gwendolen indicate just how complex a creation she is. They are as various as the New Testament, Greek tragedy, Arthurian legend; even, as we shall see, the Kabbalah. If ever a novel defied adequate synthetic reconstruction from 'sources', it is this one. However, it is clear that Gwendolen is described from at least three perspectives. One, which might loosely be termed Freudian, is patently diagnostic. George Eliot uses a characteristically unsubtle flash-back technique to account for certain conditioned structures of assumption and response in her heroine. Hence episodes studiously recalling the strangling of a canary, youthful inattendance upon the girls' sick mother and importunate questions about the parental marriage (i.3, p. 20). More pointedly 'Freudian' is the sexual detail that is so reminiscent of the descriptions of Isabel Archer in *The Portrait of a Lady*. As Rex discovers, Gwendolen has 'a certain fierceness of maidenhood in her'; 'a sort of physical repulsion, to being directly made love to' (i.7, p. 63). She feels 'passionately averse' to Rex's 'volunteered love' (p. 73), and prefers the 'absence of eagerness' in Grandcourt's 'mere incarnation of delicate homage' (iii.27, p. 279). Wondering at this, the post-Freudian reader receives a recognisable explanation: 'the life of passion had begun negatively in her' (i.7, p. 73). It seems that Gwendolen's early emotional identification with her parents has been impaired (her father is all but absent, of course) and that this has inhibited the formation of adult emotional structures. In this novel, as in James's, sexuality serves as a form of existential notation, and it is teasingly poised between metaphor and metonymy in representing various aspects of the relational will. Moreover, Gwendolen has an 'under-consciousness' (iv.31, p. 327) that haunts her acknowledging self: masochistic and grandiose fantasies exert a gratuitous pressure on her consciousness, generating that form of 'dread' that Freud termed 'guilt'. Before considering George Eliot's technique for rendering such veiled insecurities, a second perspective is worth noting, and this involves the novel's rather censorious presentation of gambling and the ethos of self-dramatising risk.

We know that one source for Gwendolen was Byron's grand-niece, an addicted gambler described in an appalled George Eliot letter.[64] K. M. Newton is surely right to emphasise the connection. Gwendolen is indeed an instance of the 'egotistic' Byronic romanticism he finds in Eliot's fiction.[65] We first meet her (through Deronda) at the gaming-table, depositing her stake with 'an air of firm choice' (i.1, p. 5). That 'choice' is, however, deceptive: it is desperate and despairing and George Eliot profoundly disapproves of it.[66] Here again the existential view provides a revealing contrast. According to the anti-organicist Sartre, what keeps the gambler going is a 'permanent rupture in determinism'.[67] Because the self is a sequence of quasi-discreet choices, yesterday's decision to stop exerts no real pressure upon the present. George Eliot takes a less sanguine organicist view: gambling is the expression of a cumulative ethical negligence. It has a history in the individual's past; it is damaging to self and other; and it substitutes the speculative teleology of sated desire for the proper social completions of the rational will.[68] All of Gwendolen's early life goes on in this mode. Marrying Grandcourt is a 'great gambling loss' (v.36, p. 411) from which only the providential contingency of his drowning can ultimately deliver her. Hence Deronda's disapproval, 'terrible-browed angel' (vii.54, p. 627) that he is.

Gambling, then, is the novel's negative example of choosing and it is roundly condemned. Less confident, however, is the work's treatment of its central themes concerning essence, relation and system, genetics and typology. Gillian Beer notes that Gwendolen resembles other Eliot heroines (Romola, Dorothea) in exercising an essentially negative genetic prerogative. She has no children.[69] But beyond this her place in the novel's descriptive and evaluative framework is unclear, perhaps unsatisfactory. Beer believes that the ending is optimistically inconclusive. Gwendolen finally externalises her destructive fantasies during the drowning episode[70] and faces a future in which choices need not necessarily be circumscribed: 'At the end of the book she remains, isolated, unpredictable, entering the indeterminate future, in which not all choices are constrained and mapped.'[71] This indeed seems to be the implication of the quotation from Shakespeare given at the beginning of Chapter 53: 'My desolation does begin to make / A better life'. But it is the *kind* of 'life' once again that is in question. Is it really so 'unpredictable' as Gillian Beer's appealing reading would suggest, or has Gwendolen been confined to that platitudinous, constricting, life of compromise that awaits Dorothea, Romola and (had she lived) Maggie Tulliver? The proposed 'unpredictability' is perhaps more characteristic of James; the horizon of Gwendolen's future would seem to be limitingly social. It is the interminable moral vigilance urged in Deronda's pedagogic blueprint. If so, Gwendolen is doubly a loser in the risky business of essence, gene and typology. Her (allegedly) trivial attempt to exercise femininity as a form of self-assertion has failed. She is left with a confining experience of womanhood in which convention and self-construction supposedly coincide. George Eliot apparently believes her now to be in good faith. Sartre would disagree.[72] What is more, Gwendolen must be content with a static concept of her self as genetic core whilst her mentor Deronda enters an altogether different world in which self is dynamic and destined. Unlike Gwendolen's, his soul proceeds towards a source apparently unavailable to Victorian, Christian womanhood.

This is the novel's version of the teleology of ascent. Deronda proceeds towards a transcendental relation. As Robert Preyer has argued, George Eliot's fiction here moves 'beyond the liberal imagination';[73] ultimately, perhaps, beyond the ethical humanism of her earlier novels. Deronda's journey to the East is what no phase of Gwendolen's life can ever be: it is a self-sacrificing risk underwritten by a god. At best Gwendolen must settle for what the existentialists call 'situated freedom', for a sense of freedom that depends upon the experience of limitation. According to Sartre, 'the paradox of freedom' resides in there being 'freedom only in a *situation*'.[74] Quite so, but Gwendolen's 'situation' apparently permits none of the questing self-transformation available to Sartrean man.

Not surprisingly, *Daniel Deronda*'s evaluative and philosophical confusions are reflected in its narrative techniques. In the case of Gwendolen, these apparently seek at once to liberate and to 'map' character. Henry James sensed the tension and gave it definitive expression. In '*Daniel Deronda*: A Conversation' Constantius says that in gaining knowledge Gwendolen's mind is made to 'ache with the pain of the process', and it is indeed just this conflict between a formulaic sense of destiny and a feeling of psychic lawlessness that infuses the depiction of this heroine. At best something like Lewes's unchartable 'symptomatic' unconscious is powerfully suggested, but the novel's narrative commentary constantly seeks to assert the claims of process. And here an ironic but characteristic feature of George Eliot's creative greatness emerges. Character in *Daniel Deronda* is most suggestive where its dramatic and metaphoric selectiveness elude the claims of the generalising narrative commentary.

The novel's corrective and comprehensive analysis of character will be familiar to all readers of the commentary in *Daniel Deronda*: 'Surely a young creature is pitiable who has the labyrinth of life before her and no clue' (iii.24, p. 254). As Barbara Hardy has demonstrated, this is but one tone among many. It is also the least suggestive. A reading of Gwendolen might close on what is by contrast perhaps the most suggestive method of all: George Eliot's use of narrated monologue* to render the 'unmapped country' of her heroine's mind.[75] One instance – Gwendolen's capitulation to Grandcourt – has been cited; another occurs after Grandcourt has cut Lydia Glasher at Rotten Row. The young woman is consumed by the feelings of hopelessness:

> No! she foresaw him always living, and her own life dominated by him; the 'always' of her young experience not stretching beyond the few immediate years that seemed immeasurably long with her passionate weariness. The thought of his dying would not subsist: it turned as with a dream-change into the terror that she should die with his throttling fingers on her neck avenging that thought. Fantasies moved within her like ghosts, making no break in her more acknowledged consciousness and finding no obstruction in it: dark rays doing their work invisibly in the broad light.   (vi.48, p. 564)

Here an elliptical rendering of consciousness and the cognisance of the commenting narrator interweave. The first clause is given in

---

* I use the term as it is defined by Dorrit Cohn. It refers to a technique whereby the consciousness of a character is given in the guise of the narrative discourse.

narrated monologue, something approaching the fictional idiom of the character: 'No! she foresaw him always living . . .'; but 'the "always" of her young experience' announces the evaluative perspective of external report. Words such as 'subsist' are again clearly extrinsic to character; but in the final sentence the externality of appraisal merges with Gwendolen's appalled subjectivity: 'Fantasies moved within her like ghosts, making no break in her more acknowledged consciousness and finding no obstruction in it. . . .' Psychological realism aspires here to the 'contextual privacy' of self 'known' both contextually and empathetically. George Eliot here finds an 'appropriate form' for a traumatically dissociated state. Freud, who so admired *Middlemarch* and *Daniel Deronda*,[76] might have seen here the evidence for the unconscious he often sought in literature.

III

'Character . . . is a process and an unfolding' – the formulation from *Middlemarch* with which this study begins no doubt reflects the tensions James had in mind when he wrote that Gwendolen was made to 'ache with the pain of the process'. For, if 'unfolding' suggests that character is fluid and unpredictable, 'process' implies that, at some level, it moves in, or is to be understood according to, a pattern. In fact, the 'real complex human being' of George Eliot's aesthetic seems at once to embody and to elude such patterns, to both mirror and subvert strategies for understanding individuals. In *The Portrait of a Lady* Henry James was to term these strategies 'the categories of the human appeal' (III.6, p. 221). The phrase is deeply paradoxical: it suggests a gap between the unmediated impact other selves make upon us (their 'appeal'), and the 'categories' society gives us for making sense of them.

An Eliot or James novel will often simulate this paradox. Even as *Daniel Deronda*, for example, sets given social limits upon the romantic freedoms Gwendolen can have and upon our conception of her, it attempts to liberate her as an aesthetic creation, to make the reader feel that she possesses a margin of self that neither social 'categories', nor the aesthetic structures that constitute her, can entirely rationalise. George Eliot's humanist novel needs, it seems, to confer an illusion of freedom and depth upon character in order to make its theme of necessary social limitation and definition appear continuous with the reader's extra-literary experience. This paradox will require further discussion, but let us for the moment consider the interplay between freedom and constraint in two other of *Daniel Deronda*'s characters: the Princess Leonora and Daniel himself.

The Princess reads now as a kind of existential prototype. She seizes the freedoms Gwendolen cannot have, repudiating motherhood for art, Judaism for Christianity, duty for personal authenticity, tradition for a more personalised sense of destiny. This is an act of heroic self-construction that George Eliot cannot ultimately countenance, and it is significant that she uses a notion of racial essence to punish it. Having denied a genetic core that is female (maternal) and Jewish, the Princess is dying the proper death of moral melodrama: her cancer is an agent of organic retribution, destroying the genetic self she had sought to deny. Or rather *chosen* to deny: 'I am still the same Leonora . . . here within me is the same desire, the same will, the same choice', she insists. But what has the 'choice' been about?

> 'Oh – the reasons of our actions!' said the Princess, with a ring of something like sarcastic scorn. 'When you are as old as I am, it will not seem so simple a question – "Why did you do this?" People talk of their motives in a cut and dried way. Every woman is supposed to have the same set of motives, or else to be a monster. I am not a monster, but I have not felt exactly what other women feel – or say they feel, for fear of being thought unlike others.'   (vii.51, p. 586)

The emphasis here on self-shaping 'actions' is familiarly existential. Again, in not feeling thus 'for fear of being thought unlike others' she chooses to reinterpret her given self in a way not sanctioned by the social categories for understanding others upon which George Eliot here depends. The Princess possesses an essence which she wishes to transform through choice and action. The famous Sartrean existential slogan, 'existence comes before essence',[77] seems apt for this tortured and portentous woman. Like Gwendolen, Leonora has 'wanted to live a large life, with freedom to do what everyone else did' (p. 588), 'everyone else' here being non-Jews; but, unlike Gwendolen, she has seen her choices through. According to George Eliot, two tragic consequences follow. One is that Leonora, having repudiated a self-defining tradition, has liquidated her character into a series of discontinuous, self-conscious roles.

> The speech [to Deronda] was in fact a piece of what may be called sincere acting: this woman's nature was one in which all feeling – and all the more when it was tragic as well as real – immediately became matter of conscious representation: experience immediately passed into drama, and she acted her own emotions.　(p. 586)

This is the 'sincerity' whose transformation to a more radical 'sincerity' Lionel Trilling charts in *Sincerity and Authenticity*.[78] Well may feminist critics such as Gillian Beer find in this portrait 'a thrillingly sustained argument for the right of a woman to vary in motives, passions, needs, and not to subserve always the assumptions of society or the demands of race and inheritance: the stories of her culture'.[79] But Beer's verb is equivocal. In what sense can it be said that George Eliot 'advances' such an 'argument'? Not, it would seem, to endorse it. She attributes to the Princess a torment also attributed to Latimer, the blighted visionary of 'The Lifted Veil': a 'double consciousness' (p. 586); but this is apparently not the existential bad faith that may ultimately issue in authenticity. Heidegger believes that 'anxiety individualizes',[80] but in neither Gwendolen's nor Leonora's case is it ultimately permitted to do so. One is overpowered by a conventionalised understanding of womanhood; the other, having chosen to deny it, by the irrefusable genetic Jewish identity that, as it were, names her from within. As George Eliot sees it, the tragic consequence is that the dying mother is somehow compelled by a logic of genetic retribution to pass on to her son the genetic truth of his own identity: 'I am forced to be withered, to feel pain, to be dying slowly. Do I love that? Well, I have been forced to obey my dead father. I have been forced to tell you that you are a Jew, and deliver to you what he commanded me to deliver' (p. 588). She has, then, no choice in the matter; but the 'tragedy' is that she can only now pass on to Deronda a designation: the 'incarnate history' of Judaism, the transmission of cultural practice from person to person, may in George Eliot's view connect essence and typology, self and culture. Leonora's choice, however, has precluded this sacred entitlement. Daniel must seek the emotional riches of his rightful inheritance elsewhere. He turns to Mordecai, a man who has chosen Judaism. Indeed, a man who has chosen it to the exclusion of almost everything else.

IV

Among George Eliot's many fictional 'experiments' the Princess Leonora is surely one of the most revealing, for Eliot has here apparently fashioned a critique of the romantic essentialist image of self that informs most of her novels. It is an image that has been anathema to existentialism. Sartre terms it 'the ontological mirage of self',[81] and Heidegger (in rebuttal of Descartes and Kant) 'the ontical priority of the isolated subject'.[82] The self so conceived cannot, they believe, effect its own transformations. Yet the portrait of the Princess pulls up well short of the 'divine absence'[83] Sartre associates with existentialism's alternative image of the individual. Having granted the Princess a hypothetical freedom to choose and change, George Eliot visits upon her a retributive genetic radicalism. For reasons that no doubt ran deep in her own life and psychology, Eliot could not here concede the freedoms she has imagined.

Deronda is intended as the charismatic counter-example. The point and extent of the proposed contrast between him and his mother is apparent in the many passages about his origins, motivation and his capacity to choose:

> Might there not come a disclosure which would hold the missing determination of his course? What did he really know about his origin? Strangely in these latter months when it seemed right that he should exert his will in the choice of a destination, the passion of his nature had got more and more locked by this uncertainty. The disclosure might bring its pain, indeed the likelihood seemed to him to be all on that side; but if it helped him to make his life a sequence which would take the form of duty – if it saved him from having to make an arbitrary selection where he felt no preponderance of desire?
>
> (v.37, p. 437)

The uncommitted Deronda here described resembles the figure of Clennam in the early stages of Dickens's *Little Dorrit*. In both characters the ethical will is strong,[84] yet each is paradoxically excluded from wholly committed action by the past. Each man intuitively knows himself to be the issue of a concealed origin. Clennam is racked with guilt; Deronda experiences an anxious, expectant passivity. His mother has chosen out of egoistic 'passion'; his instinct is to wait and to align 'passion' with 'duty'. This way, the novel asserts, lies true heroism. Deronda does not have to settle for the 'unhistoric acts' (III, Finale, p. 465) of *Middlemarch*; nor does he actively have to choose in the first instance. His fate is that of Zarca in 'The Spanish Gypsy': 'I choose not – I *am* Zarca' (p. 146). Like the gypsies of the poem, he partakes 'Of heritage as inevitable as birth' (p. 145); indeed of a 'heritage' that is radically continuous with 'birth'. His calling is at one and the same time that of tradition and of heredity. He is George Eliot's quintessential Jew.

Like Gwendolen, Deronda is many things by implication: a Moses or Christ figure; a biblical prophet; a Jewish Messiah; a quester from the world of medieval romance; a Kabbalistic journeyer. He is also the embodiment of that sympathetic and self-effacing receptiveness so dear to George Eliot's moral idealism. The narrator asserts that the evolving individual eventually attains a state in which 'our self is a not-self' (iv.22, p. 349), and Deronda, who desires a 'choice that might come from a free growth' (ii.16, p. 164), achieves precisely the sympathetic capacity that George Eliot had found so appealing in Feuerbach's conception of human relationships. But this exemplary status can pall. Deronda enjoys a kind of enchanted loving accompaniment in the narrative. Thus we are told that 'there was hardly a delicacy of feeling this lad was not capable of' (p. 153). This prompts reservations. One is, superficially at least, a matter of 'technique': neither Deronda nor the other Jewish characters are depicted in the powerfully suggestive combination of psychonarration* and narrated monologue that is used for Gwendolen. These portraits rely more heavily upon self-revelation through dialogue (Mirah, for example) or the kind of stilted inner report quoted above, where a stylised psychonarration predominates. Interior views of

---

* Again Cohn's term. I mean by it the narrator's discourse about a character's consciousness.

other Jews are seldom given; Deronda's are extensive but anxiously and intrusively orchestrated.

But a problem in technique is seldom merely that; it generally reflects a deeper unease. In *Daniel Deronda* unease arises from the choice to write about Jews, not just in the obvious sense that they are unfamiliar, but in a more specifically philosophical one. George Eliot's Judaism dramatises a Kabbalistic neoplatonism which conceives of the self as centred, present, substantial and teleological: its genetic Jewish core entails its proceeding either towards or away from its transcendental source. Deronda thus has a soul and the privilege of a radical designation. 'Jew' accounts for his being with a completeness that the designation 'woman' cannot have for Gwendolen and Leonora. Self, code, tradition and type coincide in Deronda, Mirah and Mordecai. A beneficent typology compensates for the wrath of history.

William Baker reviews many of the sources for this genetic mysticism. One he does not mention appears only by ironic implication: having translated a work in which the 'essence of Christianity' – that is, of man – was actually predicated upon the excrescence of Judaism, George Eliot now reverses the Feuerbachian scheme and contemplates a sublime and superior separateness for the Jewish soul. She may have derived this idea from many places but two obviously influenced it. One was the medieval Spanish Jewish poet and philosopher Halevi, whose notion of election 'intensifies the distinctiveness of Israel by ascribing a specific religious faculty lacking in all other nations'.[85] The depiction and disquisitions of Mordecai are redolent with allusion to Halevi. A second source is the Kabbalah, a tradition recently revived for an ecumenical criticism by Harold Bloom, especially in *Kabbalah and Criticism* and *The Breaking of the Vessels*. Bloom offers a selective review of this vast and varied tradition in *Kabbalah and Criticism*, but this is by his own admission largely drawn from Gershom Scholem's famous account in the *Encyclopaedia Judaica*,[86] probably the best scholarly introduction for the general reader.

Scholem concedes that he is tracing not a unitary tradition but rather 'a multiplicity of different approaches', and he charts these in great detail. Two strains are generally recognised: a 'practical school', mystical and magical in emphasis, deriving initially from ninth-century German Judaism; and a 'speculative', more systematically philosophical, one with roots in twelfth-century

Franco-Spanish culture. It is to the latter tradition, especially to the so-called 'Lurianic Kabbalah', that the portraits of Mordecai and Deronda owe their principle allegiance. Several fundamental implications for *Daniel Deronda* may be suggested here. First, the Lurianic Kabbalah assumes a kind of postlapsarian 'human condition'; again, it pictures the self as teleological, proceeding towards or away from its divine source; further, its concept of the self is essentialist: the self possesses a mystical 'soul' that is teleologically destined either for reunion or for separation. This destiny determines a certain narrative and ethical structure for earthly life: duty, tradition and transmission are its hallmarks. Significantly, this Kabbalistic tradition proposes what deconstruction terms a 'logocentric' view of language: divine intention is immanent in words and finds appropriate expression in symbolism and symbol systems. Finally, the world vision offered is essentially Manichean: good is the path of teleological ascent; evil is dramatically opposed (though variously formulated).

It is impossible to know how far George Eliot in fact consciously intended a Kabbalistic interpretation of *Daniel Deronda*, but in so far as she did it must give rise to certain misgivings. Such a reading might suggest, for instance, that Gwendolen, because a non-Jew, is by divine preordination denied access both to Deronda and to the plenitude that is his birthright. (Such an implication is at odds with Judaism's traditional acceptance of conversion.) Again, it might imply a radical epistemological split in the fictional 'reality' offered, with some characters 'centred' and others not; some spiritually destined, others in a state of irremediable ontological exile. In this sense Leavis was characteristically acute but impressionistic in sensing a quite freakish unevenness in the novel. It is a long way from the Kabbalah to 'The Great Tradition', and Leavis's organicist moral conception of the novel could not begin to penetrate the philosophical discontinuities with which George Eliot was working.

One critical method that specialises in such discontinuities is deconstruction, and *Daniel Deronda* has attracted a formidable example of this kind of reading. Cynthia Chase's celebrated essay 'The Decomposition of the Elephants'[87] deftly exposes contradictions within the novel between a proto-existential crisis plot on the one hand, and its mystical neoplatonism on the other.

However, deconstruction's inability to give an account of lived and felt social practices and traditions is apparent in Chase's demonstration. Her reduction of the novel's conflicting accounts of personal identity to a 'logical principle: if $b = A$ and $B = b$, then $B = A$ (since A cannot at the same time equal b and not equal B, which equals b)'[88] points up a discontinuous (deconstructive) textual logic, but in so doing it ignores what typically concerned George Eliot: spiritual life – in this case Judaism – as an 'incarnate' tradition. However conflicted, *Daniel Deronda* is not this 'decentred';[89] it tries to envision an accord between the subjective spiritual lives of individuals and the larger social structures within which, and through which, they unfold. Self and system are mutually entailing. However, the novel does seem to privilege the Jewish soul, to suggest that it can have both essence (the experience of being and feeling Jewish) and transcendence (an extra-social access to divinity). Deconstruction diagnoses the muddle but makes nothing of the cultural inwardness that is George Eliot's theme. But neither, it is often argued, can George Eliot herself.

The Jews in *Daniel Deronda* have struck many readers as lifeless incarnations; indeed, many Jewish readers have been disappointed, even offended. Thus, while the American Jewish critic Lionel Trilling finds in the novel 'a genuine, inner, intimate quality',[90] Edgar Rosenberg, in his extended study of the Jew in English literature, *From Shylock to Svengali*, finds nothing but 'stereotypes'.[91] Generations of such disagreement suggest that it cannot be resolved simply through the imposition of someone's taste, be it Leavis's or anyone else's. Clearly this novel reveals as much about the reader as it does about its characters, and for a number of reasons. One is simply that Judaism is too culturally multifarious to elicit overwhelming consensus from anyone, Jews or non-Jews. The other is perhaps more interesting and more complex. George Eliot's Jews are persons in whom character and code coincide to a degree unfamiliar in the conventions of novelistic realism. Yet such a coincidence is quite familiar among religious Jews (and others) who have chosen – or believe themselves to be chosen for – a highly codified life. The individualistic liberal self is here an irrelevancy.

It seems pointless to revert to Leavis or his disputants in assessing *Daniel Deronda*. More promising, perhaps, is an approach such as Alasdair MacIntyre's. In *After Virtue* MacIntyre insists that the relationship between character and self, personal and cultural narratives, is tied to specific cultural practices, and that we must understand this relationship in order to chart versions of the self.[92] This is perhaps the best implication to be drawn from George Eliot's well-intentioned but misguided geneticism. It might indeed 'widen' our 'vision' of Jews and others intelligently. Equally, the 'reception' of such a novel may provide important clues to our patterns of typology, tolerance and persecution, and the 'reception theory' of cultural and historical analysts[93] (Mukarovsky, Vodicka, Gardamer, Jauss and others) may be of real value here.

So also might the less historically specific reception theory of Wolfgang Iser.[94] Iser's version of textual phenomenology rests on the now familiar claim that literary texts are not finalised forms of an author's intention; rather, they are incomplete statements whose signals and sentiments are completed in a process of co-creation by the reader. In so completing a text the reader draws partly on learnt forms of competence that are distinctively 'literary' (for instance, recognising a lyric poem as lyric and so paying particular attention to lineation, rhyme, meter and other features associated with this form of writing), but also on more general cultural 'thought systems'[95] that society uses to interpret and constitute the world it takes to be 'real'. Such a theory as Iser's of course raises the problem discussed in our first chapter: how far is what we take to be 'real' in fact so, and how far is it an unverifiable social fiction? Iser insists that sign systems, literary and other, are 'a means of telling us something about reality',[96] that our world is not in any simple sense a social or textual fabrication. Indeed, he even ventures the now unfashionable claim that we learn from various forms of social narrative something about 'basic dispositions of human nature'.[97] Such apparently universalist assumptions have left Iser open to charges of political naïvety or conservatism, the objection being that notions of 'human nature' or 'dispositions' are often expedient fictions promulgated to maintain the *status quo*. This need not, however, be the implication – concepts of 'human nature' can as much secure political change as impede it – and Iser's theory has the virtue of steering a course between two extreme views of character in fiction: one which insists that characters are determinate, 'life-like' creations about whom we can achieve unambiguous moral consensus; the other, that characters are merely ideological constructions whose ostensible reference to real or generalised human characteristics ought to be refused by the critic. If, as Iser claims, reading is a process of co-creation, reading complex character will always be a somewhat variable thing, for we complete texts not only through learnt forms of social and literary competence, but also out of our own necessarily subjective experience. Readers will agree on much, but some divergences are inevitable. This such a critic as Leavis seems often unable to concede. This does not, however, mean that characters are signs with no real or stable referent. If certain 'human dispositions' are sufficiently generalised to enable or prompt us to designate a thing 'human', literary texts may indeed refer us to relatively stable features of human 'reality' that are not simply textual or ideological. Reading character can thus tell us something of general validity about persons, but also, if we read self-consciously, about the narrative strategies we employ to render meaningful the world in which we live.

Daniel Deronda reflects often upon its own narrative procedures and it also insistently contrasts different kinds of narrative assumption and convention – literary, social, mystical, historical. As we have seen, its characters reflect these multiple perspectives. If the reader is tempted to relate Gwendolen to literary predecessors in the realist novel of education, Deronda seems oddly removed from her ambience, a character conceived within a quite alien set of conventions. His 'Englishness' is a case in point. Superficially, he is Anglicised according to the logic of George Eliot's customary stress upon the developing character's environment; yet the novel's genetic mysticism undermines this premise: having been born Jewish, Deronda is radically and unalterably that. Hence what many readers have thought his implausibly untroubled conversion from the status of English gentleman to that of Kabbalistic quester. Gillian Beer rightly points out that this is the stuff of fairy-tale metamorphosis[98] rather than of novelistic realism, and the novel's choice-plot shifts accordingly. Unlike Gwendolen's, Deronda's choices are preordained: he has essentially to accept that he has been chosen. George Eliot's point seems to be that character can be understood in an atemporal prophetic way, not merely in the progressive manner of psychological realism; and *Daniel Deronda* enforces the point by trying to retrieve historically a tradition whose understanding of the self is structured in this way.

Kabbalistic mysticism too, it urges, has its codes and its terms of human assessment; but what, the novel seems to ask, remains common beneath these widely divergent perspectives on the self?

The novel's answer is equivocal and critics have been quick to seize upon the contradictions involved in a concept of human identity that veers between biologism, mysticism and Kantian moralism. Such reservations would not however have surprised George Eliot. Her little-known late essay on the Jews, 'The Modern Hep! Hep! Hep!', reveals her to be deeply troubled about the relationship between self, typology, essence and relation, and she knew well, generations before National Socialism, the dangers of hypostatising the postulates of race.

Daniel Deronda remains, nevertheless, an aberration among the major English novels. Thus did Leavis feel compelled to edit and retitle it *Gwendolen Harleth* in order that it might better conform to the contours of his Great Tradition.[99] Yet the truth is that *Deronda* looks forward less to Leavis's exemplar Lawrence than to the humanist mysticism of such a writer as Martin Buber. Buber acknowledges a debt to the same Feuerbach George Eliot translated[100] and follows the German in proposing an other-centred transactional image of human personality. In his great ecumenical work *I and Thou*, Buber repudiates Descartes, Kant and Sartrean existentialism,[101] arguing that ' "I" is the true shibboleth of humanity':[102] that we live 'Inscrutably involved' in 'currents of universal reciprocity'[103] the tendency of which is always *relational*. The resemblances to George Eliot's legendary 'need to be loved' are strong. He writes of the 'innateness of the longing for relation',[104] of the encoded 'dynamics of the soul'[105] for which 'All actual life is encounter.'[106] However, like George Eliot herself, he declines wholly to empty the self of essence: 'the *a priori* of relation' is an 'innate You':[107] The other is a mystical emanation, a substance not wholly spoken for in transaction or socially constituted. He joins two other prominent figures in this study in seeing the self as thread-like. This is Buber:

> Whether it lives in relation or outside it, the I remains assured of itself in its self-consciousness, which is a strong thread of gold on which changing states are strung.[108]

This is Sartre:

> The For-itself rising into being as the nihilation of the In-itself

constitutes itself simultaneously in all the possible dimensions of nihilation. From whatever point of view it is considered, it is the being which holds to itself by a single thread, or more precisely it is the being which by being causes all the possible dimensions of its nihilation to exist.[109]

Finally, George Eliot on Casaubon's 'experience' and 'soul':

it was that proud narrow sensitiveness which has not mass enough to spare for transformation into sympathy, and quivers thread-like in small currents of self-preoccupation or at best of an egoistic scrupulosity. (*Middlemarch*, II.29, p. 11)

For Sartre (who goes on to adopt the term 'Diaspora' for the 'For-itself'[110]), the self is a transitive gathering of negations, an absence; for Buber it is a relational propensity that somehow knows itself to be *essentially*, substantially, that;[111] for George Eliot it also possesses substance: it possesses mass which may or may not be relationally actualised or transformed through relationship.

A heavily scored personal copy of Christian D. Ginsburg's *The Kabbalah* suggests that the Kabbalism of *Daniel Deronda* owes much to a Victorian account. Ginsburg writes at length about the soul – 'that which constitutes the real man is the Soul'[112] – and about choice. According to the famous Kabbalistic doctrine of the 'transmigration of souls', the frail soul may thrice inhabit the body of another in its quest for transcendental reunification. Thus does Mordecai choose Deronda. But both have of course already been chosen. Deronda confides to his mentor:

'It is quite true that you and Mirah have been my teachers', said Deronda. 'If this revelation had been made to me before I knew you both, I think my mind would have rebelled against it. Perhaps I should have felt then – "If I could have chosen, I would not have been a Jew."' (viii.63, p. 698)

But it is of course the problematic contention of this strand of the novel that choice and chosenness are one and the same thing.

THE PORTRAIT OF A LADY

I

Henry James wrote one of the earliest reviews of *Daniel Deronda*; in fact he wrote a short notice of the first instalment of the novel for the *Nation* in February 1876.[113] It is clear from this and from his letters at the time (he tells Alice James that, despite its weaknesses, 'I enjoyed it more than anything of hers'[114]) that the novel held a particular fascination for him. This fascination was to issue ten months later in the classic '*Daniel Deronda*: A Conversation'.[115] The 'Conversation' remains one of the great appreciations of the work, and its urbane exchanges probe many of the issues that were to exercise later criticism. However, the urbanity can be deceptive. Behind it lies James's pessimistic – and characteristic – verdict on George Eliot's creative method: her conception may be sublime, but, precisely *because* it dwells so much in the realm of conception, 'brain', the 'abstract', it fails to achieve the expansion of vision and sympathy George Eliot seeks. Pulcheria, one of the three participants in the dialogue, is offered as a sort of living proof of *Deronda*'s failure to 'widen the English vision'. Having read the novel, she remains an avowed (though, it would seem, essentially benign) anti-Semite: she jokes about Jewish noses, sympathises with Leonora's having 'hated' not just 'the Jewish race', but also its 'manners and looks', and pronounces herself ostentatiously (to her lap dog) 'not convinced', either by George Eliot's art or her altruism. Thus does the inartistic squander, in James's view, the sacred offices of art.

If the novel is to amount to 'moralised fable, the last word of a philosophy endeavouring to teach by example', it seems doomed to move only the already-converted. One such is Constantius, the male representative in the dialogue. He is himself a writer and reviewer, one of those Jamesian characters 'on whom nothing is lost'.[116] (Significantly, George Eliot uses almost exactly this phrase for the musician Klesmer in *Deronda*, iii.22, p. 221.) Constantius is the James surrogate in a discussion which by implication must take a 'fictional' form in order to subtilise and advance George Eliot's ponderous creative cause. His manner is Jamesian and his judgements generally authorial. The third character, Theodora, is a more dispassionate thinker than Pulcheria but a more derivative one than Constantius. She is yet another incipient Jamesian artist. The dialogue opens with her seated 'on her verandah with a piece of embroidery, the design of which she made up as she proceeded, being careful, however, to have a Japanese screen before her, to keep her inspiration at the proper altitude'. True creativity is beyond her.

James's disquiet at the genetic mysticism of *Daniel Deronda* is clear in the 'Conversation', but it is handled with characteristic tact. The 'race-passion' is acknowledged as a problem, but Constantius is every inch the English gentleman in feigning puzzlement at George Eliot's intentions: 'There is something very fascinating in the mission that Deronda takes upon himself. I don't quite know what it means. . . .' He is also very much the Jamesian critic in highlighting two weaknesses in the novel, one the 'poor illusion' achieved in the Jewish sections, the other the more general problem of choice. The latter is in part a creative difficulty. Constantius echoes James in regretting that George Eliot 'has chosen to go into criticism'; that is, that she has made of the novel a forum for a speculative, humanist metaphysics. She writes for 'critics of the universe'; she is one herself. But the requirements of the reader's imagination are thereby all too often, in James's view, ignored. Choice is also a thematic problem. Gwendolen is a brilliant creation but 'a little childish for the weight of interest she has to carry'. Like so many of George Eliot's heroines, she is, James feels, too thin to concede choosing its proper thematic and aesthetic centrality.

The range and penetration of James's appreciations of *Daniel Deronda* can only be intimated here, and a reading of the 'Conversation', together with James's review of the Cross *Life* and the second volume of Edel's edition of the *Letters*, is necessary for a just appraisal. Certain salient – and again characteristic – features must suffice here.

One concerns narration – more specifically, the narrative structure George Eliot adopts to express an imaginative and intellectual outlook. In so far as it concedes inherent elements of tragedy and irony in (for want of a better phrase) the human condition, James applauds this outlook. Constantius notes that

> George Eliot always gives us something that is strikingly and ironically characteristic of human life; and what savours more of the essential crookedness of our fate than the sad cross-purposes of these two young people? Poor Gwendolen's falling

in love with Deronda is part of her own luckless history, not of his.

'The essential crookedness of our fate' – it is as much Isabel Archer's phrase as Gwendolen's, and James knows that its presence in *Deronda* derives from an achieved 'sense of the universal'.[117] The novel fuses the elevation of 'romance' and the reflective reach of 'brain' ('intellectual brilliancy') in at times achieving the illusion of a 'complete' fictional 'world'. When it succeeds, narration – the 'threads of the narrative' – resembles 'wires capable of transmitting messages from mysterious regions'; it offers that 'lateral extension into another multitudinous world'[118] that James so cherishes in great fiction. But here, as elsewhere in George Eliot, he finds success all too occasional. *Deronda* enters more into 'views' of life than the thing itself; it seems divided between the 'spontaneous' and the 'artificial'. It lacks dramatic momentum, is sometimes ponderous in style and is structurally fragmented. What is more, it lacks humour. In short, narration proceeds from the 'abstract to the concrete'.

This, with the resultant aesthetic discontinuities, implicates character. The novel, James believes, contains 'a vast amount of life' but too 'little art', and its want of 'tact' is reflected in the 'importunity of the moral reflections' that surround and interpret character. In part this is owing to the displaced perspective of the narrator-as-Judaic-historian who 'takes' the Jews 'as a person outside of Judaism – aesthetically.' Something is wrong with the portrait: it is too didactic and knows its subjects by 'apparatus' rather than 'grace'. Some of these characters are 'described and analysed to death', but 'we don't see them or hear them nor touch them'. Deronda is a 'brilliant failure'; indeed, he and Mirah are not even 'concrete images':[119] they are 'studied' instead of 'embodied' – 'disembodied types, pale abstractions, signs and symbols of a 'great lesson'.[120] James's verdict, like his judgements upon Lawrence, Dostoevsky, Tolstoy and others, reveals the point beyond which one of the great eclectic critical spirits of the nineteenth century was not prepared to go in countenancing uncongenial aesthetic perspectives. James's 'poetics' of fiction contains an embryonic and essentially psychological theory of reader reception, but none that would yield the imaginative leniency *Daniel Deronda* so clearly demands.

Yet there are, he believes, magnificent exceptions. Theodora feels that George Eliot has unlocked some of the 'great chambers of human character'. Gwendolen is the 'most *intelligent* thing in all George Eliot's writing'. Her portrait evinces 'such a wealth of psychological detail' that the book must be counted 'a great exposé of the female mind'.[121] Even its diffuseness and inclusiveness, so different from the symbolic thinness of the Jewish sections, is applauded: 'the girl is known, inside out'. Grandcourt, too, is a triumph: a 'consummate representation' of the most detestable kind of Englishman, 'who thinks it low to articulate'. In him (as in Gilbert Osmond) 'the type and the individual are so happily met'.

In summary, George Eliot has chosen 'the possible picturesqueness' of a 'high moral tone'. This has typically divided the novel between explanation and exhibition, dramatic illusion and demonstration. But, James sees, it has also resulted in the ethical conflict already mentioned. Gwendolen chooses ill and her mind is made to 'ache with the pain of the process' of recognition. But to what end? Constantius argues that 'The very chance to embrace what the author is so fond of calling a "larger life" seems refused to her. She is punished for being narrow, and she is not allowed a chance to expand.' Gwendolen has, in James's view, been denied a second choice. To have 'embraced' 'life' afresh after Grandcourt's death might have demanded more – both of her personal stature and of George Eliot's powers of dramatic evocation.

II

Like the 'Conversation', *The Portrait of a Lady* is a creative extension of *Daniel Deronda*. But it is of course many other things as well, and it shares with the 'Conversation' a highly ambivalent attitude towards its precursor. It is at once appreciative and admonishing. Indeed, the very scope of its reworking of Eliotean materials is an unspoken indictment of a kind that must qualify the image of wholesome, inspirational influence between Eliot and James so suggestively proposed by Leavis in *The Great Tradition*. One detail perhaps sums the indictment up: Isabel Archer has already read 'the prose of George Eliot' before leaving for Europe (III.4, p. 46). The experience does not warn her off

Osmond. Like Pulcheria, she remains existentially and attitudinally unmoved by the great exemplar.

The chronology of James's own reading is revealing here. He first mentions his intention to write *The Portrait* in a letter to Howells of February 1877. *Daniel Deronda* had appeared between February and September 1876, and James's letters over succeeding months are studded with admiring and troubled references to it. Many find expression in the 'Conversation' (December 1876); most surface again, though more by implication, when *The Portrait* commences serial publication in October 1880. *Daniel Deronda* had, then, been profoundly implicated in the latter novel's creative formation. Moreover, James had in 1880 read and written about all of George Eliot's works.

The Portrait of a Lady of course lacks the visionary sweep and splendour of George Eliot's 'Jewish novel'; but it is in its own way just as preoccupied with the problems of chosenness and choice. Its characters move in a world eerily compounded of necessity and will, and in one still more riven by the brutality of crude categorising than George Eliot's own. Osmond might never say what Grandcourt thinks about the Jamaican negro – that he 'was a beastly sort of baptist Caliban' (*Daniel Deronda*, iv.29, p. 303) – but he is nevertheless a creature of categories, a psychological sadist who trades in received modes of cultural contradistinction. James's 'international theme' is not, then, the gorgeous and gallant thing it sometimes seems. *The Portrait of a Lady* is in fact about expert and exigent counterfeits of culture and about the tragic inadequacy of the codes that permit them. It images a world divided along almost every imaginable line: racial ('American', 'Italian', 'English'), national (its terms an ambiguous approximation to race), cultural (Old World and New), sexual (male, female; power, passivity), existential (innocence and experience), epistemological (the modes and proprieties of knowledge). Like *Daniel Deronda*, this novel teems with displaced persons: expatriates, willing and reluctant; suitors, collectors, children with concealed parents. Indeed, almost none escapes exile. Warburton is as 'English' as Goodwood is 'American', yet each seeks an intensity his cultural pedigree cannot confer. Their enervated quests after Isabel in foreign places are James's icon of existential desperation. They seek a choice that will deliver them

from anguish; but of course the choice – at least in this instance – is
Isabel's.

No less than *Daniel Deronda*'s this novel's concern with choice is
apparent at every turn. Its international theme in a sense parallels
George Eliot's 'Jewish' dialectic of choice and chosenness. Ralph
tells Henrietta, 'Ah, one does n't give up one's country any more
than one gives up one's grandmother. They're both antecedent to
choice – elements of one's composition that are not to be
eliminated' (iii.10, p. 125). Madame Merle, in her chilling
disquisition on self and self-expression, confides to the doubting
Isabel that 'I know a large part of myself is in the clothes I choose
to wear' (iii.19, p. 287). Her young interlocutor counters that such
choices are illusory, 'arbitrary': 'To begin with it's not my own
choice that I wear them; they're imposed upon me by society'
(p. 288). But of course this is a point about the superficiality of
certain social forms of expression, not about choice *per se*. In fact
Isabel's determination to choose in more fundamental ways
exceeds even that of Gwendolen. Yet here, typically, the two
portraits touch: each combines something like a Sartrean
commitment to self-shaping volition with a phobic disinclination
to choose. Both women are characters of dread. Osmond's
advances occasion in the young American a 'dread of having, in
this case too, to choose and decide' (iv.29, p. 18). Both are
trapped in the paradox of choosing through already given forms.
Isabel's rejection of self-imaging through clothes cannot conceal
that, although 'fond of the old, the consecrated, the transmitted',
she only 'pretended to do what she chose with it' (iv.42, p. 198).
The choice is really Osmond's and that of the society he reflects.
This is a more complex matter than Yvor Winters found in James's
treatment of choice;[122] it is also more pervasive, for almost the
entire cast – the Touchetts, Henrietta, Osmond, Madame Merle,
Pansy, the suitors – are studies in choice and in the torments of a
conventionalised freedom.

Here, indeed, even James's narrator is implicated. Ralph's
ambiguous term 'composition' raises the fundamental question: is
one's self one's own 'composition' or someone else's? If the latter,
whose? In either case, by what forms and proprieties does it
proceed? An early letter in which James suggests that the idea of a
god – 'some application of the supernatural idea' – is desirable
rather than plausible[123] perhaps indicates the depth and
implications of the problem. Without a belief in a god, the

question of authority, in art and in life, becomes critical. The house of fiction metaphor discussed in Chapter 2 proposes certain answers, but it is a typically equivocal performance. The watcher at the window (that is, the artist) resembles his characters in being at once determined and free. Ideally at least, he is free to choose his perspective and so his vision; yet so imperious is his calling that the Preface to *The Portrait* can according to James at best be an 'apology for a motive'. Still, he recalls that Isabel (and the others) had been 'curiously at my disposal': like Turgenev, he may shape his blessed apparitions. This indeed is the 'challenge', the 'charm of the problem'.[124] He has the novelist's gift for inquiry – that 'grouping instinct for the right complications' – and may choose an appropriate form. Such a choice he terms, with an obfuscating and false modesty wonderfully his own, a 'trick'. Given that James is here recalling the creation of a world rife in cultural counterfeits and bogus artists, this is an audacious choice of word. What, after all, distinguishes him from the frauds he so mercilessly exposes?

One answer is tradition, though not the bracingly vitalistic one of Leavis. Dedicated writers learn from precursors in a manner unavailable to despairing narcissists such as Osmond. But they must refract what they receive through their own subjectivity. The creative present is both a bridge and a breach with the past. The Preface to *The Portrait of a Lady* acknowledges a great debt to George Eliot, but it also confirms a deviation from a writer who could, James thought, never conceive of fiction as an indulgence in the 'great game of art'. The 'trick' signals a refusal of an inhibiting seriousness. It is a kind of prior choice compelled by a predecessor who also, paradoxically, renders the choice possible. George Eliot's attempt to centre the sentient heroine is a 'deep difficulty braved' which elicits in the 'addicted artist' James a 'pang' for a greater perfection. Again, he adopts the idiom of risk and imaginative adventure to reflect the urgency of the challenge. He wishes to have the creative 'danger intensified' so that George Eliot's thing may be done 'so much better'. This 'danger' can seem a rather precious business, but it apparently entails at least three kinds of threat: the threat of failure *per se*; of a loss of coherence arising from a break with the past; and of a loss of contact with the untransmuted 'reality' or substance to which, according to James, fiction addresses itself. Beyond this, there is surely a burden of guilt: having learnt so much from George Eliot, he is now in a sense turning against her and, in so doing, turning her against herself.

The discussion centres on the 'delicate vessels' to which George Eliot refers in Chapter 11 of *Daniel Deronda*: 'In these delicate vessels is borne onward through the ages the treasure of human affections'. James's gloss is as follows:

> Challenge any such problem with any intelligence, and you immediately see how full it is of substance; the wonder being, all the while, as we look at the world, how absolutely, how inordinately, the Isabel Archers, and even much smaller female fry, insist on mattering. George Eliot has admirably noted it – 'In these frail vessels is borne onward through the ages the treasure of human affection.' In 'Romeo and Juliet' Juliet has to be important, just as, in 'Adam Bede' and 'The Mill on the Floss' and 'Middlemarch' and 'Daniel Deronda', Hetty Sorrel and Maggie Tulliver and Rosamond Vincy and Gwendolen Harleth have to be; with that much of firm ground, that much of bracing air, at the disposal all the while of their feet and their lungs. They are typical, none the less, of a class difficult, in the individual case, to make a centre of interest; so difficult in fact that many an expert painter, as for instance Dickens and Walter Scott, as for instance even, in the main, so subtle a hand as that of R. L. Stevenson, has preferred to leave the task unattempted.

Like Shakespeare, George Eliot has attempted to diffuse the 'difficult' 'centre' through a dispersion of interest. Competing foci of attention enable the 'slimnesses' involved to have their 'inadequacy eked out with comic relief and underplots'. The resultant crisis of form precipitates two of the great compensations of James's aesthetic: the pivotal and self-conscious protagonist whose greater sentience integrates and structures the work; and the novel conceived as an architectonic whole:

> The difficulty most worth tackling can only be for him [the artist], in these conditions, the greatest the case permits of. So I remember feeling here (in presence, always, that is, of the particular uncertainty of my ground), that there would be one way better than another – oh, ever so much better than any other! – of making it fight out its battle. The frail vessel, that

charged with George Eliot's 'treasure', and thereby of such importance to those who curiously approach it, has likewise possibilities of importance to itself, possibilities which permit of treatment and in fact peculiarly require it from the moment they are considered at all. There is always the escape from any close account of the weak agent of such spells by using as a bridge for evasion, for retreat and flight, the view of her relation to those surrounding her. Make it predominantly a view of *their* relation and the trick is played: you give the general sense of her effect, and you give it, so far as the raising on it of a superstructure goes, with the maximum of ease.

This 'superstructure' is the summation of James's 'experiments of form', and the shift from 'experiments in life' displaces primary concern from unmediated 'feelings and emotions' to the act of mediation itself. In so far as this is permitted by transmission – say, an appreciative but somewhat antagonistic reaction to George Eliot – it suggests the kind of decentring of the text to which Harold Bloom draws attention: texts are defensive responses to other texts and their progenitors; aesthetic structures prove to be intertextual.[125] However, James anticipates and qualifies just such a claim: the Preface gives us *The Portrait of a Lady* 'reduced to its essence'. The work is in his view radically 'present', despite its debts, its daring and its apparently terminal irony. Yet, as the Preface concedes, this presence is no simple thing. The house of fiction again:

> The spreading field, the human scene, is the 'choice of subject'; the pierced aperture, either broad or balconied or slit-like and low-browed, is the 'literary form', but they are, singly or together, as nothing without the posted presence of the watcher – without, in other words, the consciousness of the artist.

'Choice' is here cited provisionally in order to suggest an almost involuntary engagement: 'life', like 'literary form', is too generalised a feature of the novelist's undertaking to admit of pointed description. Only when a particular writer chooses to convey his unique view of things does art begin to epitomise a sacred sentience and selectivity. But in a sense this choice, too, is illusory: since it resides in the writer's 'consciousness', it has arguably already been made. James's point is that vision is, as the phenomenologists have it, 'situated': meaning and authority are profoundly – perhaps radically – individual. But an obligatory choice is a thing of dubious authority. What kind and degree of creative agency does it confer? How far can a 'situated' moral authority be generalised? How 'individual' can a communicable 'vision' be? Even as it intones the categorical imperative, *The Portrait of a Lady* flirts with an existential humanism in order to expose central problems in post-Kantian ethics and epistemology. The existential image is offered: 'consciousness' collapses categories: subject/object, 'singly'/'apart'. But Isabel is to discover the hazards of this enchanted dynamism. There is a fine line between mutuality and a manipulated absorption into another mind. Indeed, the novel suggests that it is precisely the creativity of the other's perception that necessitates certain codes and categories of personal entitlement. Even as *The Portrait*'s narrator seeks to liberate his subject through form, another portraitist – Osmond – frames her with a deadly and derivative expertise.

III

The formal correlative of situated authority in *The Portrait* is the limited omniscience of its narrator. James fashions out of the divided narrative structure he has received a less voluble form than George Eliot's. His novel accords substantially with his theory: exhibition predominates over 'luminous brooding' and expatiation; the empirical 'I' of Eliotean commentary recedes and is replaced by an unstable and uncertain narrative authority. Whose 'portrait', the reader wonders, is it? What truth value does it have? James anticipates Joyce, Wilde and others in using the practice of portrait painting to focus larger problems of agency, truth and authority in narrative. Alasdair MacIntyre has remarked upon the aptness of the metaphor, for 'good' portraiture, at least in James's and Joyce's period, requires a special accord between virtue and virtuosity, freedom and form. The artist employs convention in order to evoke a life-like individuality. In so doing he participates in the 'good life', not simply because he pays his subject the compliment of an avowedly 'true' report, but also because the skills of portraiture entail an initiation into certain modes of knowing. Mastering these is laudable; possessing the power to combine exactitude and inquiry is a form of 'virtue'. 'Good' – 'realistic' – portraiture is, like fiction, heuristic: it deepens as it describes. Certainly, James proposes a complimentary kind in which 'resemblance has usurped' an 'iconic relationship'.[126] But Osmond's is another matter. Though a painter by repute, his true medium is a kind of manipulative fictionalising that trivialises and brutalises its subjects. His arts are those of appropriation.

It is significant that James so often proposed portraiture as an analogy for the writing of novels. The analogy is clearly inexact: not only because words and paint differ fundamentally, but also because a portrait arrests a narrative sequence while a novel charts it in inquiring detail. Characters develop in fictions as they cannot in paintings. To write a novel about a portrait may well, therefore, be an admission that the reader's expectation of narrative coherence and development is impossibly exacting; it may perhaps also be a way of saying that the writer no longer has a generally accepted set of social assumptions about selves and their artistic representation to which he can appeal. In this sense *The Portrait* is an implicit concession to narrative desuetude, and its narrative structure reflects this paradox.

Like George Eliot's, James's narrator is torn between solicitude and impersonality. *Daniel Deronda* contrasts a 'bird's-eye reasonableness' with a 'reverential interest'. Its accent is on the latter. *The Portrait* inverts the emphasis: the 'imagination of loving' (III.5, p. 54) is besieged by an encroaching and often invidious impersonality. The introduction to Isabel is an obvious example:

Her life should always be in harmony with the most pleasing impression she should produce; she would be what she appeared, and she would appear what she was. Sometimes she went so far as to wish that she might find herself some day in a difficult position, so that she should have the pleasure of being as heroic as the occasion demanded. Altogether, with her meagre knowledge, her inflated ideals, her confidence at once innocent and dogmatic, her temper at once exacting and indulgent, her mixture of curiosity and fastidiousness, of vivacity and indifference, her desire to look very well and to be if possible even better, her determination to see, to try, to know, her combination of the delicate, desultory, flame-like spirit and the eager and personal creature of conditions: she would be an easy victim of scientific criticism if she were not intended to awaken on the reader's part an impulse more tender and more purely expectant.   (III.6, p. 69)

This segment of what is in fact a more diffuse introduction than any in George Eliot exemplifies the massive and momentous ambivalence of James's fictional humanism. The question of 'presenting' or 'producing' self, of substance and appearance, may wait; here it is the ambience of paradox and contradiction that requires emphasis. Isabel is given as a cluster of contradictions ('meagre knowledge'/'inflated ideals'; 'innocent'/ 'dogmatic'; and so on). In a sense the uncertainty is bogus – the narrator is leading us on. But not entirely. Isabel is psychologically and circumstantially unresolved at the end of the novel, both for herself and for the reader. Her obscurity is tragic and genuine and the narrator does not dispel it. Indeed, his presence dwindles as the novel proceeds. In place of the Eliotean sublime the portrait offers the unembellished epigrammatic asides of an uncommitted observer: 'There are deep-lying sympathies' (III.23, p. 362). Like Ralph, the narrator seems often 'restricted to mere spectatorship at the game of life' (III.15, p. 210); certainly the confident appeal to a moral consensus is a luxury upon which he seldom presumes. Earlier in the introduction he suggests, 'It may be affirmed without delay that Isabel was probably very liable to the sin of self-esteem' (III.6, p. 67); but 'probably' qualifies the confidence of 'without delay' and in order to preserve the 'dignity of his subject' the 'biographer' must 'shrink from specifying' her frailties (ibid.). Later we are told,

> She was a person of great good faith, and if there was a great deal of folly in her wisdom those who judge her severely may have the satisfaction of finding that, later, she became consistently wise only at the cost of an amount of folly which will constitute almost a direct appeal to charity.
>
> (III.12, pp. 144–5)

'Good faith' is another suggestive, if approximate, anticipation of existentialism; 'almost a direct appeal to charity' recalls the 'impulse . . . more purely expectant' of the earlier passage. Such phrases reflect important shifts in the novel's evolution from

George Eliot to James. Her byword is 'sympathy'; he opts for the more restrained 'charity'. Moreover, he makes care dependent upon narrative structure in a fashion that would have aroused her fear of 'calculation'. In a passage that must figure in any comparative reading of her fiction and James's, George Eliot writes that, in addition to 'prudent calculation', 'the generous leap of impulse is needed too to swell the flood of sympathy in us beholders, that we may not fall completely under the mastery of calculation, which in its turn may fail of ends for want of energy got from ardour'.[127] However tender, 'impulse' in James becomes a function of the 'expectant' process of reading and fictional duration. We are here, in the late revision of the masterwork of his middle phase, on the threshold of the late phase. In *The Golden Bowl* Maggie Verver finds that in order to negotiate her situation she must exercise the 'foredoomed ingenuities of her pity' (xxiv.vi.1, p. 330). Charity and calculation fuse. But this is to anticipate.

'*Almost* a direct appeal to charity' – James acknowledges that it cannot be entirely direct. It must be mediated. Just so, the diffident narrator cannot simply give or naturalise his protagonist's mind: 'The working of this lady's spirit was strange, and I can only give it to you as I see it, not hoping to make it seem altogether natural' (iii.29, pp. 21–2). Herein, perhaps, lies the central problem for the evaluating humanist critic of James's novel. Is this disclaimer just another 'trick', an expedient sleight of hand; or does it sincerely concede a fact of portraiture, fictional and other – that self possesses a privacy at which the codes can only gesture? James's elaborately rationalised narrative procedures seem in spirit to encroach upon contextual privacy; but, as we shall see, *The Portrait* in fact both assumes and asserts the existence of an unassimilable essence in each individual.

Isabel's introduction also constitutes a tonal break with the more effusive Eliotean medium through which we meet Maggie Tulliver, Dorothea and Gwendolen. James's uneasily remote conviviality implicitly corrects George Eliot's 'high moral tone'. James's narrative voice is by contrast urbane, distilled, almost enervated. The narrating persona edges embarrassedly out of the picture, his formal displacement an eerie analogue of the circumstantial and spiritual displacement he narrates. For *The Portrait of a Lady* is also a map of 'the land of consideration' (iv.39, p. 45) – that blighted region, in this case Osmond's Italy, in which conventional self-consciousness cripples individual powers of expression and response. Osmond is its epitome, but the other journeyers share with him the status of unwitting phenomenologists. Having bracketed or suspended the indigenous cultural narratives within which their selves have taken shape, the Touchetts, the Countess Gemini, Madame Merle and the rest have consigned themselves to an eternity of speculation. 'Who are you? – what are you?' Isabel asks the appalling Merle (iv.49, p. 326). It is just this question that haunts the novel's cast of exiles.

Madame Merle, indeed, seems to Isabel to lack a certain 'tonic wildness' (iii.19, p. 274). In *The Portrait*'s open debate about nature and culture she is a casualty of the kind James was again to dramatise in *The Golden Bowl*. 'The forms . . . are two thirds of conduct', says Fanny Assingham in that novel (xxiii.iii.11, p. 390). James, who had taken careful note of George Eliot's attempt to 'present a struggle between nature and culture' in 'The Spanish Gypsy',[128] questions the proportions in *The Portrait*. But, even granted Fanny's statistic, what, he may be said to be asking, makes up the other third? One answer lies in philosophising the self. We shall see that *The Portrait* does this at length. Another answer, or perhaps the same one by other means, arises from a tough review of established culture. And this *The Portrait* also undertakes.

James's Europe is as rotten as the England of *Daniel Deronda*. Indeed, George Eliot here obviously provided a polemical model. However, there is no Palestine in *The Portrait of a Lady* and the 'fearful self'[129] is everywhere in peril. Like Dorothea Brooke in *Middlemarch*, Isabel finds herself anguished and alone in Rome, and what she learns there is of the first importance for an understanding of *The Portrait of a Lady*. It is in Rome that she admits into consciousness an awareness that is profoundly Eliotean: it is a 'haunting sense of the continuity of the human lot' (iv.49, p. 327). This is James's way of saying that human kind is not just a series of dissociated cultural episodes. Its experience bridges disparate times and places. Indeed, travelling fascinates Eliot and James precisely because it so exposes the culturally provincial self to just this recognition, especially in the greatest and oldest places. In this sense *The Portrait* unmasks the myth of culture's monopoly of the self. Something in the self transcends its local cultural conditioning. Isabel must integrate certain learnt social assumptions with things that exist existentially, 'Deep in her soul' (iii.6, p. 71). Her self is not wholly spoken for by any particular form of culture she knows or encounters.

The pervasive loss of cultural authority about which both Eliot and James write renders Isabel's challenge at once more urgent and more plausible. It makes everyone a potential New Englander: 'exposed', as James had written in his biography of Hawthorne, both to suffering and to knowledge. The challenge requires careful discriminations between negative examples: the naked 'will' of Madame Merle (iv.40, p. 155); the manipulative passivity of Osmond; the tragic detachment of Mrs Touchett; perhaps even Ralph's fated failure of total commitment. It means perfecting a power of humane 'construction' and interpretation in a world glittering with partial portraits. Behind these, of course, lies the ultimate fear. *The Portrait*'s existential imagery of drifting, floating, sailing and journeying repeats the question of agency: is there a purpose, or are we adrift in a universal and godless contingency?

Typically, James on the whole explores the metaphysical issue through human relationships. The ubiquitous practice of portraiture frames the question in terms of self, system and agency. It may be, the novel suggests, that we are in a sense the authors of what we see; but this view risks exhausting the reality of the other person. James's code-rich creation ultimately recoils from the loss of individual essence that can result either from unbridled subjectivity in the way we perceive others, or from the homogenising powers of signification itself. And well it might, for James sees the threat that the denial of essence may entail the denial of the moral agent, even the suppression of moral entitlement.

In this, indeed, James and George Eliot agree, but again James feels the need to revise Eliotean materials in narrating a quest for the essentialist self. Gwendolen has been made 'narrow' and 'not allowed a chance to expand' – Constantius's verdict is James's own. What then of Isabel Archer, the young American so desirous of 'free expansion' (iii.5, p.68)? Let us delay the inevitable catalogue of circumstantial similarities between the novels and note for the present certain obvious affinities and discrepancies between the two heroines. In general terms they clearly share an existential configuration that painfully compounds free-seeking and fear. Both are characters of 'dread'; both wish to live a concept of freedom: Gwendolen's is drawn from 'genteel romance', and Isabel, an impercipient reader of George Eliot, also holds 'romantic views' (III.20, p. 311) on the subject. She is also accorded a tendency that is the hallmark of the Eliotean egoist: she reposes too much trust in 'theories' (III.6, p. 66) and has lived too little. Moreover, each woman possesses the power of imaginative 'construction', and therefore the capacity at once for error and for growth. Their pasts have not helped, however: each has had an absent father, a lack of restraint in childhood and has suffered a disorienting psychic insularity. Eliot and James chart the resultant vertiginous insecurities through an existential notation of sea, space and exile, and through an apparently binary (almost Fichtean) conception of self: the 'best self' must be wrested from the 'worst' and self-assertion corrected by a sense of social obligation.

Of the two, James's narrative method is the more cryptic and metaphoric. In *The Portrait* George Eliot's late themes are stripped of much of what James saw as their messy, metonymic contingency. As the Preface indicates, delegated omniscience is his weapon for rewriting. He centres the besieged hero or heroine. Thus, the epigraph to *Daniel Deronda* refers attention to Gwendolen:

> Let thy chief terror be of thine own soul:
> There, 'mid the throng of hurrying desires
> That trample o'er the dead to seize their spoil,
> Lurks vengeance, footless, irresistible
> As exhalations laden with slow death,
> And o'er the fairest troop of captured joys
> Breathes pallid pestilence.

Yet its title redirects interest to Daniel. Gwendolen's is a displaced portrait. Isabel, by contrast, is the undisputed subject of the work in which she appears. Even so, the two heroines are in a sense equally abandoned: Gwendolen cannot (apparently) have Judaism; Isabel is mercilessly duped by the appearances of Art.

Significantly, both works are rich in semiotic convention. *Deronda*'s narrative Judaism, music, painting and symbolism are paralleled in *The Portrait* by portraiture, journalism, music, the theatre and one of the greatest of all Jamesian arts – conversation. Eco's contention that the sign resides where there is the possibility of lying[130] perhaps in part explains the ethos of risk that pervades each novel. Both picture life as more than merely semiotic, but where, they ask, is truth in a world whose purpose eludes human understanding? One answer is that it resides in human interaction; another is that we meet it through a certain incorrigible 'condition' that assails each and every soul. A third possibility is that we bring about certain truths in our lives by the choices we make, and this in turn involves the individual's attitude to fate, circumstance and change.

No less than *Daniel Deronda*, *The Portrait of a Lady* depicts a gambling world. Gwendolen, Mirah and Isabel are all daughters of gamblers, and the novels both allude to 'the game of life' (*Deronda*, iv.31, p. 326; *The Portrait*, iii.15, p. 210). This is of course tragically apt for Isabel, for she is in part the victim of an enchanted bet. Ralph is too sick to submit to the risks he persuades his father to bequeath to her, but his 'amusement' (iii.18, p. 243) at her daring sours when she chooses to marry Osmond: 'He had played the wrong card, and now he had lost the game' (iv.39, p. 141). Isabel's recognition comes later, but in the same key. She has failed in 'an attempt to play whist with an imperfect pack of cards' (iv.53, p. 391). In a sense she is the dupe of everyone's game: of Ralph's, of Osmond and Merle's, certainly; but also of her creator's, for James too is a gambler: he is the 'addicted artist' who courts 'danger' at a creative remove. The Preface joins Ralph in wishing to see Isabel 'affront her destiny'.[131] It is a characteristically ambiguous verb. James's 'experiment of form' is also in this sense an 'experiment in life'. 'Affront' fuses 'submit', 'confront' and 'refuse' in response to an equivocal 'destiny'. Is it Isabel's to fashion or to face? How far does it determine the 'self' that may choose, or choose to refuse? Like *Daniel Deronda*, *The Portrait* asks how far individuals choose their destinies and how far destiny is a matter of submission to choices already and obscurely made.

IV

It must be conceded that as a fictional creation Isabel is something of an exhibition. She is quintessentially Jamesian in being an emanation of the sublimated intensities of art. Certainly, her portrait lacks the metaphysical ominousness and resonance of

Gwendolen's, though there are teasing allusions to metaphysics in
the novel. In conversation with Madame Merle, Isabel is
ironically (though not entirely patronisingly) said to be 'fond of
metaphysics' (III.19, p. 266), and at home in post-Puritan
America she contemplates 'cosmic treacheries' (III.3, p. 31). Her
late vision of Ralph's ghost, and indeed the catharsis of his death,
confirm what transcendence there is in James's world. Yet her
limits are in some fundamental way James's own. However
tendentious, George Eliot's mystical Judaism constitutes an
otherworldly intensity against which spiritual privation can seem
authentically tragic. In *The Portrait* James cultivates the tragic
atmosphere for all it is worth ('It's not absolutely necessary to
suffer; we were not made for that', asserts Isabel – III.5, p. 65), yet
it is an altogether thinner thing. Ultimately, Gwendolen's lack
appears the greater because her world, postulating as it does the
possibility of true spiritual deliverance, is potentially the more
rich.

In both novels, the terrible tenuousness of the ego registers in
the heroine's phobic ambivalence about experience. Isabel greets
the news of her benefaction with 'Yes, I'm afraid; I can't tell you.
A large fortune means freedom, and I'm afraid of that' (III.21,
p. 320). As so often in James, experience is archetypally imaged as
a poisoned cup. Thus Ralph: 'You want to drain the cup of
experience.' And, in the reply, Isabel: 'No, I don't wish to touch
the cup of experience. It is a poisoned drink! I only want to see for
myself' (III.15, p. 213). It is this adolescent paradox that James's
high refinement so brutally exposes. Indeed *The Golden Bowl*'s
chilling and memorable phrase, the 'high brutality of good
intentions' (XXIII.ii.4, p. 169) is not too strong for this novel of
charmed but tortured disenchantment.

Isabel is of course more vulnerable to charm because she is
more sophisticated than Gwendolen. Her 'discourse of
imaginative fears' is in a sense narrowed by virtue of her knowing
more of the world. Yet she is a Kantian innocent. According to
Kant, 'Innocence is a splendid thing, only it has the misfortune
not to keep very well and to be easily misled.'[132] James's use of
Genesis (and of Milton's use of it) in charting Isabel's innocence
reveals much about his highly analogical creative method. The
'unmapped country' of Gwendolen's mind, with its 'gusts and
storms', compares interestingly with an early image of Isabel
introspecting:

It often seemed to her that she thought too much about herself; you could have made her colour, any day in the year, by calling her a rank egoist. She was always planning out her development, desiring her perfection, observing her progress. Her nature had, in her conceit, a certain garden-like quality, a suggestion of perfume and murmuring boughs, of shady bowers and lengthening vistas, which made her feel that introspection was, after all, an exercise in the open air, and that a visit to the recesses of one's spirit was harmless when one returned from it with a lapful of roses. But she was often reminded that there were other gardens in the world than those of her remarkable soul, and that there were moreover a great many places which were not gardens at all – only dusky pestiferous tracts, planted thick with ugliness and misery.   (III.6, p. 72)

'Conceit' enters the late revision of the novel and is typically pointed in its ambiguity: it suggests an act of vision that is generically imaginative but also arrogant in its presumption. This is not the garden of worldly knowledge. She has yet to meet that in the 'garden' that is Osmond's mind (IV.42, p. 196), and in the physical surroundings that are its iconic and claustral correlative. The passage may seem to question the virtues of self-consciousness, but it is of course James's aesthetic determination that Isabel should possess just that. Thus, although she is an Eliotean 'egoist', she possesses a superior and artistically expedient capacity for knowing herself to be one. George Eliot is seldom this deft; indeed, in such passages' curious fusion of intimacy and aloofness, of lucid surface and opaque depth, James seeks a narrative technique for character that can give more adequate artistic expression to his precursor's great themes.

By analogically connecting the gardens of Genesis, Osmond's Florence and the psychic landscape of post-Puritan New England, James of course raises again the question of nature and culture. The novel's resounding warning is roughly this: you are in the most primitive peril precisely when you think the inner life – either your own or another person's – a thing prior to evil or wholly reclaimed and rationalised by culture. The self is here seen as a fallen thing; it does not so much encode rational structures as require their endless, vigilant renewal. Like *Daniel Deronda*, *The Portrait* asks how the self ought to be conceived. It is – despite T. S. Eliot's famous disclaimer about James and ideas – a philosophical fiction.[133]

The best introduction to self in *The Portrait* is the early speculative exchange between Isabel and Madame Merle. It needs to be quoted at some length. Isabel has declared a lack of interest in Caspar Goodwood's house. Madame Merle replies,

> 'That's very crude of you. When you've lived as long as I you'll see that every human being has his shell and that you must take the shell into account. By the shell I mean the whole envelope of circumstances. There's no such thing as an isolated man or woman; we're each of us made up of some cluster of appurtenances. What shall we call our "self"? Where does it begin? where does it end? It overflows into everything that belongs to us – and then it flows back again. I know a large part of myself is in the clothes I choose to wear. I've a great respect for *things*! One's self – for other people – is one's expression of one's self; and one's house, one's furniture, one's garments, the books one reads, the company one keeps – these things are all expressive.'
>
> This was very metaphysical; not more so, however, than several observations Madame Merle had already made. Isabel was fond of metaphysics, but was unable to accompany her friend into this bold analysis of the human personality. 'I don't agree with you. I think just the other way. I don't know whether I succeed in expressing myself, but I know that nothing else expresses me. Nothing that belongs to me is any measure of me; everything's on the contrary a limit, a barrier, and a perfectly arbitrary one. Certainly the clothes which, as you say, I choose to wear, don't express me; and heaven forbid they should!'
>
> 'You dress very well,' Madame Merle lightly interposed.
>
> 'Possibly; but I don't care to be judged by that. My clothes may express the dressmaker, but they don't express me. To begin with it's not my own choice that I wear them; they're imposed upon me by society'.   (III.19, pp. 287–8)

Madame Merle's platitudinous 'When you've lived as long as I' travesties the idea of the self's narrative intelligibility. Like the Princess Leonora, she has been too much an actress, too much a self liquidated into exigent roles, to make profound sense of her experience. Isabel sees her as 'something of a public performer, condemned to emerge only in character and costume' (IV.31, p. 39); yet she also senses the presence of a tragic residue in Merle's personality, where a 'corner of the curtain . . . never was lifted' (ibid.). As we shall see, just such an image is central to George Eliot's fictional explorations of personal concealment and disclosure. The 'shell' has, however, other implications. Madame Merle here proposes an image of the self as absent, decentred; indeed, the self so conceived is a sort of vacant potentiality capable only of transactional or discursive actualisation (possessions, other people, convention). In the claim that 'There's no such thing as an isolated man or woman' lies the seeds of Isabel's late movement of pity – 'Poor, poor Madame Merle!' (IV.49, p. 331) – for it is precisely this lady's loss of faith in the deepest possibilities of relationship that isolates her from true mutuality and care. Her emphasis on *'things'* is the hallmark of what MacIntyre terms the 'manipulative mode of moral instrumentalism';[134] it substitutes transaction for interaction, possessions for people. 'Where does [the self] begin' and 'end', indeed? Her answer is that it does neither: it is dispersed across and constituted through an impersonal network. Isabel's analysis of these things predates Saussure's by three decades, but it is surprisingly acute. She sees that Madame Merle is doing what we should now think of as semiotics: ' "What's language at all but a convention?" said Isabel. "She has the good taste not to pretend, like some people I've met, to express herself by original signs" ' (III.19, p. 274).

She also gauges the cost of the semiotic view of self. Madame Merle is a depersonalised casualty of the myth of culture's monopoly of the self. Isabel thinks her 'too perfectly the social animal' (ibid.); 'not natural' (p. 273); 'so cultivated and civilised' (p. 272). In short, 'her nature had been too much overlaid by custom and her angles too much rubbed away' (pp. 273–4). 'Angles' are a favourite Jamesian metaphor for an unassimilable personal essence or residue. They reflect the contextual privacy that Madame Merle seems to lack. 'Isabel found it difficult to think of her in any detachment or privacy, she existed only in her relations, direct or indirect, with her fellow mortals' (p. 274). In a sense Isabel is right. It is Merle's appalling fate to be subsumed by the 'system' as it is, paradoxically, embodied in another person; indeed, in her most intimate 'relation', Osmond. Yet, no matter how wanting in personal authenticity, the novel suggests that the self is never merely a 'shell'. Isabel discovers to her cost that

Madame Merle is a creature of opaque intention and an expert manipulator of the codes. Survival for Isabel is to require penetrating this woman's motives, her past and her personality.

Against Merle's semiotic view Isabel pits her own. She insists in effect that a person's essence exceeds the codes : 'nothing else expresses me'; that the cultural sign is indeed 'arbitrary' and therefore at best a 'barrier' to self-expression. Merle by contrast presages Barthes, Culler and Eco on clothes: since the self is conventional, the conventions of fashion may express it: 'a large part of myself is in the clothes I choose to wear'. For Isabel such a choice is meaningless precisely *because* it is conventional: 'To begin with it's not my own choice to wear them; they're imposed upon me by society'. What, then, is she urging? The answer appears to be a rough (and rather implausible) amalgam of Emersonian essentialism and existential self-creation. She is here what Lionel Trilling terms 'the opposing self': she has made a prior choice – or so she thinks – to reject the codes that to a large extent structure her character, and so her power of choosing.

This paradox all but breaks her; yet the novel insistently commends her position above the view to which she almost succumbs. 'I'm convention itself', says Osmond (iv.29, p. 21). It is his wish that his life be a 'work of art' (p. 15). His is the ethos of appearances, of empty and enervated forms and structures. In Osmond, self and role click so precisely into agreement that nihilism gets itself disguised as style. Unlike Madame Merle, no corner of the Osmond curtain conceals the suggestion of a soul.

Perhaps the most plausible image of self in *The Portrait* is offered by Ralph, so clearly Osmond's spiritual counterpoint in the novel. Again: 'Ah, one does n't give up one's country any more than one gives up one's grandmother. They're both antecedent to choice – elements in one's own composition that are not to be eliminated' (iii.10, p. 125). This is as close as *The Portrait* comes to actually formulating an organicist image of self: Ralph sees it as unity of past and present, and as the upshot of an interplay between culture, nature, choice and heredity. This is the image that ultimately prevails in the novel. It reads essence back into Osmond's cultural absolutism, and intersubjectivity into the solipsism of Isabel's existential disjunction of essence and expression.

But the cost of its attainment is enormous. Like Gwendolen's, Isabel's education in self comes through an agonising education in choice. Having sought 'liberty', 'expansion' and 'freedom', she too is made to 'ache with the pain of the process' of being 'narrowed'. Only in this instance it is a much more conscious choice. She actually decides to 'choose a corner and cultivate that' (iv.34, p. 65); to seek in Osmond a more hedonistic form of what Dorothea seeks in Casaubon: a life rich in 'knowledge' that 'will give one a sense of duty', but also the 'liberty' of a 'sense of enjoyment' (iv.42, p. 198). Here again is the conflict between a teleology of personal satisfaction and of Kantian 'duty'. 'A girl in love was doubtless not a free agent', she tells herself (iv.40, p. 160); yet in Isabel's case, as in Gwendolen's, the romantic sentiment has been conceptual rather than carnal: their marital choices are utterly derivative, a mere reordering of social priorities. Thus do Isabel's existential yearnings founder on convention and precedent. Ironically enough, this is another version of Madame Merle's discovery. James's reworking of Genesis reminds us that evil too is an enactment of precedent.

What then can transcend the enervated and entropic structures of personal appropriation? *The Portrait* gives no clear answer to this question; indeed, James's entire creative career is in a sense an attempt to formulate one. This he does through repeated reworkings of expatriation, appropriation and, of course, choice. His first important novel, *Roderick Hudson* (1875), centres on an American artist in Europe who believes that his 'power to choose is destined to snap like a dry twig'. Roderick's lack of originality is a self-fulfilling prophecy – and a self-destructive one. His mentor, Rowland, sums up for James: 'The power to choose *is* destiny' (Ch. 7, p. 122). Another early prototype of the international theme is *The American* (1876), where the pointedly named Christopher Newman chooses to leave America in search of a subtler self-image in Europe. But his mid-Western mercantile mind is incurably keyed to transaction, and he is as implausibly innocent as the novel's Parisians are grossly iniquitous. Newman's choice proves to be chasteningly corrective, but he lacks the sentience really to learn. *Washington Square* (1880), too, centres on choice, but in its negative form. Catherine Sloper's ultimate renunciation of Townsend presages the theme of the life not lived in later reworkings such as 'The Beast in the Jungle' (1903). The great explorations of choice in the middle period are *The Portrait* itself, *The Bostonians* (1886) and the sinister *What Maisie Knew* (1897). This, perhaps the most ruthlessly calculating of all James's novels, focuses the problem through the mind of a child. '*Can* you choose?' (xi.30, p. 338), Sir Claude asks Maisie. Initially she cannot, but a dawning sense of self and of adult entitlement issue finally in the choice of Mrs Wix. The late phase again reworks the problem of choice in an ambience of international disorientation. *The Golden Bowl* and *The Wings of the Dove* occupy later chapters; here is Lambert Strether's great disquisition on freedom and consciousness in *The Ambassadors*. Life, he urges, is

> at the best a tin mould, either fluted or embossed, with ornamental excrescences, or else smooth and dreadfully plain, into which, a helpless jelly, one's consciousness is poured – so that one 'takes' the form, as the great cook says, and is more or less compactly held by it: one lives in fine as one can. Still, one has the illusion of freedom; therefore don't be, like me, without the memory of that illusion. . . . Do what you like so long as you don't make *my* mistake. For it was a mistake. Live!
>
> （xxi.v.2, p. 218)

Strether is yet another of James's surrogates, and his advice to Little Bilham reflects the belief in a combination of free will and determinism that informs the Preface to *The Portrait*.

How far does James's notion of choice resemble George Eliot's? Whence does it derive? James is notoriously difficult to pin down on such matters. Dorothea Krook believes that his 'essential view of reality' does not derive from 'anywhere, or anybody, in particular'; Stephen Donadio's *Nietzsche, Henry James, and the Artistic Will* can offer no external evidence that James read Nietzsche, but argues for close philosophical parallels with James; J. H. Raleigh finds in the fiction a 'poetics of empiricism'; William Gass detects echoes of Kant; Paul Armstrong associates James with phenomenology; and in *Henry James and Pragmatic Thought* Richard A. Hocks explores the best-documented source of all, the tradition of pragmatism pioneered by Henry's brother, William.[135]

It is no accident that William James is counted the first of the indigenous American existentialists, nor that as late as 1905 Henry could tell him that 'Philosophically, in short, I am "with" you, almost completely.'[136] William's 'teleological view of mind'[137] resembles the novelist's own in elevating experience above *a priori* truths and in conceiving life as an experiment that might validate assumptions upon which actions are predicated. To believe in the freedom of choice is, in this view, to render freedom possible. This is what Henry means when he determines to exercise a 'will to act'[138] and when he writes to a bereaved Grace Norton that 'I don't know *why* we live' and urges her to attend to the 'terrible algebra' of her 'own life'.[139] It is to this 'algebra' that James addresses himself as he fashions seductive simulations of freedom in his fiction.

In *The Portrait* Isabel chooses on the assumption of freedom and is brutally denied it. James's famous phenomenological dictum 'consciousness is an illimitable power'[140] is here unequal to the stupefying 'system' that is Osmond's mind. Like Gwendolen, she is enslaved by the illusion of mastery. She imagines herself 'his providence' (IV.42, p. 192) and he flawlessly promotes the illusion. After declaring his love he gives her Strether's advice, but it is from demonic lips: 'Go everywhere . . . do everything; get everything out of life. Be happy – be triumphant' (IV.29, p. 16). Gradually, however, after marrying him, she feels the 'rigid system close about her' (IV.42, p. 199). His 'beautiful mind' seems to 'mock at her' (p. 196); she strikes the young Rosier as 'framed' in a 'gilded doorway' (IV.37, p. 105). There is nothing subtle here, either about James's method or Osmond's masterly marital portraiture. A horrific 'gulf' (IV.42, p. 189) divides the 'land of consideration' from the novel's vision of a Kingdom of Ends.

Yet, as she tells Henrietta, 'I married him before all the world' (IV.47, p. 284) and the status of marriage further focuses the problem of choice in the novel. Marriage is, after all, *par excellence* a public expression and validation of a private choice, and, though the novel leaves unresolved the question as to its proper claims, it grimly fulfils James's stated intention in writing the book: Isabel is indeed 'ground in the very mill of the conventional'.[141] For James, as for George Eliot, marriage epitomises the paradox of contractual freedom: 'It's to make you independent that I want to marry you', explains the importunate Goodwood (III.16, p. 228), but it is not this simple. Marriage is an intersubjective, and so an ultimately unverifiable, convention. Eliot and James explore the possibilities of the I–Thou relation, and in James they fare much the worse. Gwendolen and Isabel are cognate studies in the terror of dissolution of identity in intimacy, possession or unreflective pleasure, but in *The Portrait* no one makes a marriage like Deronda's.

V

Like George Eliot's ambivalence about freedom and choice, James's pessimism threatens the cogency of his realist technique. Though a less plural creation than Gwendolen, Isabel is nevertheless subject to a surprising array of descriptive and evaluative norms. Here indeed a characteristic Jamesian aesthetic logic is at work, for such norms – categories, indices of personal value – are also a central thematic concern of the novel. Technique and theme converge. An example is what the narrator calls 'the categories of the human appeal'. His point about these is that categories are needed to order and make sense of the intersubjective world. Needless to say, no individual is entirely without such categories, but *The Portrait of a Lady* is about the tragic paucity of many of our available norms and about the disastrous choices that flow from inadequate forms of human appraisal. Osmond seems to Isabel 'a specimen apart' who does not belong 'to types already present to her mind' (iii.24, p. 376), and so in a sense he is; but he gets through the net less because Isabel is in some vague allegorical sense 'innocent' than because the 'types' she possesses do not permit her adequately to sift the experience she has.

Creatively rethinking the 'types' is George Eliot's and James's chosen task as novelists and they employ a variety of narrative techniques in its service. Some of James's methods in *The Portrait* – the strategic personal flash-back, for example – closely resemble George Eliot's; others, however, reflect shifts both in technique and outlook. The treatment of sexuality is a case in point. James's greater dependence upon metaphoric modes of characterisation is apparent in the way he specialises Isabel's sexual fear into a sovereign, at times almost a singular, psychological trait. This fear comes to symbolise much about her existential orientation – her strength of will, her attitudes to commitment and, importantly, her attitudes to choice. And the same metaphoric technique extends to other characters, especially to Osmond. Osmond is clearly modelled in part on George Eliot's study in male perversity, Grandcourt. In both characters sexuality has become pathologically entangled in the need to dominate. Both are psychological sadists in whom libido has been displaced into will. Isabel discovers just how deep the confusion between the erotic and the despotic runs when she enters a plea for a life of shared liberty to her husband. Her plea for 'the cause of freedom, of doing as they chose', elicits an extraordinary response: 'Then it was that her husband's personality, touched as it never had been, stepped forth and stood erect' (IV.42, p. 199). The sexual imagery is typically blatant. Osmond is most aroused when his dominance and his enormous powers of repression are most threatened. Here as elsewhere, the novel hints at an eerie interplay between carnality and choice. Like Gwendolen, the audacious Isabel is subjected to a kind of psychological rape. In either case, this begins disarmingly, since their suitors' reticence appeases their fears of profound emotional commitment. Gwendolen is reassured by the 'absence of all eagerness' in Grandcourt's approaches, Isabel by the want of any 'eagerness to shine' (III.26, p. 400) in Osmond. But marriage proves to be another matter.

If Isabel's loss of her child is, like Gwendolen's childlessness, a symbolic denial of the ruthless sexual stereotyping to which she has been subjected, her alternatives seem almost as threatening. Her late encounter with Caspar at Gardencourt is itself a kind of rape, and together with the novel's accumulation of menacing sexual detail (pushing, thrusting, hardness, yielding, unlocking, parting petals), it exceeds in violent literalness anything in *Daniel Deronda*. Caspar's 'kiss'

> was like white lightning, a flash that spread, and spread again, and stayed; and it was extraordinarily as if, while she took it, she felt each thing in his hard manhood that had least pleased her, each aggressive fact of his face, his figure, his presence, justified of its intense identity and made one with this act of possession.   (IV.55, p. 436)

The moment is at once orgasmic and phobic, his 'identity', expressed in his power of sexual 'possession', a disintegrating force upon hers. But his 'love' too is a violation. She realises that

> she had never been loved before. She had believed it, but this was different; this was the hot wind of the desert, at the approach of which the others dropped dead, like mere sweet airs of the garden. It wrapped her about; it lifted her off her feet, while the very taste of it, as of something potent, acrid and strange, forced open her set teeth.   (pp. 433–4)

'Acrid' registers the repugnance Isabel feels both in her lovelessness and in her loss of liberty. Though Isabel tears herself away, the encounter seems either to confirm or to tell her something fundamental about herself. Yet this scene of ravishment (greatly heightened in the New York revision) cannot be interpreted with any certainty and it contributes to the insoluble ambiguity of the novel's conclusion. What, after all, does it mean to return to Rome after such an experience? The most humane reading must surely concede that Isabel herself may not know. And it is of course entirely consistent with James's aesthetic that we should be left in doubt. His premise is that the onus of meaning-creation should be left with the reader. *The Portrait*'s sexual descriptions thus suggest a great deal about the existential condition of its characters but resolve little with certainty. The novel leaves crucial aspects of its own story unnarrated.

The same is in a sense true of some aspects of *Daniel Deronda*. Its ending is also inconclusive: we know little more of Gwendolen and her future at the close than we do of Isabel. Yet there are significant differences. Isabel seems to have achieved a more personalised sense of duty than does Gwendolen. We do not know what choice Isabel will ultimately make, but there is an impression that her choices must now – and will now – be made unaided. This impression is partly circumstantial; but it is also a reflection of James's narrative technique, for he is prepared to abandon characters to their fates without the anxious narrative accompaniment that is a compelling need for George Eliot.

James's admission that *The Portrait* is 'before all things a study in character'[142] captures nicely his capacity to withhold compassion. A 'study' – this is what we sense Isabel to be. As the novel progresses and her crisis deepens, the narrator in fact increasingly withholds comment and recedes into impersonality. This involves the deletion of certain familiar Eliotean intensities, and also a suppression of information that she would think indispensable to a just and full account. Here again, the treatment of choice in the novels reflects differences in narrative outlook and technique. George Eliot had rendered Gwendolen's moment of marital choice in all its subtle sophistry and self-deception. But Isabel's moment of choice is never described. Instead we are given the nebulous symbolism of further travels with Madame Merle. When we next encounter Isabel, after these travels, she is married. As Leavis says when comparing Eliot and James, 'the difference is in what James leaves out'.[143] But, once again, more is involved. Typically, James prefers registration – both the character's and the reader's – to be retrospective. Isabel's 'vigil of searching criticism' in Chapter 62 is James's favourite thing in the book.[144] It epitomises what Ruth Bernard Yeazell calls the 'syntax of knowing'[145] in James, consciousness's minuet of evasion and acknowledgement in response to the crises choices have wrought.

A comparison with *Daniel Deronda* is revealing here, though, since one cannot parallel the moments of choice, it will be less misleading to compare those in which the two women recognise the magnitude of their mistakes. Gwendolen's dread intensifies at Grandcourt's slighting of Lydia Glasher:

> What possible release could there be for her from this hated vantage-ground, which yet she dared not quit, any more than if fire had been raining outside it? What release, but death? Not her own death. Gwendolen was not a woman who could easily think of her own death as a near reality, or front for herself the dark entrance on the untried and invisible. It seemed more possible that Grandcourt should die: – and yet not likely. The power of tyranny in him seemed a power of living in the presence of any wish that he should die. The thought that his death was the only possible deliverance for her was one with the thought that deliverance would never come – the double deliverance from the injury with which other beings might reproach her and from the yoke she had brought on her own neck. No! she foresaw him always living, and her own life dominated by him; the 'always' of her young experience not stretching beyond the few immediate years that seemed immeasurably long with her passionate weariness. The thought of his dying would not subsist: it turned as with a dream-change into the terror that she should die with his throttling fingers on her neck avenging that thought. Fantasies moved within her like ghosts, making no break in her more acknowledged consciousness and finding no obstruction in it: dark rays doing their work invisibly in the broad light.   (vi.48, pp. 563–4)

Isabel, as yet unaware of the role of the 'other woman', Madame Merle, in her life, reflects after a disagreement with Osmond about Pansy's future. She thinks of Osmond's house:

> Between those four walls she had lived ever since; they were to

surround her for the rest of her life. It was the house of darkness, the house of dumbness, the house of suffocation. Osmond's beautiful mind gave it neither light nor air; Osmond's beautiful mind indeed seemed to peep down from a small high window and mock at her. Of course it had not been physical suffering; for physical suffering there might have been a remedy. She could come and go; she had her liberty; her husband was perfectly polite. He took himself so seriously; it was something appalling. Under all his culture, his cleverness, his amenity, under his good-nature, his facility, his knowledge of life, his egotism lay hidden like a serpent in a bank of flowers. She had taken him seriously, but she had not taken him so seriously as that. How could she – especially when she had known him better? She was to think of him as he thought of himself – as the first gentleman in Europe. So it was that she had thought of him at first, and that indeed was the reason she had married him. But when she began to see what it implied she drew back. . . .　　(*The Portrait*, iv.42, pp. 196–7)

Both passages are centrally concerned with psychic death: the horror of one's own and the desire to transfer its 'suffocating' 'power' to the oppressor. However, while the desire is explicit in Gwendolen, it is sublimated and unconscious in Isabel. Her response is a kind of typologising or arranging of Osmond, who had once seemed 'a specimen apart', under conventional 'categories' of 'human appeal'. The activity is at once agonised and organised; a highly cerebral sifting of the data of her life. It finds expression in the almost surgical precision of James's middle style. The sentences are shorter than George Eliot's; a kind of composure-in-recognition is suggested by the way in which knowledge unfolds through balanced and parallel qualifying clauses: 'Osmond's beautiful mind . . . Osmond's beautiful mind indeed . . . .' Yet the deadly imagery – the house, the serpent – is a scenic, an almost hypnotic, objectification of a state, a measured transcription of unconscious horror for conscious consideration that gives the lie to the assurance, though at this stage more for the reader than for the character. The vigil sequence is remarkable for the extent to which consciousness is its own reflector. James's peerless sense of psychic privacy quite remarkably confers upon what is in fact a manifestly *written* and stylised passage of interleaved psychonarration and narrated monologue a sense of solitude that seems magically – though of course deceptively – to exclude the narrative voice.

The Eliot passage is by contrast far more uneven in all respects – linguistic, formal, psychological, epistemological. Gwendolen's awareness is less edited than Isabel's, more a case of the whole being in panicked and instantaneous reaction. Needless to say, character here cannot articulate as it can in James, and the narrator wrenches discourse from quirkily punctuated narrated monologue ('What release, but death?'), to a subtilised narrative rendering of the character's formulations ('The thought of his dying would not subsist'), thence to a position of acknowledged experiential superiority: 'the 'always' of her young experience'. Here parallel clauses or phrases actually trigger imbalance: 'the double deliverance from the injury' denies the symmetry created in 'The thought that his death was the only possible deliverance for her was one with the thought that deliverance would never come. . . .' Such strategies also of course *reflect* imbalance, the veerings of consciousness in agonised registration, its intensities expressed in a greater dependence on narrated monologue than James's requires. Nor does James require the sense of the body that is so apparent in George Eliot. While the body and its death throes (suffocation) are in James a metaphor for the mind, in George Eliot they are also an actuality – Gwendolen's horror rends her nerves; feeling is powerfully physical and physical death seems a plausible extension of the moral depravity she is coming to acknowledge. Again, Gwendolen's 'large discourse of imaginative fears', and the contingent inclusiveness of George Eliot's method, create an atmosphere of mind quite unlike James's. Each writer of course acknowledges the presence of mental 'process', of the systematic and rationalising activities of the psyche; and each (though James far more than George Eliot) would assume that narrative convention is in a sense analogous in its systematic activity, its mediation through structure and form. Yet, by comparison with George Eliot's, James's sense of mind seems articulated, censored to a degree that excludes the admission of the primitive energies of the unconscious. Seldom in James do unconscious 'phantoms' well up into consciousness as they do here in Gwendolen; nor does he generally concede this degree of riotous discord within the psyche. His is the language of displacement and repression. It is not, of course, that he does not perceive the discord; rather that the inchoate, the unaestheticised, is of less interest to him than it is to Eliot, and that it is the deadly game in which consciousness enacts its minuet of evasion and sentient objectification that constitutes his central subject. To this extent, Isabel's consciousness is never made 'quite natural' in an Eliotean sense. She remains what many readers sense her to be on a first reading: something of an absent character.

The contrast is apparent in the treatment of portraits in the two novels. In *Deronda* we are told,

> Some faces which are peculiar in their beauty are like original works of art: for the first time they are almost always met with question. But in seeing Gwendolen at Diplow, Deronda had discerned in her more than he had expected of that tender appealing charm which we call womanly. Was there any new change since then? He distrusted his impressions; but as he saw her receiving greetings with what seemed a proud cold quietude and a superficial smile, there seemed to be at work within her the same demonic force that had possessed her when she took him in her resolute glance and turned away a loser from the gaming-table. There was no time for more of a conclusion – no time even for him to give his greeting before the summons to dinner.   (v.35, pp. 378–9)

The passage bristles with 'Jamesian' words – 'charm', 'impressions', 'appealing', 'change' – and George Eliot implies that for Deronda Gwendolen's 'wonderfully mixed consciousness' (vii.56, p. 647) remains a portrait paradigmatically incomplete. Yet *Daniel Deronda* takes transparency far enough for Daniel to frame and typify our sense of Gwendolen's spiritual possibilities. Isabel learns not simply that she possesses a personal essence, but that it must somehow find articulation and protection within the codes. But it is more radically a novel of incompletion than George Eliot's, for the lessons of self-expression, self-preservation, and indeed the state of the codes themselves, are all in the end left unresolved. The frames of the portrait close somewhat claustrally around its anguished subject.

VI

Ralph Touchett is central to any understanding of Isabel's character and fate; but, before considering James's enigmatic surrogate, let us briefly review the 'terrible algebra' of correspondences between the two novels.[146]

The Portrait teems with textual clues to confirm a deeper indebtedness and influence. There is an intriguing transposition of names: Grandcourt becomes Gardencourt, and Grandcourt's first name, Henleigh, is echoed in the name of Warburton's house, Lockleigh. Moreover, Gwendolen has a sister called Isabel. Each protagonist is in a sense displaced: Isabel from her native America, Gwendolen (the 'princess in exile') from her customary social status. Each has a flimsy notion of freedom which precipitates choices of similarly murderous (and jealous) husbands. Each is emotionally intense ('suffering, with Isabel, was an active condition' – iv.42, p. 189), prone to fear and apparently sexually diffident. Having erred, each has to negotiate the threat of egoism, both in herself and in others; they have also to face the true significance of 'another woman' in their lives (Lydia and Madame Merle) and to weigh afresh the relative claims of freedom and duty. In this Gwendolen has Deronda's counsel, whilst Isabel has the more equivocal involvement of her cousin Ralph. Circumstantially at least, each novel provides an inconclusive ending for its heroine; each also uses an existential notation of water, expanse, chariots (or coaches) and captivity. Against such similarities it may be argued that there are actually in some cases closer parallels between *Middlemarch* and *The Portrait* than between *The Portrait* and *Deronda*. Certainly, there are significant discrepancies between the plots of *The Portrait* and *Deronda*, discrepancies which reflect more general structural dissimilarities. Isabel is more central to *The Portrait* than is Gwendolen to *Daniel Deronda*; Isabel's choice does not, unlike Gwendolen's, entail a moral decision about the entitlements of a third party: Lydia rails against the marriage; Madame Merle orchestrates it. Isabel receives a fortune and, as a result, marries a man of moderate means; Gwendolen is tempted to accept Grandcourt partly because her family has been dispossessed. Again, George Eliot, enamoured of prophetic possibility, satirises the superficialities of Victorian country-house life where James, though as always ambivalent, invests it with characteristic romance and enchantment. Isabel is at the outset more sensitive, solicitous and cultured than Gwendolen and she marries a man who is also more cultivated than Grandcourt. George Eliot's novel ends, though not for the heroine, on a note of visionary expansion, with Deronda sailing for the East and Gwendolen resolving that she shall 'live'; *The Portrait* also closes with a journey, but it is a journey back to the face and place of bondage. Isabel's intentions at this point are perhaps even less accessible to us than Gwendolen's, though much here depends upon one's understanding of her relationship with Ralph and of her vision of his ghost.

Unlike Gwendolen, who somewhat begrudgingly welcomes Deronda's grand corrective benignity into her life, Isabel is inclined to feel that she does not 'need the aid of a clever man to teach me how to live' (iii.16, p. 223). But of course Ralph offers precisely that when he urges her not to marry Osmond. Moreover, in arranging the nearly fatal freedoms of his father's bequest, he, like Deronda, exerts an extraordinarily potent influence over her. Further, he shares with Deronda a spiritual and intellectual superiority over his female charge: Deronda has the sacred capacity of the 'transformation of self'; just so, Ralph has, in the famous phrase, 'the imagination of loving' (iii.5, p. 54). Both faculties have at their finest an impersonality that the heroines lack; however, Ralph's is in fact much the more equivocal for being deeply tied to personal gratification. He tells his father, 'I call people rich when they're able to meet the requirements of their imagination' (iii.18, p. 261); but it becomes grimly apparent that Isabel's enrichment is also to be everyone else's. The term 'requirements' attaches itself most notably to Madame Merle (iii.22, p. 345), to Osmond (iv.49, p. 324) and to Ralph himself, who admits to his father his desire to meet through the spectacle of Isabel's freedom the 'requirements of my imagination' (iii.18, p. 265). Thus does the spiritual economy of the novel's 'art' world, with its myriad 'portraits' and 'possessions', threaten to subvert generosity into gratification, ethics into exhibition. The novel's gallery of portraits of course produces a series of mirror or cognate images: Ralph and Osmond, Isabel and Madame Merle, Pansy and Mrs Touchett, Caspar and Rosier, among others; but the relationship between Ralph and Isabel is one of the more ambiguous. Clearly, Deronda is an alter ego for Gwendolen in a sense both more specific and more developed than Ralph is for Isabel, and as such Ralph has a more indirect effect upon his cousin's personal development. However, like Deronda, he is central to an interrelated set of themes concerning choice, destiny, conditioning and death.

Like Deronda, Ralph is a man whose identity has been rendered equivocal by a problem of antecedence. While Deronda's Jewishness has been concealed, Ralph has been divided between cultures. Though he chooses to settle in England, he concludes that both nationality and heredity are prior to volition: 'one does n't give up one's country any more than one gives up one's grandmother. They are both antecedent to choice. . . .' Like Deronda, then, Ralph has both an ordained genetic self and one that is the issue of a conditioning culture; however, unlike George Eliot's quester, Ralph exercises his power of choice to fashion an identity that in a sense denies both. Here the larger question of categorisation and authenticity that motivates James's international theme arises. Importantly, Ralph's voyage of self-definition runs essentially counter to his originating culture. Deronda's lies *through* his. Moreover, where Ralph actively chooses expatriation, Deronda suspends choice in anticipation of a visionary dissolution of self in genetic community. This revealed, he makes a choice that the messianic logic of the novel forbids him to decline.

If Deronda's example is as much a matter of an active mission as of an exacting message, Ralph's is to be intimately connected with passivity and death: his ghost is to tell Isabel more than anything the living man says to her. Here, indeed, the consumptive Ralph and the consumptive Mordecai may be distant analogues (it would be ambitious and forced to claim a closer relation): George Eliot's Kabbalistic doctrine proposes a transference of the energies of the dead to their refined incarnations, whilst Ralph's death, with its echoes of the crucifixion, entails a transference of tragic knowledge from the dead to the living. Each is apparently a way of insisting upon the existence of the soul. But the parallel is qualified by the fact that Deronda, and not Gwendolen, is the recipient of such knowledge in *Daniel Deronda*; also by the very different impact of life-upon-life involved in the relationships between the two heroes of sentiment and their 'frail vessels'. Though Deronda scours Gwendolen's consciousness with all the renovating sternness of George Eliot's religious humanism, Ralph's influence is in fact more potent. Deronda gestures eloquently towards a 'horizon', an ethical destiny; Ralph, enchanted benefactor that he is, actually constitutes a destiny for Isabel. He confers upon her 'freedom' and thereby freedom of choice; he becomes, like Merle and Osmond, an 'agent' in her life. If Deronda represents a transhistorical possibility, Ralph incarnates the power other people assume when life is stripped of transcendental or universal implication. His wish, like Deronda's, is to see his charge use her power of choosing; but until it is too late he does not desire to influence the choices she makes. Thereafter, of course, his belated advice avails less than Deronda's. He has sought 'amusement' (iii.18, p. 262) in a facilitated freedom; but he is to find heartbreak in the recognition that a delegation of choice is also a delegation of the capacity for tragic error. Here indeed James's more subjectivist concept of choice is apparent. In *Daniel Deronda* choice is ultimately highly circumscribed, either by the claims of tradition and heredity (Deronda), or by social convention (Gwendolen); in *The Portrait* neither will avail, and if the failure of tradition and the codes here render individual choosing more urgent, they also, and thereby, render it more problematic.

Like Deronda's, Ralph's attachment is more than merely managerial. The two relationships are suffused with sexual tension, and Ralph indeed declares his love for Isabel. But he must of course remain a spectator, the 'person upon whom nothing is lost', but upon whom, also, alas, no power of immediate engagement is conferred. He is surely the most poignant and likable version of the vicarious character in James. He is also one of the most plausible; for, unlike the culturally remote and stylised portrait that is Deronda, this one acknowledges a tragic complicity between love and manipulation, mortal wisdom and the woe it can visit upon other lives.

4 Knowledge: *Middlemarch* and *The Golden Bowl*

ELIOT, JAMES AND KNOWLEDGE

The theme of choice in *Daniel Deronda* and *The Portrait of a Lady* is much complicated by the problem of personal displacement; for a displaced person, be it an unwitting Jew or an expatriate American, must often choose at a certain self-conscious remove from coercive or consoling cultural norms. This may mean that no clear guidance emerges from a dominant traditional perspective on conduct; that narratives linking the youthful and adult, or the public and private, personality are absent or insufficient; or, in a more general sense, that certain fundamental assumptions about the authority of the individual moral agent cease to obtain. Choices thus become either impossibly opaque or a matter of isolated and anxious existential self-determination. In George Eliot's 'Jewish novel' the prescriptive spiritual continuity of Judaism must be revealed before Deronda can choose; Isabel Archer, by contrast, marries into an indefinite exile which dictates that she must largely make unaided choices. The expatriate, poised between a native and an adopted culture, may invoke the categorical imperative and do what seems appropriate on a rough scale of general moral propriety, but it is a wintry prospect, especially if your husband is constitutionally incapable of the Kantian sense of conscience.

However, these novels do not reserve displacement exclusively for those who are physically abroad. Expatriatism, like dispersed forms of Judaism, is also, as James knew so well, a state of mind. Caspar Goodwood and Warburton possess it at home. So too, of course, does Gwendolen. In fact George Eliot makes roughly this point in the famous Prelude to *Middlemarch*. Though more sophisticated and spiritually intense than Gwendolen, Dorothea Brooke, introduced as a sort of modern St Theresa, is said to suffer the general impediments to self-expression that other English women of the nineteenth century experience. For these latter-day Theresas, even indigenous culture can be a form of exile. Such women 'were helped by no coherent social faith and order which could perform the function of knowledge for the ardently willing soul' (I, p. 2). Whether *Middlemarch* entirely sustains this claim in relation to Dorothea is open to question. But such judgements can wait. For the moment the important qualification to George Eliot's anxious humanist account is the word 'knowledge'. The Prelude joins *Deronda* and *The Portrait of a Lady* in arguing that a loss of general cultural coherence results in far-reaching forms of psychological and epistemological disequilibrium. Accepted parameters of knowledge, be it of intellectual disciplines or of other people, are threatened, blurred or overturned. Thus does *Middlemarch* repeatedly test the proper limits and configurations of knowledge against a background of rapid historical change and transformation. It asks not just what one can know about mythology, human anatomy, human psychology, but *how* knowledge is constituted and with what authority.

This chapter centres on knowledge, for both *Middlemarch* and *The Golden Bowl* are creative inquiries into what the philosophers call the problem of other minds. What is the status of the knowledge we claim to have of other minds? Whence does it derive? What, both in literature and in life, are its moral implications? Characteristically, however, divides between 'literature' and 'life' mock what Eliot and James have written, for it is clear that both understood the writing of fiction to be a special, but also a powerfully representative, species of intersubjective report: novels not only create, they also in a worrying sense penetrate, character. They take liberties in art about which both Eliot and James felt uncomfortable in life. This is not, needless to say, to imply that characters in novels are as it were ontologically continuous with people in life – a point to which we shall return – rather that they are sufficiently similar for writers of this kind to worry that, *qua* novelists, they run certain more general moral risks. As George Eliot's fiction, criticism and letters so often demonstrate, knowledge was for her what James in *The Golden Bowl* calls 'a fascination as well as a fear' (XXIV.iv.8, p. 180). It compelled but also appalled her, and a dread about knowing infuses everything she wrote. Often, indeed, this has significant aesthetic implications, for her writing is characteristically marked by a sense of conflict between the privileges and the presumptions of her chosen literary form.

GEORGE ELIOT ON OTHER MINDS: THE LETTERS, NOVELS AND 'THE LIFTED VEIL'

The psychological sources of this conflict run deep in George Eliot's letters. Whilst staying in Geneva with D'Albert-Durade and his wife, the young Mary Ann Evans writes home that 'I feel they are my *friends* – without entering into or even knowing the greater part of my views, they understand my character, and have a real interest in me'.[1] 'Understand', and 'real interest': the insistence upon tact and solicitude, so prominent in the fiction, is already apparent here; and, in a later letter written after the publication of *Adam Bede*, it appears more forcefully still. She wishes to write 'something that would contribute to heighten men's reverence before the secrets of each other's souls, that there might be less assumption of entire knowingness, as a datum from which inferences are to be drawn'.[2] 'Knowingness', like the oft-mentioned 'curiosity' (she writes in another letter that 'I hate hard curiosity'[3]), is anathema to the novelist who so deeply wishes to recommend sympathy, an affective participation in the feelings of others, to her reader. In the early story 'Janet's Repentance' she writes characteristically: 'Yet surely, surely the only true knowledge of our fellow-man is that which enables us to feel with him' (*Scenes of Clerical Life*, ii.10, p. 166). *Adam Bede* ostensibly endorses this sentiment through Adam's development and the selflessness of Dinah Morris. However, the novel is often ambivalent about personal knowledge, especially in relation to its implications for narrative. As this ironic aside about Arthur Donnithorne implies, there is a moral need, even an obligation, for narrators to reveal what remains hidden in life: 'It would be ridiculous to be prying and analytic in such cases, as if one were inquiring into the character of a confidential clerk. We use round, general, gentlemanly epithets about a young man of birth and fortune . . . (i.12, p. 186). Yet elsewhere character, in life and in books, is said to be extremely difficult to sound: 'Our mental business is carried on much in the same way as the business of the State: a great deal of hard work is done by agents who are not acknowledged. . . . The human soul is a very complex thing'

(I.16, p. 259). And consistent with this is the acknowledgement that, in part because of the inadequacy of language, the interior life cannot be given in any but stylised form in art: 'These were Arthur's chief thoughts, so far as a man's thoughts through hours of travelling can be compressed into a few sentences, which are only like the list of names telling you what are the scenes in a long, long panorama, full of colour, of detail, and of life' (II.44, p. 228).

The Mill on the Floss contains a number of related references. The narrator, for example, cautions against what the letter cited above calls 'knowingness': 'there is nothing more widely misleading than sagacity if it happens to get on a wrong scent; and sagacity, persuaded that men usually act and speak from distinct motives, with a consciously proposed end in view, is certain to waste its energies on imaginary game' (i.3, p. 22). Philip Wakem, talking to Maggie, is even more emphatic: 'I think there are stores laid up in our human nature that our understanding can make no complete inventory of' (v.1, p. 269). *Romola* often urges this position, stressing what it calls 'the complexities in human things' (II.52, p. 236) and the obscurity of human motives; and a revealing passage in Chapter 25 concerning Savonarola's desire for mastery of his audience echoes George Eliot's letter to Charles Bray in cautioning against precipitous inferences about the inner lives of others:

> The mysteries of human character have seldom been presented in a way more fitted to check the judgments of facile knowingness than in Girolamo Savonarola; but we can give him a reverence that needs no shutting of the eyes to fact, if we regard his life as a drama in which there were great inward modifications accompanying the outward changes.
>
> (I.25, p. 359)

Yet, rather characteristically, the rejection of 'facile knowingness' does not hold for the entire novel, and George Eliot's contrasting tendency – to trace and explain the intricacies of behaviour – surfaces revealingly when the narrator argues that 'A course of action which is in strictness a slowly-prepared outgrowth of the entire character, is yet almost always traceable to a single impression as its point of apparent origin' (II.35, p. 34). If the influence of Feuerbach registers behind many of George Eliot's exhortations to sympathise, there is perhaps a hint of Comtean positivistic confidence about explicating the processes of the mind in this almost clinical aside.

The thematic concern with personal knowledge continues in *Felix Holt*, a novel that explores George Eliot's characteristic value contrasts between egoism and sympathy, solicitude and curiosity. Harold Transome is accused of 'not caring greatly to know other people's thoughts' (Ch. 2, p. 32); Mr Lyon, on the other hand, refrains from importunate questioning from the finest sense of tact and propriety. After Esther's suggestion that she might see Felix before his trial, 'A new thought had visited him [Lyon]. But his delicate tenderness shrank even from an inward inquiry that was too curious – that seemed like an effort to peep at sacred secrets' (Ch. 44, p. 359). Again, at the end of the novel, the narrator declines to say where Felix now resides, 'lest he should be troubled by any visitor having the insufferable motive of curiosity' (Epilogue, p. 399). The limits of what in *The Mill on the Floss* is called 'sagacity' are again asserted here. Though the novel has recurrent recourse to natural-historical and scientific metaphor, the narrator significantly uses the microscope motif to argue not for human predictability but for the reverse: 'But very close and diligent looking at living creatures, even through the best microscope, will leave room for new and contradictory discoveries' (*Felix Holt*, Ch. 22, p. 197).

As we shall see, *Middlemarch* takes up these themes with a subtlety and inclusiveness seldom equalled in English fiction. But they are of course also pervasive in the discontinuous visionary world of *Daniel Deronda*, where what the narrator calls 'the wonderful mixtures of our nature' (vii.50, p. 579) constitute a constant appeal to an intuitive compassion. The force of the appeal in respect of the narrator and her characters is classically given in a passage of reflection occasioned by Gwendolen. The narrator speaks of

the iridescence of her character – the play of various, nay, contrary tendencies. For Macbeth's rhetoric about the impossibility of being many opposite things in the same moment, referred to the clumsy necessities of action and not to the subtler possibilities of feeling. We cannot speak a loyal word and be meanly silent, we cannot kill and not kill in the same moment; but a moment is room wide enough for the loyal and

mean desire, for the outlash of a murderous thought and the
sharp backward stroke of repentance.   (i.4, p. 36)

Such references to 'play' seem at times to resemble the post-
structural image of the psyche as a 'chain' of 'signifers'[4] that must
forever defer and displace 'presence' from the individual self. Yet
George Eliot would not have welcomed Lacan's logical and
clinical privileging of the public symbolic order over the substance
of individual consciousness.[5] She believed in something like
contextual privacy in the self, and her point about Gwendolen is
that her 'contrary tendencies' go deeper than conflicts produced
merely by the dynamics of language. Moreover, the narrator in
Deronda makes an important and characteristic Eliotean
distinction between the kind of obscurity that results from
category confusions in human concepts, and the much more
stubborn sort that reflects the incorrigible limits of human
understanding. Thus the following passage represents an advance
upon her earlier belief in 'the gradual reduction of all phenomena
within the shell of established law, which carries as a consequence
the rejection of the miraculous'.[6] Its emphasis is not on the power
of 'law' to subsume phenomena, but rather on the often terminal
elusiveness of the things human beings seek to know. A narrative
containing characters can, for example, never be complete.

> Men, like planets, have both a visible and an invisible history.
> The astronomer threads the darkness with strict deduction,
> accounting so for every visible arc in the wanderer's orbit; and
> the narrator of human actions, if he did his work with the same
> completeness, would have to thread the hidden pathways
> of feeling and thought which lead up to every moment of
> action . . .   (ii.16, p. 149)

This also holds for relationships between people, including the
characters in this novel. The good-natured Sir Hugo suffers from a
common 'dullness towards what may be going on in other minds'
(p. 159), but even its array of gifted and visionary spirits must
accept the limits of what the narrator repeatedly terms
'interpretation': 'all meanings . . . depend on the key of
interpretation' (i.6, p. 51). Yet here, as in *Middlemarch*, keys are
not infallible. As always, the deepest kinds of understanding are
conceived as actively yet solicitously imaginative. Catherine

Arrowpoint has 'a mind that can flash out comprehension' (iii.22, p. 221); Deronda possesses a 'reverential tenderness' (vii.51, p. 591), a disclination to impinge upon the private worlds of others.He shrinks lest 'he should obtrude his interest upon' the destitute Mirah (ii.17, p. 173), and 'from what might seem like curiosity, or the assumption of a right to know as much as he pleased' (iii.20, p. 208). His faculty for 'the transmutation of self' (v.37, p. 435) is contrasted with the 'knowingness' (i.6, p. 47) that blinds the adolescent Gwendolen to Grandcourt's ruthless perversity.

However discontinuous, the touchstone of the world of *Daniel Deronda* is divination, that loving attentiveness that cannot be simulated through system. Whence does it arise? The narrator answers, 'In many of our neighbours' lives, there is much not only of error and lapse, but of a certain exquisite goodness which can never be written or even spoken – only divined by each of us, according to the inward instructions of our own privacy' (ii.16, p. 163). The 'instructions of our own privacy' – the phrase expresses the cardinal link between George Eliot's aesthetic and her ethics. Just as one must extrapolate from introspection in order to appraise other minds, so an Eliot novel ideally offers a kind of introspection opened sensitively out to a respectful understanding. Her techniques for rendering consciousness in fiction – narrated monologue, psychonarration and others – are intended to give an exemplary and educative public access to a private world in order that readers may reconceive and repeat certain structures of solicitous knowing and inference in their own lives.

Much of the human damage done in George Eliot's novels, however, results from failures of love in just this sense; indeed, she was well aware of the tragic scarcity of true compassion. Perhaps the most dramatic and shocking admission of this fact is her remarkable short story 'The Lifted Veil', published in 1859, a story of which she was to say years later: 'There are many things in it which I would willingly say over again, and I shall never put them in any other form.'[7]

'The Lifted Veil' elevates to a scale of Gothic horror George Eliot's life-long concern with the proprieties of knowledge. Written during a time when her pseudonym was causing a crisis of secrecy and trust in her own life, it overtly images the nightmare of category collapse that haunts and impels her visions of rational and sympathetic society elsewhere. The tale describes a young man, part romantic isolate, part Swiftean misanthrope, who is cursed with total knowingness. Latimer undeservedly acquires not only clairvoyant powers (the story begins with a prevision of his own death) but also the horrific power of involuntary access to other minds. With one important exception, other minds become transparent to him: narrator-like, he penetrates the 'veil' of public personality. This 'superadded consciousness' (p. 294) is appalling in respect of casual acquaintances; but in closer relations it

> became an intense pain and grief when it seemed to be opening to me the souls of those who were in a close relation to me – when the rational talk, the graceful attentions, the wittily-turned phrases, and the kindly deeds, which used to make the web of their characters, were seen as if thrust asunder by a microscopic vision, that showed all the intermediate frivolities, all the suppressed egoism, all the struggling chaos of puerilities, meanness, vague capricious memories, and indolent make-shift thoughts, from which human words and deeds emerge like leaflets covering a fermenting heap.   (p. 295)

Passages such as these – and there are many – bristle with implication. The allusions to webs, microscopes and the inward economy of egoism indicate a deep continuity between the story and the novels, especially *Middlemarch*. Again, the image of 'leaflets covering a fermenting heap' reflects a characteristic Eliotean ambivalence towards an intuited (pre-Freudian) nihilistic nightlife in the mind. There are shades here both of the derivative triviality of Rosamond Lydgate, and of the tragic, 'unmapped' inner world of Gwendolen Harleth.

Latimer's descriptions of his state are eloquent enough to neutralise some of the story's Gothic implausibility. He complains of a 'double consciousness' (p. 307) and – in one of the most momentous phrases in George Eliot's work – of 'the fatiguing obviousness of . . . other minds' (p. 319). That the problem of 'other minds' should dwindle to the spiritual destitution of their becoming 'obvious' is her extreme formulation of the threat posed by improper – 'curious', obtrusive, knowing, indelicate – forms of knowledge. In adolescence she had written that each individual is an island;[8] 'The Lifted Veil' indicates that George Eliot feared the dissolution of personal boundaries quite as much as their power to isolate.

Latimer's solution to his situation is, like much else in the story, at once faintly absurd and psychologically plausible. He marries one Bertha, the only person to whom he does not have the power of involuntary psychic access. She is – in another striking phrase – his 'oasis of mystery in the dreary desert of knowledge' (p. 301), his salving source of obscurity. He notes that

> About Bertha I was always in a state of uncertainty: I could watch the expression of her face, and speculate on its meaning; I could ask her for her opinion with the real interest of ignorance; I could listen for her words and watch for her smile with hope and fear: she had for me the fascination of an unravelled destiny.   (pp. 296–7)

However hyperbolic, Latimer's lamentations give lurid expression to George Eliot's belief not only in the existence of veiled regions in other selves, but also in the inescapable moral implications of there being such regions in others: it is in her view simply, radically, perhaps even biologically, the case that, however passionately curious, human beings are characterised by certain limits, as well as certain powers of access, to knowledge. Thus, when the veil eventually rises upon Bertha's mind, revealing a conniving and trivial murderess, Latimer bids the reader

> Conceive the condition of the human mind if all propositions whatsoever were self-evident except one, which was to become self-evident at the close of a summer's day, but in the meantime might be the subject of question, of hypothesis, of debate. Art and philosophy, literature and science, would fasten like bees on that one proposition which had the honey of probability in it, and be the more eager because their enjoyment would end with sunset. Our impulses, our spiritual activities, no more adjust themselves to the idea of their future nullity, than the beating of our heart, or the irritability of our muscles.   (pp. 318–19)

This again demostrates how far all forms of knowledge were to George Eliot heuristic. 'Art and philosophy, literature and science' are alike 'experiments in life' that are, paradoxically, predicated upon ignorance. More precisely, George Eliot's 'meliorism'[9] pictures ignorance as a thing dwindling infinitesimally towards an ideal but unattainable limit; but also as a thing that can be actually mitigated through a participation in tradition. In 'The Lifted Veil', as in *Daniel Deronda*, Judaism joins the arts, philosophy and science in symbolising tradition. Latimer has a doleful vision of personal and cultural exclusion at a synagogue in Prague, feeling that this medieval 'remnant . . . was of a piece with my vision' (p. 309). He too is diasporic, a man in exile; only his exile goes still deeper than any in *Daniel Deronda* since he suffers from normal human limitations.

The motto George Eliot appended to the tale for publication in the Cabinet Edition makes this pivotal – but also problematic – point:

> Give me no light, great heaven, but such as turns
> To energy of human fellowship;
> No powers beyond the growing heritage
> That makes completer manhood.   (p. 276)

Here again is the fusion of a notion of biological ('human'), and tradition-bearing, cultural community ('growing heritage'). However, the tale is no more reassuring on this issue than *Daniel Deronda*. Latimer's narrative is oddly divided between culpability and determinism. The story's Gothic logic suggests that Latimer's freakish exemption from normal human 'light' is no fault of his; yet he reproves himself for his own youthful failures of sympathetic understanding towards others. He finds in himself the cardinal Eliotean flaw, 'egoism' (p. 308), and a self-pitying passivity before his fate (p. 311). At this stage the story's internal logic collapses and it becomes clear that George Eliot has here fashioned out of a moralised Gothicism a kind of residual realism in which the reader is expected to concede familiar orders of judgement and appraisal where they simply do not obtain.

In this (limited) sense 'The Lifted Veil' might be said to 'deconstruct', if George Eliot's manifest artistic intention be acknowledged. The tale may also lend some credence to George Levine's thesis about the paridigmatic status of *Frankenstein* for English realism;[10] but Judith Wilt's study of Gothic influence, *Ghosts of the Gothic*, is perhaps most illuminating in suggesting that 'the very hallmark of the Gothic' appears where 'character steps entirely out of choice into destiny, past that twilight of choice-within-destiny, wherein George Eliot and all the great English novelists normally operate'.[11] As we have seen, 'choice-within-destiny' is the prevailing imaginative ambience of *Daniel Deronda* and *The Portrait of a Lady*; in 'The Lifted Veil', however, George Eliot invests her choice narrative with a burden of circumstance that invalidates much of her moral analysis. The story's reproving ritualistic obscurantism surely suggests some of the deep personal sources apparent in the letters.

Such speculation is best pursued in the biographies,[12] but even a modest familiarity with her life reveals in George Eliot a person riven by what in *Middlemarch* she calls 'the terrible stringency of human need' (II.48, p. 313) on the one hand, and an appreciation of the necessity for a margin of self-sufficiency on the other. Perhaps Ruby Redinger is right to suggest that the 'dual solitude'[13] Eliot shared with Lewes largely resolved this tension, but certainly her fiction everywhere registers the pull between an impulse to dissolution in relationship that would sate need but denature self, and an acknowledged need for a degree of dignified detachment. The *Mill*'s famous 'need of being loved' (VI.4, p. 344) meets what resistance George Eliot can muster, but it is surely significant that, before she began writing fiction, George Eliot had complained to Herbert Spencer of being haunted by a 'double consciousness',[14] the very thing she imputes to Latimer. In a highly complex way this resistance reaches beyond her fictional themes to the structural relationships she establishes as she shapes character in narrative. As we shall see in *Middlemarch*, her omniscient technique anticipates the threat of total knowingness and transparency, even as it opens character out to seemingly unwarranted intrusions. But, as the apologetics of knowledge that threads its way through her fiction suggests, there is a guiltily self-conscious expertise at work here, a sense perhaps that the ethics of realist epistemology may be open to serious censure. Interestingly, 'The Lifted Veil' is George Eliot's only fictional attempt at first-person narration (excepting, of course, the miscellaneous *Impressions of Theophrastus Such*); indeed, the story's narrative structure is an odd hybrid that might best be termed first-person omniscience: Latimer tells his own story, but with total insight into the 'other minds' that people it.

This was perhaps what George Eliot meant when she said that there were 'many things in it which I would willingly say over again, and I shall never put them in any other form'. The story's eerie self-cancelling logic seems calculated to test the pretensions of moral realism; to incite suspected ethical incoherence into an admission of a deeper aesthetic one. This work, so thematically reminiscent of the great novels – Latimer even hears *Middlemarch*'s famous 'roar which lies on the other side of silence' (1.20, pp. 297–8) and is relieved that his old friend Charles has the 'delicacy' not to 'penetrate' into his appalling 'condition and circumstances' (p. 332) – is accorded its own 'form', never after repeated. Perhaps, however, this strangely compelling and anomalous story is prefigured in another George Eliot letter, where she admits that 'I fear authors must submit to be something of monsters not quite simple healthy human beings; but I will keep my monstrosity within bounds if possible'.[15] Such 'bounds' do not restrain Latimer. He stands as a kind of Gothic 'monster' in a moralised realist fictional world. Like George Eliot, Henry James feared the author's 'irrepressible and insatiable, his extravagant and immoral, interest in personal character and in the "nature" of a mind, of almost any mind'.[16] Latimer, himself a failed poet, seems to confess to a guilty logic that runs deep in the novelists' kindred narrative forms.

MIDDLEMARCH

I

If the appalled Gothicism of 'The Lifted Veil' serves to fetishise the problem of personal knowledge, it also asserts that the various worlds of knowledge and appraisal are not discrete. 'Art and philosophy, literature and science,' human relationships, are all alike heuristic; all depend upon a strange species dialectic of knowing and not knowing if they are to meet the requirements of human understanding. Significantly, the story reverses the *Frankenstein* pattern. In this instance it is the man of science who evinces the instinctive delicacy that the would-be poet Latimer is denied. Latimer notes that his old friend Charles, now a celebrated physician, 'repressed with the utmost delicacy all betrayal of the shock which I am sure he must have received from our meeting, or of a desire to penetrate into my condition and circumstances' (p. 332). Though by comparison a work of sober realism, *Middlemarch* again takes up the knowledge theme and images its worlds as web-like in their interconnection. The great novel's encyclopaedic inquiry bridges scholarship, science, various forms of systematics, narrative and aesthetic theory, and the world of personal relationships; indeed it insists upon the difficulty, but also the necessity, of bringing erudition to bear upon the problems of social and domestic intercourse. Casaubon's lack of delight in his marriage prompts the observation that 'It is true that he knew all the classical passages implying the contrary; but knowing classical passages, we find, is a mode of motion, which explains why they leave so little extra force for their personal application' (i.10, pp. 126–7). 'Personal application' crystallises *Middlemarch*'s concern with the assimilation of the various worlds of knowledge, and with the imperative that learnedness, no matter how remote, should have a moral and social force.

Personal knowledge – its complexities and its calls to compassion – is constantly under discussion in the novel. Casaubon, in a moment of unwitting irony, affirms its necessity by urging against it. Dorothea's disinclination to ride ought not, he thinks, to be queried: '"We must not inquire too curiously into motives," he interposed, in his measured way. "Miss Brooke knows that they are apt to become feeble in the utterance: the aroma is mixed with the grosser air. We must keep the germinating grain away from the light"' (i.2, p. 30). Rosamond and Lydgate's marriage is one of several studies in failed understanding. Rosamond 'had been little used to imagining other people's states of mind except as a material cut into shape by her own wishes' (iii.78, p. 374), and between her and her husband there occurs 'that total missing of each other's mental track, which is too evidently possible even between persons who are continually thinking of each other' (iii.58, p. 81). Casaubon's plight is again used to stress the need for candour and openness when we are told that 'His experience was of that pitiable kind which shrinks from pity, and fears most of all that it should be known' (ii.29, p. 11); and, similarly with Dorothea, that his state of mind precludes the possibility that 'the past life of each could be included in their mutual knowledge and affection' (i.20, p. 303).

Various characters are quite deliberately used to illustrate the difficulty of such 'mutual knowledge'. Fred Vincy's false surmises about Featherstone's motives prompt the observation that 'The difficult task of knowing another soul is not for young gentlemen whose consciousness is chiefly made up of their own wishes' (I.12, p. 179), and the 'difficulty' is repeatedly related to the multifariousness of personality. After discussing Casaubon in Chapter 42 the narrator remarks that 'The human soul moves in many channels' (II.42, p. 224) – that, in other words, it is not to be interpreted merely in terms of a single or simple source of motivation. Much is said about human changeability and unpredictability. In connection with Lydgate's note on the hospital chaplaincy: 'One would know much better what to do if men's characters were more consistent' (I.18, p. 273); and, on the possibility of betting on the young Lydgate's vocational prospects: 'The risk would remain even with close knowledge of Lydgate's character; for character too is a process and an unfolding' (I.15, p. 226). Or, as Farebrother puts it to Dorothea in a key passage: 'character is not cut in marble – it is not something solid and unalterable. It is something living and changing' (III.62, p. 310).

There are times indeed in *Middlemarch* when this kind of sentiment appears to threaten the novel's entire premise of personality, when George Eliot seems to be suggesting that personal knowledge is not merely 'difficult', but ultimately elusive. To adapt Mary Garth's terms, character appears 'opaque', not 'transparent' (II.33, p. 65). The narrator, for instance, cautions, 'But let the wise be warned against too great readiness at explanation: it multiples the sources of mistake, lengthening the sum for reckoners sure to go wrong' (II.45, p. 260); and it is Dorothea's lot to learn in the famous, if somewhat equivocal, twenty-first chapter of the novel that Casaubon, like any other mortal, has 'an equivalent centre of self, whence the lights and shadows must always fall with a certain difference' (I.21, p. 323). This is the terminal individuality in others that will always to some extent elude intimacy, even when it is sympathetic and well-meaning; yet we are encouraged to believe that, with Lydgate, Ladislaw, even briefly with Rosamond, Dorothea transcends its limitations through her 'incalculably diffusive' (III, Finale, p. 465) influence. Similarly, the narrator employs an astonishing range of personae – natural historian, scientist, historian, oracular moralist, confiding colleague – in order theoretically to assert what her method seems to deny: that she too is excluded from the 'equivalent centres' of her characters.

Such apparent contradictions have troubled critics since *Middlemarch* began appearing in 1873. Henry James's legendary conclusion was that '*Middlemarch* is a treasure-house of details, but it is an undifferent whole'.[17] The comment in fact reveals more about James's fiction than it does about George Eliot's; yet there is here, as in so many of his influential judgements about her, an unerring instinct for what later discussion was to deem central. Equally typical is his equivocation over precisely the main point he is making, for James cannot but concede that *Middlemarch* evokes 'that supreme sense of the vastness and variety of human life, under aspects apparently similar, which it belongs only to the greatest novels to produce'.[18] Coming from the champion of architectonic form, this is high praise indeed.

Others, however, have wished to qualify or revise James's assessment, many insisting that the 'treasure-house' effect, the sense of life-like contingency,[19] is a virtue of the novel. Quentin Anderson's memorable phrase 'the landscape of opinion' aptly reflects *Middlemarch*'s evocation of society as a code-rich miscellany in which incidental forms of social fictionalising – gossip, speculation, local mythology, fraudulence – converge in a rough and shifting consensus about the nature of 'reality'. Raymond Williams's Marxist sociological readings trace the epistemological and aesthetic instabilities involved in the fragmentation of 'knowable communities' in which knowledge is predicated upon deep personal acquaintance; Terry Eagleton's materialist account finds in the novel a jostling 'amalgam of discourses' that reveals the ideological survivals and conflicts present in George Eliot's received form of report. Structuralists, too, have been intrigued not simply by the prominence of the codes in the dramatic action of the novel, but also by its self-consciousness, the surprisingly 'modern' 'interrogation' of realism and its assumptions that mark many of the narrative intrusions.

These divergent readings suggest that the two issues that most troubled James on his reading of *Middlemarch* – its self-conscious narrative commentary and its apparent lack of unity – were more subtle, and more subtly connected, than he imagined. Typically, his admiration for the 'luminous brooding' of the commentary seems to have been qualified by his fear of 'suicidal slaps' at narrative 'credulity'; moreover, he simply does not concede that a novel, even one so epistemologically aware as *Middlemarch*, might in part be structured by a set of concerns about knowledge that are common both to the narrator and her characters. Yet this is of

course the case in *Middlemarch*: the omniscient narrator's
dialectic of knowing and not knowing is presented as a special but
recognisable case of the knowledge problem confronting
characters. Thus the commentary ranges across a tonal spectrum
from self-inclusive irony and diffidence at one end, to Olympian
detachment and sublimity at the other. Barbara Hardy's excellent
account of George Eliot's narrative tones and postures requires
only one brief illustration here.[20] This is Chapter 15's famous
statement of narrative intention:

> But Fielding lived when the days were longer (for time, like
> money, is measured by our needs), when summer afternoons
> were spacious, and the clock ticked slowly in the winter
> evenings. We belated historians must not linger after his
> example; and if we did so, it is probable that our chat would be
> thin and eager, as if delivered from a camp-stool in a
> parrot-house. I at least have so much to do in unravelling
> certain human lots, and seeing how they were woven and
> interwoven, that all the light I can command must be
> concentrated on this particular web, and not dispersed over
> that tempting range of relevancies called the universe.
>
> (i.15, pp. 213–14)

The self-inclusive 'we', together with images of omniscience as
empirical inquiry ('all the light I can command') is calculated to
diffuse the impression of transcendence, to offer the narrating
persona as an empirical rather than a transcendental presence in
the work. Similarly, emotive interjections elsewhere – 'but why
always Dorothea? Was her point of view the only possible one with
regard to this marriage?' (ii.29, p. 9) – establish the narrator as a
beleaguered character in a benighted world, sharing 'the same
embroiled medium, the same troublous fitfully-illuminated life'
(ii.30, p. 27) as her characters. So persuasive is this rhetorical
neutralising of narrative privilege in *Middlemarch* that the sublime
meditations in the commentary have a sense of situated human
limitation, even though they draw on omniscience's special
narrative dispensations. Thus can the narrator claim knowledge
of what human beings simply cannot bear to know:

> If we had a keen vision and feeling of all ordinary human life, it
> would be like hearing the grass grow and the squirrel's heart

beat, and we should die of that roar which lies on the other side
of silence. As it is, the quickest of us walk about well wadded
with stupidity.   (I.20, pp. 297–8)

Such modulations of tone and perspective, then, create a shared
problematic of knowledge between narrator and character which
unifies what seemed to James an unacceptably disparate work.
Thus does the narrator refer to 'the angle at which most people
viewed Fred Vincy' (I.23, p. 357), for it suggests that the
narrator's obligation to establish proper perspectives on persons
is an aesthetic simulation of that requirement in ethical life. But
George Eliot does not pretend that such a simulation is a simple
thing. James's belief that *Middlemarch* 'sets a limit . . . to the
development of the old-fashioned English novel'[21] no doubt
reflects his disquiet at her interrogation of realism, an
interrogation that extends to its very medium: language itself.

II

The extent of George Eliot's interest in linguistic systematics, and
indeed of her linguistic scepticism, is striking. At times she seems to
anticipate Derrida's denial of 'presence' in discourse. She writes
in a letter, for example, that 'words are helpless borrowings and
echoes, giving no description of what has gone on in the
speaker'.[22] Some of her references to the inescapably metaphoric
nature of language presage the post-structuralism of de Man.
Thus: 'intelligence so rarely shows itself in speech without
metaphor, – that we can so seldom declare what a thing is, except
by saying it is something else' (*The Mill on the Floss*, ii.1, p. 123);
'we all of us, grave or light, get our thoughts entangled in
metaphors, and act fatally in the strength of them' (*Middlemarch*,
I.10, p. 127). Moreover, there are, as the American
deconstructionist J. Hillis Miller has noted, countless references
to signs and symbol systems in her writing. As always, Latimer in
'The Lifted Veil' voices her anxiety, commenting on the
'summary medium' of words:

So much misery – so slow and hideous a growth of hatred and
sin, may be compressed into a sentence! And men judge of each
other's lives through this summary medium. They epitomise

the experience of their fellow-mortal, and pronounce judgment on him in neat syntax, and feel themselves wise and virtuous – conquerors over the temptations they define in well-selected predicates.   (p. 326)

Elsewhere, alluding to the inevitable distortions of memory, he reflects upon the elusiveness of signification: 'recollections' can 'bear hardly a more distinct resemblance to the external reality than the forms of an oriental alphabet to the objects that suggested them' (pp. 328–9). Such asides need, however, to be set in the context of George Eliot's thinking about language and narration more generally. A striking and representative statement comes in 'The Natural History of German Life':

> The historical conditions of society may be compared with those of language. It must be admitted that the language of cultivated nations is in anything but a rational state; the great sections of the civilized world are only approximately intelligible to each other, and even that, only at the cost of long study; one word stands for many things, and many words for one thing; the subtle shades of meaning, and still subtler echoes of association, make language an instrument which scarcely anything short of genius can wield with definiteness and certainty. Suppose, then, that the effort which has been again and again made to construct a universal language on a rational basis has at length succeeded, and that you have a language which has no uncertainty, no whims of idiom, no cumbrous forms, no fitful shimmer of many-hued significance, no hoary archaisms 'familiar with forgotten years' – a patent de-odorized and non resonant language, which effects the purpose of communication as perfectly and rapidly as algebraic signs. Your language may be a perfect medium of expression to science, but will never express *life*, which is a great deal more than science. With the anomalies and inconveniences of historical language, you will have parted with its music and its passion, with its vital qualities as an expression of individual character, with its subtle capabilities of wit, with everything that gives it power over the imagination.[23]

This is typical of George Eliot's thinking in that it concedes a degree of indeterminacy in language ('one word stands for many things', 'subtler echoes of association'), but without conceiving of it as terminally elusive. The 'genius' *can* 'wield' it with something like 'definiteness' and it *can* express 'individual character'. The view is, then, diachronic in that it sees linguistic difficulty as a matter of historical contingency rather than abstract logical necessity; and it proposes a version of 'contextual privacy' in which public concepts are refracted and altered through individual inner worlds. In this, in fact, even Latimer is in agreement. What makes the 'oriental alphabet' of a symbol system expressive is precisely our capacity to invest it with, and use it to *name*, the character of our own subjectivity: 'we learn *words* by rote, but not their meaning; *that* must be paid for with our life-blood, and printed in the subtle fibres of our nerves' (p. 326). This we can do better or ill and there is much to commend doing it well, for some of what we know of other minds is a reconstruction from signs, and misconstruction is the great source of tragic suffering in the world of George Eliot's fiction. Thus, in contemplating Bertha's excitingly occluded consciousness, Latimer refers to 'the language of her lips and demeanour' (p. 321) and to the fact that this fantasy image of her was conjured from 'the subtlest web of scarcely perceptible signs' (p. 319). To this extent people in Eliot's novels may be said to be 'textual', and interpersonal relationships a matter of 'readerly' 'construction' (p. 296). But George Eliot's point is that misconstruction is most likely where knowledge is formulaic and where it is a projection of egoistic desire. 'Signs are small measurable things, but interpretations are illimitable, and in girls of sweet, ardent nature, every sign is apt to conjure up wonder, hope, belief, vast as a sky, and coloured by a diffused thimbleful of matter in the shape of knowledge' (*Middlemarch*, 1.3, p. 34). Thus does the narrator in *Middlemarch* emphasise the importance of intuition and extra-linguistic intersubjectivity in relationships. Indeed, she uses the privileges of omniscience to make just this point. The moving and exemplary introduction of Lydgate images him as initially a 'cluster of signs': 'a man may be puffed and belauded, envied, ridiculed, counted upon as a tool and fallen in love with, or at least selected as a future husband, and yet remain virtually unknown – known merely as a cluster of signs for his neighbours' false suppositions' (1.15, p. 214). Like Casaubon he is in one sense a 'text' (1.5, p. 72), but he is also much more than this, for the fundamental entitlement of the individual in George Eliot's fiction is to be 'known' as a spiritual entity, as one largely but not wholly assimilable to a sign system. And the hallmarks of this kind of knowledge are of course 'tact', 'delicacy', an absence of 'knowingness', and 'sympathy'.

This account of George Eliot's language theory will not, however, satisfy a post-structuralist such as Hillis Miller, whose contention is not that George Eliot's fiction actively 'does' deconstruction, but rather that it 'deconstructs itself in the process of constructing its web of story-telling'.[24] The text is doomed to self-contradiction and disunity and deconstruction is a kind of enchanted demonstration of this fatal logic. Each text harbours a radical illogicality – its 'aporia' – which means that 'unity always turns out to be spurious, imposed rather than intrinsic'.[25] Such a view completes the long revolution against Jamesian organicism that has been in train for many decades. The 'treasure-house' replaces the 'house of fiction' as the temple of the novelist's art.

Miller's dazzling readings of George Eliot are true to his own premises about language, if not to hers. He reads *Middlemarch* as I think one ought to read 'The Lifted Veil', concentrating on its epistemological discontinuities. The novel is a 'battleground of conflicting' epistemological 'metaphors'[26] – optics, webs, currents – which ceaselessly displace one another creating an 'incoherent, heterogeneous, "unreadable", or nonsynthesisable quality'[27] in the text. Miller joins other post-structuralists in imputing this play of the signifier to the arbitrariness of the linguistic sign. Significantly, his evidence for this is empirical: 'all interpretation is false interpretation', because the 'original naming' of 'empirical data' in the world 'was an act of interpretation which falsified'.[28]

There appear to be immense methodological problems involved in claiming that anything can be deemed false in a perspective that does not concede stable referents within signs. Moreover, it is not clear that arbitrariness need entail indeterminacy. George Eliot's belief – and after Wittgenstein it remains persuasive – was that social and linguistic conventions constituted arbitrary signs as determinate within particular social contexts. The weight of evidence – literary and social – is strong in support here; and there is support, too, for the view that extra-empirical features of experience – ethical concepts, feelings, sense experience – possess a special kind of arbitrariness that post-structural theories of the sign have not been able, or inclined, to accommodate. As Altieri's account *Act and Quality* suggests, such signs in a sense link an intentional moral agent and the world of public discourse. They do not entirely constitute or elucidate such an agent. Altieri's conclusion that deconstruction 'deepens [the] drama' of signification but without giving an adequate account of the moral agent seems apt for Miller's readings of George Eliot.[29] The 'double readings' offered are exhilarating and expose real contradictions; but they do not reflect the weighting of her ethics, aesthetics or epistemology. A late meditation in *The Impressions of Theophrastus Such* is perhaps a better guide. It contemplates with horror a planet of super-beings who, having triumphed in the Darwinian battle for survival,

> will be blind and deaf as the inmost rock, yet will execute changes as delicate and complicated as those of human language and all the intricate web of what we call its effects, without sensitive impression, without sensitive impulse: there may be, let us say, mute orations, mute rhapsodies, mute discussions, and no consciousness there even to enjoy the silence.[30]

This appalled vision of the ontic, and of a language emptied of human subjectivity, perhaps suggests that George Eliot's account of language and knowledge is more powerful and persuasive than that of some of her most brilliant recent commentators.

III

Middlemarch's narrative technique, then, is designed to reveal character through the special dispensations of omniscience, but without forfeiting an authentic sense of moral difficulty. The novel tries to balance thematic unity and a sense of the unmanageable diversity of moral phenomena: the varieties of perspectives from which situations are appraised; the varieties of persons and situations that present themselves for moral appraisal; and the necessarily provisional quality of the knowledge we can have of other minds. Gillian Beer's phrase the 'double emphasis on conformity and variability'[31] is perhaps more faithful to the open-ended integrative range of *Middlemarch* than the descriptions proposed by either James or J. Hillis Miller.

The diversity of individuals and types depicted is a particularly striking aspect of the novel's social texture. Here, as in *Daniel Deronda*, there are a number of pastoral creations – highly rationalised novelistic set pieces – but there are also characters of a more opaque kind. As always, character at once motivates and reflects chosen features of narrative technique. Within the impressive spectrum of omniscient tone and attitude, the encyclopaedic cataloguing of 'the categories of the human appeal', character becomes a highly suggestive and elusive challenge to the reader's habitual modes of assumption and understanding. The novel's intense hermeneutic preoccupation is nicely captured in a narrative question: what, after all, is 'this world', the narrator asks, but a 'huge whispering-gallery?' (*Middlemarch*, II.41, p. 210).

Middlemarch's pastoral creations are given in extraordinary detail. As John Bayley notes, the classic example is Lydgate, who is introduced in Chapter 15.[32] This chapter, which was to have been the beginning of a separate narrative,[33] offers the most extensive background description in the novel: his childhood, his discovery of a vocation, his intemperate romantic experience – all are adduced with high explanatory seriousness. So, too, is a more elusive feature of his temperament, the famous 'spots of commonness' (I.15, p. 228) that are to betray an in many ways admirable and sophisticated man into fatally flawed and derivative life choices. These 'spots' appear to represent not quite temperament *per se*, but rather the way in which a vulnerable personality may absorb the tragically inadequate codes – romantic, professional and other – that betray so many characters in both George Eliot and James. In all of this the portrait of Lydgate has the virtues and failings of the self-evident. The narrator selects and interprets with that high sobriety that often marks Eliot's least suggestive mode of character creation:

> For those who want to be acquainted with Lydgate it will be good to know what was that case of impetuous folly, for it may stand as an example of the fitful swerving of passion to which he was prone, together with the chivalrous kindness which helped to make him morally lovable. (Ibid.)

To 'stand as an example' – that is very much the import of this character, though, as we shall see, the 'delicate crystal' (III.64,

p. 181) that is his marriage elicits some of the novel's most sensitive insights into knowledge and relationships.

At the other end of the narrative spectrum is such a character as Raffles, that refugee from the world of Dickensian caricature. Raffles has none of the poignant appeal of Eliotean inwardness. Like Grandcourt, he is a kind of ontological exile from the world of moral agency and as such does not elicit the customary range of solicitous interest and compassion. If many of George Eliot's creations are 'characters of love', Raffles, as his introduction illustrates, is emphatically a character of hate:

> He was a man obviously on the way towards sixty, very florid and hairy, with much grey in his bushy whiskers and thick curly hair, a stoutish body which showed to disadvantage the somewhat worn joinings of his clothes, and the air of a swaggerer, who would aim at being noticeable even at a show of fireworks, regarding his own remarks on any other person's performance as likely to be more interesting than the performance itself.   (II.41, pp. 212–13)

That Raffles is at this stage little more than 'a cluster of signs' does not in this instance discourage the narrator from categorical judgement. The 'air of a swaggerer' suffices to fix the inner man and it is noticeable how quickly and uncritically the description modulates from physical notation to a kind of accusatory psychological shorthand about unregenerate egoism (Raffles's fixation on his 'own remarks' rather than their subjects). As Lydgate reflects the metonymic inclusiveness of the Eliotean method, so Raffles is a creature of metaphor, an exile from the redemptive anxiousness of narrative attention. Yet he is, by virtue of this, oddly opaque and memorable. Raffles springs complete from authorial indignation, and, if we feel that George Eliot has here given us nothing to esteem, there is also a suspicion that much about such a man eludes even her powers of insight. A margin of self is as it were unintentionally implied: the withdrawal of sympathy infuses this, the most derivative portrait in the novel, with a special status. In *Bleak House* Raffles would be less than incidental. Here he is quite disproportionately prominent. Like Bulstrode, the narrator can 'get no grasp over the wretched man's mind' (III.69, p. 253), and the rogue's awfulness transcends the expository convenience of his entanglement in the plot.

Somewhere between the rationalised pastoral mode and the lurid picturesque, between the inclusiveness of metonymy and the selectiveness of metaphor, is the portrait of Dorothea that so captivated and exasperated Henry James. The portrait of Dorothea is an odd amalgam of inclusion and incompletion, and it derives a certain characteristic vitality from its unstable relation with the novel's proprietorial narrative commentary. Dorothea is enmeshed in a set of social and textual relations and can according to the novel's logic redeem her innocence only through relations of a superior kind. But, as Gillian Beer notes, there is here a constant tension between character-within-system, and the individual and character as an end-in-itself. Beer writes that, like Zola's, George Eliot's

> vehement fascination with individuality makes for a painful play of energies between the scrupulous disclosures of law and the passionate unanswerable needs of human beings. The writer's authority is drawn from this task of tracking and revealing the primary fixed laws of nature – with which his fiction proves to accord – but his creativity is absorbed in people.[34]

Middlemarch embeds 'individuality' in a quasi-positivistic law-governed 'nature' that *Daniel Deronda* seeks to transcend through visionary communion with the past, the future, and kindred spirits. 'Needs', then – 'the terrible stringency of human need' – infuse, but also refuse, 'relations'; social narratives and typologies find the deepest reserves of persons 'unanswerable'. Such is the recalcitrant existential logic of George Eliot's 'Study of Provincial Life'.

Like Gwendolen, Dorothea is a *Bildungsroman* study in naïvety and development. No less than Gwendolen's, her development might also be plotted in terms of choice; but in *Middlemarch* the *Bildung* choice-narrative is more insistently focused through the problem of knowledge than in the later novel. Dorothea is far more intellectual, sets a higher priority on knowledge, and seeks a role in life that will fuse knowledge's various forms: personal, scholarly, social, historical, spiritual. The marriage plot, so poignant yet also often faintly ridiculous, charts Dorothea's quest with the tough, compassionate precision that is George Eliot's hallmark as an intellectual novelist. Dorothea's stereotypical destiny is to emerge from a universal egoism, but her development is set in a highly particular social context. The Prelude's claim that 'later-born Theresas' such as Dorothea lack 'a coherent social faith and order which could perform the function of knowledge for the ardently willing soul' (I, p. 2) provides the historical background to her disastrous initial marital choice:

> The thing which seemed to her best, she wanted to justify by the completest knowledge. . . . Into this soul-hunger as yet all her youthful passion was poured; the union which attracted her was one that would deliver her from her girlish subjection to her own ignorance, and give her the freedom of voluntary submission to a guide who would take her along the grandest path. (I.3, pp. 39–40)

The narrator's 'as yet' is typically proprietorial and suggests just how far Dorothea, like Gwendolen, is foredoomed to 'ache with the pain of the process'. Moreover, like Gwendolen, Dorothea is to learn by the mistakes of misconstruction. She is initially prone to what the narrator calls 'imaginative adornment of those whom she loved' (I.1, p. 18), and her courtship with Casaubon is a matter at once (it is a fine insight) of airy obfuscation and feminine self-deprecation. Casaubon may have had his defects, but 'She filled up all blanks with unmanifested perfections, interpreting him as she interpreted the works of Providence, and accounting for seeming discords by her own deafness to the higher harmonies' (I.9, p. 110). As the desolating truth about the marriage emerges, their mutual misunderstandings, their failures of knowledge, are rendered in sensory diction: 'She was as blind to his inward troubles as he to hers: she had not yet learned those hidden conflicts in her husband which claim our pity. She had not yet listened patiently to his heart-beats, but only felt that her own was beating violently' (I.20, p. 307). Yet, before their honeymoon has concluded, Dorothea begins to realise that 'she had been under a wild illusion in expecting a response to her feeling from Mr Casaubon' (I.21, p. 323), and to discriminate, like Esther Lyon, between dream and reality. She feels – and, as is characteristic in George Eliot, a capacity for recognition and sympathy come simultaneously – 'the first stirring of a pitying tenderness fed by the realities of his lot and not by her own dreams' (p. 321). But, more than this, the narrator gathers her experience of the dawning awareness of the complexities of personal knowledge into a larger generalisation about moral process. The contrasting terms here are 'imagine' and 'feeling':

> We are all of us born in moral stupidity, taking the world as an udder to feed our supreme selves: Dorothea had early begun to emerge from that stupidity, but yet it had been easier to her to imagine how she would devote herself to Mr Casaubon, and become wise and strong in his strength and wisdom, than to conceive with that distinctness which is no longer reflection but feeling – an idea wrought back to the directness of sense, like the solidity of objects – that he had an equivalent centre of self, whence the lights and shadows must always fall with a certain difference.   (p. 323)

The two Eliotean hallmarks here are 'feeling' and 'difference'. The first, with its 'idea wrought back to the directness of sense', encapsulates the famous 'head and heart theme': knowledge in George Eliot fuses compassion and cognition; and it has, significantly, a powerful extra-linguistic dimension: the emphasis upon the 'directness of sense' suggests that much of what passes between people is primitive, intuitive, perhaps even unmediated. This is also the implication of 'difference' and the 'equivalent centre' of other people. George Eliot is not here imagining a Derridean *différance* that forever displaces 'presence', and so the possibility of reliable knowledge, from the other person; rather she is arguing for the substantial self – a subjective core of personality – which can never entirely be penetrated, but which can to some extent be known through a combination of relatively predictable expressive behaviour, personal revelation, introspection on the part of the solicitous knower and a sense of general human propensity. Had Casaubon material enough for 'transformation into sympathy', he might have been substantially released from the eternity of solipsistic suspicion that darkens his life. In a striking phrase reserved for Casaubon, *Middlemarch* too images a Gothic collapse of human communion: 'the hidden alienation of secrecy and suspicion' (II.50, p. 335) haunts and impels its argument for openness and intuition. Only when such openness has been achieved, the novel urges, can intersubjective knowledge be the kind of baptismal thing that is proposed by Feuerbach:

The presence of a noble nature, generous in its wishes, ardent in its charity, changes the lights for us: we begin to see things again in their larger, quieter masses, and to believe that we too can be seen and judged in the wholeness of our character. That influence was beginning to act on Lydgate. . . . (III.76, p. 352)

The 'wholeness of . . . character' – that is the Eliotean ideal. Paradoxically, it can never be completely formulated in relationship, yet only relationship can make it possible. These are the 'You-moments' to which Buber[35] refers, and they are hard won in the institutionalised 'It-world'[36] of George Eliot's provincial society.

Middlemarch also argues that true relation takes the individual beyond the trivial attitudes and attainments that often pass for knowledge. The narrator, objecting to 'clever' as an epithet, remarks of Dorothea that the word

would not have described her so to circles in whose more precise vocabulary cleverness implies mere aptitude for knowing and doing, apart from character. All her eagerness for acquirement lay within that full current of sympathetic motive in which her ideas and impulses were habitually swept along. (I.10, p. 128)

The passage insists that our existing vocabulary of attention is often inadequate. Here, as in *Daniel Deronda*, solicitous knowledge is conceived as an expressive form that orchestrates, reflects and provides sympathetic access to the 'wholeness' of individual character. It is to be distinguished from a 'fanaticism of sympathy' (I.22, p. 335) which 'constructs' the world after the image of its own impassioned fantasy life, and an emotionally ungenerous dependence upon systematics that cannot know the inwardness of its human subjects. Such a dependence is in *Middlemarch* repeatedly imaged as a 'key' to a unitary theory structure of knowledge. Dorothea with her 'binding theory' (I.10, p. 128), Casaubon with his 'Key' (I.7, p. 91), and Lydgate's 'knowledge of structure' (I.15, p. 223), all seek a formulaic reconstruction of knowledge from signs. Of the three, only Dorothea emerges with any certainty from such a dependence and it is she who, at the end of the novel, is said to have had an 'incalculably diffusive' influence (III, Finale, p. 465) on other people, to have been both available and intuitive in human relationships.

It is a measure of the chastened tragic ambience of the novel that that influence does not extend to the unregenerate Casaubon. In *Middlemarch*'s tragic economy there are profound, even absolute, human failures, and even marriage to Dorothea cannot save Casaubon. But there are, too, moments of partial mutual enlightenment whose quality is said to mitigate what may remain circumstantially impoverished lives. A case in point is Lydgate, whose great intellectual and marital ambitions are stifled by his 'commonness' and the 'embroiled medium' in which he lives, but who nevertheless shares with the 'diffusive' Dorothea a 'cry from soul to soul' (ii.30, p. 27). If it is difficult to see in such 'You-moments' the degree of mitigation that George Eliot proposes, it is at least important to understand her logic of consolation.

Ultimately, *Middlemarch*'s immense social pessimism deems this logic the only one available. George Eliot does not generally countenance forms of social and political disruption that might radically recast the terms of personal relationships.[37] Lydgate must settle for a qualitative and momentary deliverance from the paucity of provincial social institutions, and here the case of a qualifying 'political' reading of George Eliot must inevitably rest.

Her implicit reply is always that 'What has grown up historically can only die out historically';[38] that gradual change is preferable to the incoherence resulting from a dramatic rupture with the past. Felix Holt's 'Address to Working Men' expresses a profound and characteristic conservatism. But *Middlemarch* replies, too, in another way: it offers itself as art, and as an aesthetic simulacrum of life, that can qualitatively improve 'individual lots'. George Eliot's doctrine of the extension of sympathy insists that art can activate reserves and structures of feeling in the reader, and the narrator in *Middlemarch*, like those in the other novels, attempts to promote this process by exemplification. Thus Lydgate comes to be 'known' beyond 'the cluster of signs' that initially designate him, both by the narrator and the intuitive Dorothea. However, George Eliot does not suggest that Lydgate is thereby rendered an ontologically 'real person'. On the contrary, her assumption is that concepts linking the opaque inner world and that of public – ethical, social, political – discourse can be named and exemplified in texts and that this naming activates certain sympathetic structures in the reader.

What George Eliot does not give, but what is strongly implied in this position, is a developed form of so-called 'reader-response theory' that will specify the structures involved, their social and psychological derivation and their power to shape the possibilities of personal and collective experience. A reader-response theory such as Iser's, described in Chapter 2, might, however, join with more political versions in completing George Eliot's account; for a plausible theory of character in fiction cannot rest on the absurd claim that characters in novels are ontologically like, or in any simple way reflect, 'real people'. They are in fact highly speculative and selective images of self that depend upon creative completion by the reader. Such completion is in part a function of unique subjectivity in the reader; but it is also a function of conditioned literary and social response. The great creators of character appear to replicate in texts aspects of a social grammar that shapes and facilitates our understanding of persons. Characters in novels are in this sense continuous with those in life and they trigger in readers completions that are similar to those we make in our extra-literary experience. Thus does fiction permit the individual to recognise, name and creatively extend ethical, spiritual and psychological concepts involved in his interpretations of other selves. To say that the concept 'love' is arbitrary is in this view less important than to suggest that it is an intersubjective construct that enables individuals creatively to co-ordinate their subjective and their social lives, and to use language in order to extend individual perception and experience.

This is how George Eliot conceives of language. 'Love' is not for her 'immanent' in the black marks on the page; neither is it entirely knowable; but it does name a recurrent, private experience, and it can be used in fiction not only to reflect, but also to extend our understanding of that experience. In a novel it takes on contextual relationships with other signs, and is pictured in carefully contrived human situations. Omniscience can thus open it out as social life cannot: it can embed 'love' in a linguisticised psychological continuum – in narrated monologue, for instance – which explores interrelations, achieved and possible, with words such as 'will', 'sympathy' and 'knowledge'.

Omniscience, then, can amend and explore the authority of ethical words, but it can do so only selectively. The structures of fiction set significant, though flexible, limits; but the greatest limit of all is, of course, the unmanageable plurality of human experience. This George Eliot's word for Gwendolen Harleth – 'iridescence' – openly acknowledges. She was not so naïve as to suppose what Sterne had notoriously disproved a century before: that realism can be a complete report on anything. In general her reports are more inclusive than James's, but a more or less effective process of selection and intimation is always at work in her creation of character.

Middlemarch's description of Dorothea in Rome is a revealing example:

> To those who have looked at Rome with the quickening power of a knowledge which breathes a growing soul into all historic shapes, and traces out the suppressed transitions which unite all contrasts, Rome may still be the spiritual centre and interpreter of the world. But let them conceive one more historical contrast: the gigantic broken revelations of that Imperial and Papal city thrust abruptly on the notions of a girl who had been brought up in English and Swiss Puritanism, fed on meagre Protestant histories and on art chiefly of the hand-screen sort; a girl whose ardent nature turned all her small allowance of knowledge into principles, fusing her actions into their mould, and whose quick emotions gave the most abstract things the quality of a pleasure or a pain; a girl who had lately become a wife, and from the enthusiastic acceptance of untried duty found herself plunged in tumultuous preoccupation with her personal lot. The weight of unintelligible Rome might lie easily on bright nymphs to whom it formed a background for the brilliant picnic of Anglo-foreign society; but Dorothea had no such defence against deep impressions. Ruins and basilicas, palaces and colossi, set in the midst of a sordid present, where all that was living and warm-blooded seemed sunk in the deep degeneracy of a superstition divorced from reverence; the dimmer but yet eager Titanic life gazing and struggling on walls and ceilings; the long vistas of white forms whose marble eyes seemed to hold the monotonous light of an alien world: all this vast wreck of ambitious ideals, sensuous and spiritual, mixed confusedly with the signs of breathing forgetfulness and degradation, at first jarred her as with an electric shock, and then urged themselves on her with that ache belonging to a glut of confused

ideas which check the flow of emotion. Forms both pale and glowing took possession of her young sense, and fixed themselves in her memory even when she was not thinking of them, preparing strange associations which remained through her after-years. Our moods are apt to bring with them images which succeed each other like the magic-lantern pictures of a doze; and in certain states of dull forlornness Dorothea all her life continued to see the vastness of St Peter's, the huge bronze canopy, the excited intention in the attitudes and garments of the prophets and evangelists in the mosaics above, and the red drapery which was being hung for Christmas spreading itself everywhere like a disease of the retina.   (I.20, pp. 295–7)

The experience described is less consoling than Isabel Archer's moment of revelation in Rome in *The Portrait* (III.27). It is also more inclusive. Characteristically, it assumes an interplay between heredity ('nature') and culture ('a girl who had been brought up in English and Swiss Puritanism'), fusing the two in an existential orientation towards knowledge: 'a girl whose ardent nature turned all her small allowance of knowledge into principles, fusing her actions into their mould, and whose quick emotions gave the most abstract things the quality of a pleasure or a pain'. Again the interaction of 'head' and 'heart' is emphasised, and as always the question is how far this orientation may be transformed by acts of will. At this stage the overwhelming and fragmented givenness of Rome stands as an icon for entrenched habits of perception and response. There is nothing in *Middlemarch* to match the existential daring of the portrait of Deronda's mother – the novel rests upon what Sartre dismisses as liberalism's 'extra-empirical communication between consciousnesses'[39] – but it urges that a kind of evolution through accommodation is possible in the self. This is a slow, painful and only partially willed process and it involves a reconstruction within the ego of what we should now term conscious and unconscious regions of the mind. The 'forms' which 'fixed themselves in her memory even when she was not thinking of them' signal something like the unconscious, and the entire portrait suggests that certain narrative structures can assimilate unconscious to conscious and present to past experience. Thus can Dorothea reconceive her identity as a social being.

This assumption registers in the passage's narrative technique, which revolves the consciousness of the character through a series of more and less intimate perspectives. 'Let them conceive' sets character at a distance and establishes an analytic rapport between narrator and reader; 'ardent nature' is an item of psychological detail again given from an omniscient perspective and in the narrator's idiom; but Dorothea's 'impressions' (a familiar Jamesian word) are given in something closer to narrated monologue: the balancing conjunctions and emotive adjective of 'Ruins and basilicas, palaces and colossi, set in the midst of a sordid present' sounds more like the idiom of Dorothea's mind and draws the reader closer to its atmosphere. Elsewhere, occasionally, consciousness achieves that impression of an excluded narrative origin that is loosely termed 'stream of consciousness': 'thoughts became vague and images floated uncertainly' (1.5, p. 62). Such description is reminiscent of the 'unmapped country' of Gwendolen's mind, but it is seldom sustained in *Middlemarch*: 'she could but cast herself . . . in the lap of a divine consciousness which sustained her own' (ibid.) is typically less spontaneous. Similarly, in the Rome description, the narrator's desire to exemplify and generalise elsewhere disrupts the subjective flow of mind: 'Our moods are apt to bring with them images which succeed each other like the magic-lantern pictures of a doze' postulates an exemption from conscious awareness but does not render it. Like the minds in James's late novels, those in *Middlemarch* are habitually and oppressively vigilant. But, of course, *Daniel Deronda* was to refine and extend this aspect of George Eliot's techniques of characterisation.

The rhapsodic and cloying imposition of narrative understanding characterises many of the descriptions of Dorothea. However, there is the occasional 'oasis of mystery in the desert of knowledge'. One such, discussed at length by Barbara Hardy, is the implication, through imagery and omission, of sexual frustration and repression in the young woman.[40] Another is the curious – but, in the world of this metonymic novel, suggestive – silence about Dorothea's past. She is yet another Victorian orphan, thrust into a situation of existential crisis, and there are fleeting allusions to her childhood. We are told that in Lausanne 'Dorothea had never been tired of listening to old Monsieur Liret' (1.5, p. 67); we have an image of her as a child 'showering kisses on the hard pate of her bald doll' (1.20, p. 303); we are told of her 'early troubling her elders with questions about the facts around her' (II.37, p. 149); she herself tells Will that 'I have always been finding out my religion since I was a little girl' (II.39, p. 180); and, in an interestingly enigmatic moment that is not pursued, she avoids comparing her own background with that of her interlocutor, Will: ' "Ah, what a different life from mine!" said Dorothea, with keen interest, clasping her hands on her lap. "I have always had too much of everything. But tell me how it was . . ." ' (II.37, pp. 140–1).

Little, however, is done with these details and the narrator invests most authority and interest in the introductory account of Dorothea's past given in Chapter 1. The account is in many ways a Victorian set piece, and it offers a familiar combination of information about heredity and circumstance. Heredity in this case involves 'the hereditary strain of Puritan energy' that Dorothea has received through the family (I.1, p. 10); circumstance amounts – one would suppose centrally – to this: the sisters

> had both been educated, since they were about twelve years old
> and had lost their parents, on plans at once narrow and
> promiscuous, first in an English family and afterwards in a
> Swiss family at Lausanne, their bachelor uncle and guardian
> trying in this way to remedy the disadvantages of their
> orphaned condition.   (p. 9)

That 'and had lost their parents' is not syntactically separated is both striking and significant; for George Eliot's interest in Dorothea's past scarcely extends – as it does with a Maggie Tulliver – to the psychological determinations of familial circumstance. *Middlemarch*'s silence about Dorothea's 'orphaned condition' is remarkable; the more so because we are told that for the young lady 'the really delightful marriage must be that where your husband was a sort of father' (p. 12).

Much of the critical disagreement about the character of Dorothea revolves around this temporary exemption from narrative analysis. It is in a sense immensely suggestive, implying not only uninterpreted regions of Dorothea's mind, but also unknown ones, and it may indeed be a tactful concession to opaqueness in character. However, there is, as Leavis sensed, something unsatisfactory about *Middlemarch*'s attempt to modulate in and out of Dorothea's subjective world. The shifts in narrative distance and point of view create a tension between knowingness and solicitude that subtly undermines the novel's exemplary commitment to just these values. George Eliot had written in *The Mill on the Floss* that 'Jealousy is never satisfied with anything short of an omniscience that would detect the subtlest fold of the heart' (vi.10, p. 390). There is no doubt a tremendous temptation to jealousy in the kind of self-portraiture she attempts in the figure of Dorothea, and the novel's awkward tone of loving elucidation in this instance surely has deep personal roots.

IV

'Sympathy is one of the great psychological mysteries – and as a psychologist I am bound to explain it, but can't'.[41] This admission in a late George Eliot letter stands as a self-conscious corrective to the knowingness of a jealous omniscience. It suggests that, within the conventional narrative structures she employed, her great theme of sympathy had ideally as its formal correlative a kind of reticence. Having inherited from Kant and others an image of human society as an individual centred Kingdom of Ends without a knowable transcendent God, the fictional humanist had somehow to divest omniscience of its apparently alien and distracting privileges. She could argue for a 'sympathy' that would acknowledge the individual as an end-in-itself, but she had also to replicate it in language. Casaubon and *Middlemarch*'s narrator share the negative Eliotean imperative of not entirely knowing Dorothea; feeling 'bound to explain' and capitulating to the feeling are in George Eliot's world significantly different things.

Casaubon, of course, cannot concede to others the status of ends-in-themselves. The narrator poignantly notes on Dorothea's behalf that 'She was always trying to be what her husband wished, and never able to repose on his delight in what she was' (ii.48, p. 306). This dignified and simple observation must explain some of the immense appeal and importance of *Middlemarch* for female readers. It suggests how urgently the novel attempts to get a sophisticated female protagonist across that familiar threshold of a self-acceptance not rooted in masculine approval. Here, indeed, women readers are often understandably unwilling to accept the novel's Finale, in which Dorothea is said to have made a sober but satisfactory compromise with existing social and domestic roles. It seems to me, as to many others, that this compromise is a disappointment and that again its roots are as much personal as social. By the time George Eliot wrote *Middlemarch* she had, after all, enjoyed with George Henry Lewes a much more creative and emancipated life than she permits any of her heroines. One can only speculate that forms of guilt and self-deprecation constrained her attempts to imagine in fiction freedoms she actually knew in her own private life.

What she does, however, evoke with immense power and precision is the human constraint that certain kinds of male jealousy and self-cancelling drive set upon the emotional reserves of women. Casaubon, that fictional progenitor of the sterile and stupefying Osmond, is the great creation of *Middlemarch*. Whether he is based upon Herbert Spencer, Mark Pattison or other suggested models is surely unimportant here. More revealing is the reticent technique that confers upon him his tortured and poignant presence as a character. Casaubon eludes the claims of Eliotean pastoral. The 'dead hand' of his will is this novel's icon for a shockingly possessive individualism; but his exemption from authorial expertise ironically affords him an opaque privacy that other characters do not possess. Here we need to review character in *Middlemarch* more generally.

Like any novel, *Middlemarch* establishes certain dominant characterological structures to which particular figures conform in varying degrees. Roger Fowler's theory of 'characterological semes' in *Linguistics and the Novel* offers the structural linguistic version of this phenomenon; Robert Langbaum's *The Mysteries of Identity* a more historical, liberal-humanist account.[42] The terms of *Middlemarch*'s concept of identity are by now familiar from the description of Dorothea in Rome. But they will bear repetition before turning to the strikingly metaphoric methods of characterisation used in the creation of Casaubon.

In broad terms Eliot conceives of developed personality here as an organic thing. It is the upshot of a combination of circumstance, choice and heredity; is capable of change but continuous with its past; it can integrate affective and rational levels of experience; and it comprises both conscious and unconscious levels of mind. Thus on the unitary nature of the self: 'A human being in this aged nation of ours is a very wonderful whole' (II.40, p. 206); on temperament and circumstance: 'For there is no creature whose inward being is so strong that it is not greatly determined by what lies outside it' (III, Finale, p. 464); on choice: 'We are on a perilous margin when we begin to look passively at our future selves' (III.69, p. 384); in connection with Bulstrode, on the past: 'Even without memory, the [past] life is bound into one by a zone of dependence in growth and decay' (III.61, p. 126). This is Farebrother (with authorial approval) on change: 'character is not cut in marble – it is not something solid and unalterable' (III.72, p. 310). With reference to affective and rational orders of experience, Dorothea, we remember, begins 'to conceive with that distinctness which is no longer reflection but feeling – an idea wrought back to the directness of sense' (I.21, p. 323); and, affirming both unconscious and conscious areas of the psyche, the narrator explains that Bulstrode's 'misdeeds were like the subtle muscular movements which are not taken account of in the consciousness' (III.68, pp. 235–6). Sartre's characteristic existential objection to this image of self is that it is inherently conservative: it pictures personality as determined by such an 'ensemble' of forces that self-authenticating choice and change become almost inconceivable. And in practice this is often the case in George Eliot's novels. But the image is also organicist in the more specifically aesthetic sense that various features of characterological description become interdependent within fictional convention. 'What is character but the determination of incident? What is incident but the illustration of character?' asks Henry James, making just such an assumption. Yet in James and George Eliot alike, the great suggestive creations often partake selectively and unpredictably of this seamless fictional web. Aberrant details, and especially strategic descriptive omissions, set many of these characters apart. Organicist expectations provide a background against which the opaque oddity of the special case assumes a particular power.

The epigraph to Chapter 25 of *Daniel Deronda* makes with reference to Grandcourt the point that so obviously applies to Casaubon: 'How trace the why and wherefore in a mind reduced to the barrenness of a fastidious egoism, in which all direct desires are dulled, and have dwindled from motives into a vacillating expectation of motives . . . (ii.25, p. 3). 'How trace' concedes a failure of authorial understanding: so recalcitrant is Casaubon's mental state, and so unregenerate his egoism, that the 'pain of the process' seems a profound irrelevance. He is as close to a true romantic solitary as any George Eliot character, though his obsessions, like Osmond's, are of course tragically derivative. *Middlemarch*'s narrative technique here evokes an existential exile that the divided logic of 'The Lifted Veil' had been unable to contrive without recourse to the pseudo-romanticism of Gothic horror.

A good deal of anxious commentary is of course devoted to making Casaubon accessible to the reader. (George Eliot tells John Blackwood in a letter that 'Mr. Collins has my gratitude for feeling some regard towards Mr. Casaubon, in whose life I lived with much sympathy'.[43]) Phrases such as 'like the rest of us' (II.42, p.221) are used to avert a sense of incomprehensible oddity in the character; the narrator pleads fervently on his behalf, urging intelligent sympathy for him: 'I protest against any absolute conclusion, any prejudice derived from Mrs Cadwallader's contempt for a neighbouring clergyman's alleged greatness of soul' (I.10, p. 125); and again: 'Dorothea – but why always Dorothea? . . . Mr Casaubon had an intense consciousness within him, and was spiritually a-hungered like the rest of us' (II.29, p. 9). In a particularly revealing passage in which Casaubon's resentment towards Ladislaw threatens to alienate the reader, the narrator resorts to precautionary parentheses in an attempt to restore or ensure involvement: 'Poor Mr Casaubon felt (and must not we, being impartial, feel with him a little?) that no man had juster cause for disgust and suspicion than he' (II.37, p. 156). Yet the rhetorical question seems unequal, precisely, to the intensity of Casaubon's feelings at this stage – 'disgust and suspicion' – and he manages repeatedly to elude the novel's sympathising strategies; also, as an interesting passage in Chapter 37 reveals, its generalising strategies. Casaubon is displeased at Mr Brooke's intention to promote Will, and we are told,

> That is the way with us when we have any uneasy jealousy in our disposition: if our talents are chiefly of the burrowing kind, our honey-sipping cousin (whom we have grave reasons for objecting to) is likely to have a secret contempt for us, and any one who admires him passes an oblique criticism on ourselves. (II.37, p. 131)

The effect here is complex. The passage attempts, through an obscure fusion of character's and narrator's points of view, to assimilate Casaubon's anguish to a hypothetical norm familiar to the reader ('That is the way with us'); however, in so doing it has both to represent his thoughts as achieving a degree of articulation inconsistent with his very limited mode of self-awareness ('if our talents are chiefly of the burrowing kind'), and to render them in a tone almost arch in its knowingness, a tone quite remote from any normally associated with Casaubon. The result of this explanatory tonal and psychological falsification is that the character, already successfully established in the work, seems to decline the preferred plural 'us', and to evade the presumptive expertise of the narrator.

The word 'disposition' may further help to account for Casaubon's elusive quality, for he, like many of George Eliot's hardened egoists, evinces a certain fixity of character which – and this, of course, is partly her point – will not yield to the novel's sense of moral process. We are in fact told that his recessive and anxious 'characteristics' are 'fixed and unchangeable as bone' (1.20, p. 303), an observation that casts doubts upon the claim late in the novel that 'the effect of her [Dorothea's] being on those around her was incalculably diffusive' (III, Finale, p. 465). The effect upon Casaubon seems negligible: almost untouched by Dorothea's force of 'fellow-feeling', he seems to live not just beyond the novel's affective social sources but, challengingly, and with a powerful fictional autonomy, beyond certain of its registers of understanding.

Significantly – and the contrast here with Lydgate is striking – he is accorded only the most sketchy of pasts. Though the miniatures at Lowick and some of the intricacies of the plot give oblique intimations about his background, it is never dramatised and never used for psychologically explanatory purposes. Indeed, a good deal of his opaque fascination as a character derives from George Eliot's having (whether deliberately or not it is hard to say) maintained a suggestive silence about Casaubon as a younger man. At times the novel projects an implied psychic past for him, alluding to 'this mental estate mapped out a quarter of a century before' (II.29, p. 13), or to 'something deeper, bred by his lifelong claims and discontents' (II.37, p. 132); but precisely what the 'something deeper' is, or why his unhappiness should have begun so early, we are not told. It is striking that the only image of Casaubon as a younger man offered in the novel comes through

Dorothea, after his inquiry as to whether she will obey his wishes in the event of his death:

> And here Dorothea's pity turned from her own future to her husband's past – nay, to his present hard struggle with a lot which had grown out of that past: the lonely labour, the ambition breathing hardly under the pressure of self-distrust; the goal receding, and the heavier limbs; and now at last the sword visibly trembling above him!   (II.48, p. 313)

That the narrator does not venture this image has the effect of suggesting an intriguing lack of certainty about the character, and a region of this experience closed even to its creator.

Casaubon's air of detachment and obscurity may be attributed to one further facet of the novel's technique: George Eliot's brilliant manipulation of interior views of his character. It is significant that proportionally he is presented less from within than the other protagonists; but, more than this, it is the kind of interior portraiture used that influences the reader's relationship with him. With very few exceptions, accounts of Casaubon's inner life are restricted to psychonarration: to, that is, a distanced reporting of his thoughts that does not presume the kind of intimacy with, or immersion in, character that we associate with narrated monologue. Only in Chapters 37 and 42 are we permitted intimacy with the idiom of Casaubon's inner life: 'It was as clear as possible that she [Dorothea] was ready to be attached to Will and to be pliant to his suggestions . . .' (II.42, p. 222). Casaubon's 'power of suspicious construction' (p. 221) is disclosed, briefly, with great force and immediacy; yet by this stage the distancing impact of George Eliot's presentation has had its effect: Casaubon's social isolation (his first name is not spoken until Chapter 29) has been corroborated, formally, by the remove at which the reader has been compelled to perceive him, and the abiding impression is of a man both in fact, and in the creative power of fiction, apart.

This apartness and alienation is in a sense a refusal of George Eliot's great theme of sympathetic understanding. Yet Casaubon is far from alone in so resisting the Eliotean ethic. Though Will likens his feelings for Dorothea to a 'crystal' without a 'flaw' (II.47, p. 297), *Middlemarch* presages James's masterpiece *The Golden Bowl* in imaging many relationships as a fractured crystal. It is true of the Bulstrodes, of the Casaubons and of the Lydgates. The Lydgates indeed are a particularly pointed study in the corruption and perversion of knowledge within relationship. They lack 'mutual understanding and resolve' (III.75, p. 347), suffer from a 'total missing of each other's mental track' (III.58, p. 81) and make of marriage a place to pool their derivative immaturities. Thus as the reality of his union draws upon Lydgate he reflects, 'It was as if a fracture in delicate crystal had begun, and he was afraid of any movement that might make it fatal' (III.64, p. 181). The fatality that eventually besets the marriage is nothing so violent as a complete rupture; it is, rather, that slow corrosive form of enervation and ebbing commitment that is seen as a kind of death-in-life in George Eliot's fiction.

Though her novels hold out the prospect of renewed 'understanding and resolve', of knowledge that may rekindle the creative individual, it is a reflection of her tragic outlook prior to *Daniel Deronda* that remarkably few sophisticated sexual relationships between men and women in her novels actually succeed. This is 'the element of tragedy which lies in the very fact of frequency', the appalling actuality of 'ordinary human life' that can scarcely be abided. Yet it is George Eliot's intention in *Middlemarch* and elsewhere to make audible the growing grass and the 'squirrel's heartbeat', to penetrate the conspiracy of silence upon which so many social fictions rest. *Middlemarch* registers as few other novels can the inveterate waste of human potentiality, the trivialisation of the life of the spirit. Its 'cry from soul to soul' is in a sense the 'roar that lies on the other side of silence'.

Middlemarch of course focuses this sense of loss and waste through marriage. Indeed, the novel in a sense bridges the world of Jane Austen, where dramatic action ceases at the threshold of marriage, and that of Lawrence, where intimacies only intimated in Eliot become the indices of personal and spiritual possibility. *Middlemarch* on the whole conceives of marriage as an intensification of other, asexual relationships: a general sense of process and of propriety is assumed to obtain even in the atavistic inner world of sexual love. Yet the novel is also drawn to marriage because there the scale of tragic human gratuity is so immense and so obvious. Casaubon's 'unresponsive hardness' to his young wife occasions one of the novel's great meditations on marital failure. Characteristically, the narrator insists that such failures are at heart a refusal of the possibilities of knowledge:

That ['horrible'] is a strong word, but not too strong: it is in these acts called trivialities that the seeds of joy are forever wasted, until men and women look round with haggard faces at the devastation their own waste has made, and say, the earth bears no harvest of sweetness – calling their denial knowledge.   (II.42, p. 231)

JAMES ON KNOWLEDGE

Henry James believed that George Eliot erred artistically in trying to 'recommend herself to a scientific audience' and that '*Middlemarch* is too often an echo of Messrs Darwin and Huxley'.[44] Such judgements typically signal the limits of James's aesthetic. They also caution against unduly selective readings of the novel more generally. As Gillian Beer so persuasively demonstrates in *Darwin's Plots*, no comprehensive account of knowledge in *Middlemarch* can rest, as the one above largely does, at intersubjective knowledge. Too many other forms are under discussion in the novel; and, in any case, the issues that we have construed as 'psychological' and 'personal' – questions about systems, relations, structural signification and the self, authority, origin, social taxonomy and individual 'difference' – reflect the scientific and philosophical climate of the time. Darwin, Huxley and Spencer are properly major influences in *Middlemarch*. Like her other 'experiments in life', this one explores the post-Kantian possibilities of humanist description. What relation does the ethical will bear to the natural causality that is the subject of positivistic science? How far is moral life an exigency in a natural selective world? To what extent can a systematics penetrate individual consciousness, motivation and the extra-empirical 'innerness' of human relationships? What, after all, are we to say of the 'species' if we abandon received myths of its 'origin'?

As a matter both of psychology and of aesthetic policy James was generally disinclined to ask such questions in an explicit fictional form. His tendency is usually to restrict them to the personal, to seal the eerie fascinations of the inner world off from empirical analysis. Indeed, his 'experiments of form' increasingly discourage not only comment of this kind, but also overt comment *per se*. In the remarkable Preface to *The Golden Bowl* he conjures one of those classic, faintly histrionic, phrases of deprecation for the

intrusive omniscient structure he finds without favour in George
Eliot and other Victorian realists: 'the mere muffled majesty
of irresponsible "authorship" '[45] is one of James's last
designations for what he saw as the obsolete quasi-scientist,
philosopher and Johnsonian moralist of the 'old-fashioned
English novel'. In James's hands George Eliot's great knowledge
theme remains a 'fascination and a fear', but early modernism's
disenchantment with scientific positivism – a mood already
apparent in *Daniel Deronda* – is reflected in a dramatic change in
emphasis.

The knowledge theme, of course, goes far back in James's work,
fictional and other. The novelist who so admired the 'rare
psychological penetration' of George Eliot's fiction shares with
her an uneasiness about just such pretensions. It is in the Preface
to *What Maisie Knew* that he voices his disquiet at 'the author's
irrepressible and insatiable, his extravagant and immoral,
interest in personal character and in the 'nature' of a mind, of
almost any mind'. In fact James's own interest was rather more
selective than this might suggest. Certain minds were not in his
view intrinsically interesting. Hence his strictures upon the
thinness of Emma Bovary as a central consciousness in Flaubert's
novel. Yet one of James's appraisals of Flaubert, written in 1893,
raises in more general and sympathetic terms the problem of
knowledge: its temptations and its properties. Wondering 'if the
time has not come when it may well cease to be a leading feature of
our homage to a distinguished man that we shall sacrifice him
with sanguinary rights on the altar of curiosity', he continues,

> Flaubert's letters indeed bring up with singular intensity the
> whole question of the rights and duties, the decencies and
> discretions of the insurmountable desire to *know*. To lay down a
> general code is perhaps as yet impossible, for there is no doubt
> that to know is good, or to want to know, at any rate, supremely
> natural. Some day or other surely we shall all agree that
> everything is relative, that facts themselves are often falsifying
> and that we pay more for some kind of knowledge than those
> particular kinds are worth.[46]

Here in close concentration are the issues that so exercise George
Eliot. The unease at mere 'curiosity'; the ethics ('rights and
duties') of personal knowledge; a certain ambivalence, apparently

enacted in 'The Lifted Veil', about the voracity of one's interest ('the insurmountable desire to *know*'); the sense, so reminiscent of *Middlemarch*, that there is a need in life to discriminate between different *kinds* of knowledge; and finally the suspicion, again prominent in 'The Lifted Veil', that the price of certain of these kinds may be too high.

Many of these concerns carry over into James's comments about other writers. In writing about Trollope he seems persuaded that 'to know is good': fiction can help man to understand himself.

> Trollope will remain one of the most trustworthy, though not one of the most eloquent, of the writers who have helped the heart of man to know itself. The heart of man does not always desire this knowledge; it prefers sometimes to look at history in another way – to look at the manifestations without troubling about the motives.[47]

Similarly, Turgenev's comprehensive grasp of the lives of his characters 'has the immense recommendation that in relation to any human occurrence it begins, as it were, further back. It lies in its power to tell us the most about men and women'.[48] Yet the 'power to tell' must not, and in Turgenev does not, degenerate into clinical curiosity. James is fascinated by Hawthorne in this respect. He sees in his great American predecessor a 'constant struggle . . . between his shyness and his desire to know something of life; between what may be called his evasive and inquisitive tendencies.' Hawthorne's inquisitiveness has certain advantages over that characteristic English 'mistrust of analysis', and James admires in him – it stands indeed as something of an ideal for the young critic – a certain 'imaginative interest and contemplative curiosity' towards others. This would seem closely akin to George Eliot's notion of sympathetic understanding, and, as we have seen, James alludes memorably to some such faculty in both Trollope and Balzac. Of the former: 'If he was a knowing psychologist he was so by grace; he was just and true without apparatus and without effort'; and of the latter and his characters: 'It was by loving them . . . that he knew them; it was not by knowing them that he loved.' For James, then, as for Eliot, there is in human relations a profound difference between knowledge and knowingness. Yet the high sobriety of *Middlemarch*'s tragic sense is a thing markedly more sanguine than James's customary outlook. James in fact credited himself with 'the imagination of disaster'.[49] As *The Portrait of a Lady* so unrelentingly demonstrates, his world is, for all its allure, a place of torment, and it teems with treacherous – manipulative, prurient, possessive – knowers.

Long before *The Portrait* James had opened his great theme out with some explicitness. The credulous Newman in *The American* finds himself 'swimming in a sort of rapture of respect' (II.2, p. 39) for the expatriate Mrs Tristram, who confesses that 'curiosity has a share in almost everything I do' (II.25, p. 512). The opaque Parisians he meets are however far more troubling. His intended wife, Claire, seems 'enveloped in triple defences of privacy' (II.6, p. 114), and this early version of the international theme, heavily revised for the New York Edition, turns on Newman's inability to intuit a caprice that eludes his simple mid-Western modes of understanding. *The Portrait* of course takes up the theme with far greater sophistication. Incidental allusions to intersubjective knowledge reflect the importance of the concern. Daniel Touchett has a 'fine ivory surface, polished as by the English air, that the old man had opposed to possibilities of penetration' (III.5, p. 50); Isabel discovers of Pansy in Chapter 41 that 'Her transparent little companion was for the moment [after a visit from Warburton] not to be seen through' (IV.41, p. 178). Typically, the novel considers contrasting attitudes to the hazards of knowing other people. Hence Madame Merle's immortal confession: 'I don't pretend to know what people are meant for . . . I only know what I can do with them' (III.22, p. 345). Ralph, on the other hand, possesses 'the imagination of loving' (III.5, p. 54). Isabel (who, Ralph feels, 'would take, as he said, a good deal of knowing; but she needed the knowing' – III.7, p. 86) exhibits a familiar Jamesian ambivalence in the whole matter. Like his Hawthorne, she is torn between the 'evasive' and the 'inquisitive'. She likes to understand people, certainly: 'Isabel was fond, ever, of the question of character and quality, of sounding, as who should say, the deep personal mystery' (IV.30, p. 26); yet, 'With all her love of knowledge she had a natural shrinking from raising curtains and looking into unlighted corners. The love of knowledge coexisted in her mind with the finest capacity for ignorance' (III.19, p. 284). And it is in part, of course, that 'capacity for ignorance', that failure appropriately and clear-sightedly to sound 'the personal mystery', that precipitates her disastrous choice of Osmond. For her, as for Dorothea, a deeper understanding comes too late:

> But she had seen only half his nature then [during courtship], as one saw the disk of the moon when it was partly masked by the shadow of the earth. She saw the full moon now – she saw the whole man. She had kept still, as it were, so that he should have a free field, and yet in spite of this she had mistaken a part for the whole.   (iv.42, p.191)

Other works of the middle period echo the theme. Miss Henning in *The Princess Casamassima* is a 'daughter of London' who represents its 'immense vulgarities and curiosities, its brutality and its knowingness' (v.4, p. 61); others ('The Aspern Papers', *The Reverberator*, *The Bostonians*) are particularly concerned with the problem of privacy and the public person that exercises James in his assessment of Flaubert. Still others explore the unofficial politics of power in relationships. The telephonist in the short story 'In the Cage' derives a familiar Jamesian feeling of psychic mastery from her possession of secrets:

> There were the brazen women, as she called them, of the higher and the lower fashion, whose squanderings and graspings, whose struggles and secrets and love-affairs and lies, she tracked and stored up against them till she had at moments, in private, a triumphant vicious feeling of mastery and ease, a sense of carrying their silly guilty secrets in her pocket, her small retentive brain, and thereby knowing so much more about them than they suspected or would care to think.
>
> (xi.5, p. 387)

But it is in the 'dramatic' novels immediately prior to the final phase that a peculiarly sinister interplay between a thematic preoccupation with knowledge and its formal correlatives enters James's fiction. The most chilling instance is perhaps that calculating novel of innocence and awfulness *What Maisie Knew*, which explores (and, through its rigid management of point of view, utilises) the vision of a young girl in depicting a transition from innocence to knowledge. Knowledge here, as it so often is in James, is a matter of discerning what is 'going on' between people;

but this in turn entails some measure of understanding of them. The narrator notes with implied regret that Maisie's irresponsible parents 'had really not been analysed to a deeper residuum' than mere appearance (xi.1, p. 7), and he laments, while describing a moment of deep – if strategic – intuition between father and daughter, the poignancy of the girl's early exposure to the troubling obliquities of personal knowledge. If Beale

> had an idea at the back of his head she had also one in a recess as deep, and for a time, while they sat together, there was an extraordinary mute passage between her vision of this vision of his, his vision of her vision, and her vision of his vision of her vision. What there was no effective record of indeed was the small strange pathos on the child's part of an innocence so saturated with knowledge and as directed to diplomacy. (xi.19, p. 182–3)

The Sacred Fount, James's only attempt at a first-person novel, explores (if that is the word) the question of personal knowledge through a nameless prurient and self-absorbed narrator whose omnivorous curiosity about the private lives of fellow guests at Newmarch has, in the absence of a corrective internal perspective, led critics to wonder if James has not here lost some grasp of the ethics of his own theme. Occasionally the narrator raises the ethical issues. He feels he is suffering from a 'ridiculous obsession' and deems it 'absurd to have consented to such immersion, intellectually speaking, in the affairs of other people' (Ch. 6, p. 72); and, when he and Mrs Brissenden find Guy Brissenden and May Server together, he observes, somewhat dubious at Mrs Brissenden's reaction, that 'It [his thought] even felt a kind of chill – an odd revulsion – at the touch of her eagerness. Singular perhaps that only then – yet quite certainly then – the curiosity to which I had so freely surrendered myself began to strike me as wanting in taste' (Ch. 3, p. 44). Such concern with 'taste' and 'curiosity', however, is very much the exception in a novel largely given over to quite perverse inquisitiveness about the emotional lives of others.

In the novels of the late phase James takes the knowledge theme up with greater subtlety and suggestiveness. Ruth Bernard Yeazell has rightly found in the final elaborations of early concerns 'a world where the boundaries between unconscious suspicion and certain knowledge, between pretense and reality, are continually shifting – a world in which the power of language to transform facts and even to create them seems matched only by the stubborn persistence of facts themselves'.[50] As we shall see, the strange translucency of these works reflects a reticence in narrative structure and an extraordinary sense of moral difficulty that ought not be reduced to Leavis's charge of 'a loss of sureness' in James's 'moral touch'.

The Wings of the Dove refrains from overt denunciation, but it again depicts knowledge as a thing under threat. Curiosity, uncertainty and suspicion infuse the relationships that surround Milly Theale, herself tragically excluded from common understanding. After her fateful interview with Sir Luke Strett the narrator reflects that 'No one in the world could have sufficiently entered into her state; no tie would have been close enough to enable a companion to walk beside her without some disparity' (XIX.v.4, p. 247). Milly leaves Mrs Stringham moving 'in a fine cloud of observation and suspicion; she was in the position, as she believed, of knowing much more about Milly Theale than Milly herself knew' (XIX.iii.1, p. 104); and their acquaintance ('They had met thus as opposed curiosities') convinces her early on that 'the key of knowledge' of Milly is the fact that she has been 'starved for culture' (p. 109). Importantly, Milly's opaque and intriguing presence is conceived as a puzzle not merely for other characters, but for the reader as well:

Such a matter as this may at all events speak of the style in which our young woman could affect those who were near her, may testify to the sort of interest she could inspire. She worked – and seemingly quite without design – upon the sympathy, the curiosity, the fancy of her associates, and we shall really ourselves scarce otherwise come closer to her than by feeling their impression and sharing, if need be, their confusion. She reduced them, Mrs Stringham would have said, to a consenting bewilderment; which was precisely, for that good lady, on a last analysis, what was most in harmony with her greatness. (pp. 116–17)

And Milly herself is not without curiosity about others. Mrs Lowder strikes her as 'a person of whom the mind might in two or three days roughly make the circuit' (XIX.iv.1, p. 149), but not so

Kate Croy, whom she cannot but think of as having an 'other side', one 'not wholly calculable' (xix.iv.3, p. 190). Milly indeed experiences a 'sense, which sprang up at its own hours, of one's being as curious about her as if one had n't known her' (xix.v.1, p. 212). It is a sense shared by Densher who 'did n't want her [Kate] deeper than himself' (xx.vi.2, p. 19), and by other characters in respect of one another in the intensely calculating world of the book. Lambert Strether's ambassadorial mission in *The Ambassadors* further extends the theme. His undertaking entails mounting moral complexity, yet he admits to Maria Gostrey that his interest in Chad's and Madame de Vionnet's private affairs entails a vicarious quest for youth:

> But nevertheless I'm making up late for what I didn't have early. I cultivate my little benefit in my own little way. It amuses me more than anything that has happened to me in all my life. They may say what they like – it's my surrender, my tribute to youth. One puts that where one can – it has to come in somewhere, if only out of the lives, the conditions, the feelings of other persons. (xxii.vii.3, p. 51)

Amusement at 'the feelings of other persons' is not, however, Strether's response to his climactic encounter with Chad and Madame de Vionnet in Book xi; indeed, Chapter 3 movingly reveals his sense of regret not only at the falsities of the meeting, but also at the indelicacies of his involvement in the situation. His mission has taken him deep into the opaque landscape of human relations, just as a rather different situation exposes Maggie Verver in *The Golden Bowl* to the perils and the necessities of knowing.

THE GOLDEN BOWL

I

The Golden Bowl takes to a lavish extreme the characteristic late Jamesian exemption from the conditions of what George Eliot calls 'ordinary life'. Beside her quasi-positivistic 'study of provincial life', James's last completed novel seems to image a world of gorgeous gratuity. Her urge to explain and evidence conduct in social and historical terms, to give a full metonymic account, is in marked contrast to the charmed suggestiveness of

James's late metaphoric method. *The Golden Bowl* takes its title from a symbol, and the parameters of knowledge shift accordingly: knowing becomes more privileged, more specialised and in many ways less honest. The novel reflects James's belief that fictional interest must depend upon the 'really sentient' rather than the 'stupid' character. Significantly, it was not long after the publication of *The Golden Bowl* that he wrote disapprovingly of the sociological focus of Thackeray, Dickens and George Eliot. He tells H. G. Wells, author of *Kipps*, that 'You have for the very first time treated the English "lower middle" class etc., without the picturesque, the grotesque, the fantastic and romantic interference of which Dickens, e.g., is so misleadingly, of which even George Eliot is so deviatingly, full'.[51] To the end, James's preference was to be for 'experiments of form' rather than the less mediated social actuality that George Eliot termed 'life'. His late appraisals of Hardy and Lawrence are consistent with the limiting and limited account he gives of *Middlemarch*.

The magnificent pluralism of *Middlemarch*, its interest in the various worlds of knowledge, again contrasts strikingly with the enchanted formalişm of James's Preface to *The Golden Bowl*. Here knowledge is conceived as a means of revealing and concealing the personal facts, for characters in relation to one another, and for all in relation to the reader: 'It is the Prince who opens the door to half our light upon Maggie, just as it is she who opens it to half our light upon himself'.[52] The pattern of revelation and concealment is reflected in James's portentous claims about character and narration in *The Golden Bowl*. The first is that 'We see very few persons in "The Golden Bowl", but the scheme of the book, to make up for that, is that we shall really see about as much of them as a coherent literary form permits'.[53] And the second: '*no* refinement of ingenuity or of precaution need be dreamed of as wasted in that most exquisite of all good causes the appeal to variety, the appeal to incalculability'.[54] 'Incalculability', the opaque suggestiveness of the fictional subject, vies, then, with the novelist's impulse to penetrate and exhibit the inner lives of characters. This is one of James's final pronouncements on the perennial problem of fictional humanism, and it renders knowledge an extraordinarily equivocal thing. What, after all, does knowledge amount to in so rarefied and obscurely coded a world as the one James envisages in *The Golden Bowl*?

One answer, as always, is that it entails knowing what, in a world of opaque implication, is actually 'going on'. Such knowledge is by no means trivial in late James: as his jungle imagery – 'The pathless wild of the right tone' (xxɪv.v.1, p. 212) – suggests, survival is a high priority even amidst all the subtlety, and survival can necessitate penetrating motives, confidences, machinations, so far as this is possible. But this will aid only those who understand just how unpalatable much of what there is to find out really is. Real knowledge rests upon a sense of tragedy. Thus Fanny Assingham talks of Maggie's having to waken to 'what's called Evil – with a very big E: for the first time in her life. To the discovery of it, to the knowledge of it, to the crude experience of it' (xxɪɪɪ.iii.11, p. 385). But this is by no means particular to Maggie. On the contrary, as J. H. Ward points out in his book on evil in James's fiction, evil is a kind of 'common denominator'[55] in the novels that awaits the unsuspecting initiate in the arts of worldly entrapment.

Like *Middlemarch*, *The Golden Bowl* repeats the word 'knowledge' with striking frequency, and its force can at times seem Eliotean. Thus the narrator appears to distinguish between what George Eliot would call 'sympathy' and 'curiosity' when describing Fanny at Fawns: 'her sympathy had ventured, after much accepted privation, again to become inquisitive' (xxɪv.vi.1, p. 325). Similarly, the Maggie–Adam relationship occasions many references to the power and purity of an empathetic understanding. Adam's letter to Maggie announcing his plan to marry Charlotte prompts in him 'his imagination of her prepared state' (xxɪɪɪ.ii.7, p. 229), a phrase echoed by Maggie to Adam at Fawns: 'One must always, whether or no, have some imagination of the states of others' (xxɪv.v.3, p. 258). Later again she feels that 'he had read his way so into her best possibility' (p. 269). No less than George Eliot's, James's world is steeped in the hermeneutics of human intercourse; no less than she, James emphasises the importance of 'divination' in reading and responding to the signs. Maggie's 'fantastic flight[s] of divination' (xxɪv.v.4, p. 282) eventually enable her to intuit a good deal of what is passing between Amerigo and Charlotte, and of what they are thinking about her. Indeed it is upon such 'real knowledge' (xxɪv.iv.10, p. 201) that she depends in her desperate struggle to retrieve her marriage. Thus does she enter a charmed circle of intuitive relation, for the illicit couple share 'identities of impulse' (xxɪɪɪ.iii.9, p. 356) that are as deeply private as they are passionate. This is the 'relation of mutual close contact' (xxiii.iii.4, p. 289) into which Charlotte tells herself that she and Amerigo have been coerced.

That there are various orders of mutuality – familial, romantic, merely social – is a matter that the novel raises but does not apparently take to be central. Fanny tells Bob that

> a person can mostly feel but one passion – one *tender* passion, that is – at a time. Only that doesn't hold good for our primary and instinctive attachments, the 'voice of blood,' such as one's feeling for a parent or a brother. Those may be intense and yet not prevent other intensities. (xxiii.iii.11, p. 395)

In fact the line between 'instinctive attachments' and others is far from clear in *The Golden Bowl*: Adam and Maggie, after all, have a 'passion' amounting almost to incest. But neither is the line between knowing and not knowing, sympathy and curiosity, as clear as it is in George Eliot; and this is both a matter of moral and epistemological uncertainty. The self in late James is often quite nightmarishly opaque. Typically, Fanny seems to speak with a certain histrionic authority when she tells Bob that 'One can never be ideally sure of anything. There are always possibilities' (xxiii.i.4, p. 86). Amerigo urges the human point in conversation with Maggie, insisting that he has an 'unknown' 'single self' about which she has discovered nothing. Fanny later echoes it to Maggie. Of Amerigo and Charlotte she asks, 'Ah who can say what passes between people in such a relation?' (xxiv.iv.9, p. 173). As her crisis mounts, Maggie herself feels the 'need not to be penetrable' (xxiv.v.1, p. 226), and she has increasingly to depart from what in George Eliot's fiction is the proper response to duplicity and need. The novel's moral evolution from Eliot to late James is reflected in one of *The Golden Bowl*'s memorable moral epithets. The increasingly strategic Maggie must observe the 'foredoomed ingenuities of her pity' (xxiv.vi.1, p. 330). Mere beneficence is inconceivable; she cannot but put knowledge to darker uses.

Knowledge in *The Golden Bowl* thus reflects that late Jamesian fusion of sordidness and solicitude that has troubled so many critics.[56] It is exigent and enchanted, exquisite and base. Thus does Fanny ponder the marital predicament in 'all its ugly consistency and its temporary gloss' (xxiv.iv.7, p. 126). Such a formulation, however, does not entirely reflect the tragic achievement of the book, for *The Golden Bowl*, no less than *Middlemarch*, images knowledge as a gift richly alluring enough to render failure tragic in its waste and its ineptitude. Indeed, one of the novel's special features, its epigrammatic brilliancy, seems designed to sustain a sense of ideal value even whilst life's finest possibilities are being wasted by the characters concerned. The narrator reflects on 'the high luxury of not having to explain' (xxiv.iv.8, p. 145), on 'the large freedoms only of others' (xxiv.iv.2, p. 26) and, in a phrase again reminiscent of George Eliot, on 'the possible heroism of perfunctory things' (xxiv.v.4, p. 288). Such phrases convey, in typically understated form, the elusive ideals of James's late fiction.

Charlotte's first visit to the solitary Amerigo at Portland Place typifies the novel's moral ambience:

'Is n't the immense, the really quite matchless beauty of our position that we have to "do" nothing in life at all? – nothing except the usual necessary everyday thing which consists in one's not being more of a fool than one can help. That's all – but that's as true for one time as for another. There has been plenty of "doing," and there will doubtless be plenty still; but it's all theirs, every inch of it; it's all a matter of what they've done *to* us.' And she showed how the question had therefore been only of their taking everything as everything came, and all as quietly as might be. Nothing stranger surely had ever happened to a conscientious, a well-meaning, a perfectly passive pair: no more extraordinary decree had ever been launched against such victims than this of forcing them against their will into a relation of mutual close contact that they had done everything to avoid. (xxiii.iii.4, p. 289)

If there is something familiarly diabolic about Charlotte's subtle displacement of motive and responsibility ('what they've done *to* us'), the situation is by no means thus clearly defined. But all the central characters are thus exercised by the need to plot, interpret and rationalise, and there is indeed a 'matchless beauty' in the exemption from unspoken constraints that the couple enjoy. The narrator's 'well-meaning' and 'perfectly passive' are of course typical in their reticent irony: Charlotte *is* rationalising. Yet the resultant 'relation of mutual close contact' is allowed a substance and dignity to which a censorious view of James's 'moral touch' cannot do justice. James here contemplates the morality of mutual relation with a kind of accepting sophistry that George Eliot will not countenance.[57]

A further and related scene describes Maggie and Adam alone for the last time at Fawns:

> They were husband and wife – oh so immensely! – as regards other persons; but after they had dropped again on their old bench, conscious that the party on the terrace, augmented as in the past by neighbours, would do beautifully without them, it was wonderfully like their having got together into some boat and paddled off from the shore where husbands and wives, luxuriant complications, made the air too tropical. In the boat they were father and daughter, and poor Dotty and Kitty supplied abundantly, for their situation, the oars or the sail. Why, into the bargain, for that matter – this came to Maggie – could n't they always live, so far as they lived together, in a boat? She felt in her face with the question the breath of a possibility that soothed her; they needed only *know* each other henceforth in the unmarried relation. That other sweet evening in the same place he had been as unmarried as possible – which had kept down, so to speak, the quantity of change in their state. Well then that other sweet evening was what the present sweet evening would resemble; with the quite calculable effect of an exquisite inward refreshment. They *had* after all, whatever happened, always and ever each other; each other – that was the hidden treasure and the saving truth – to do exactly what they would with: a provision full of possibilities.
>
> (xxiv.v.3, p. 255)

A 'provision full of possibilities' – however surprising the intensity between father and daughter, it is the sense of 'possibility', of emotional richness, that prevails here. This richness is doubtless erotic in some degree: 'the breath of a possibility' soothes the anxious Maggie. Yet it would be misleading to see this as the central concern of the passage. That concern is reflected in the italicised '*know*': like the meeting between Amerigo and Charlotte, this one turns on the quality of mutuality achieved. The extraordinary sense of shared, inviolate privacy evoked here is the best 'possibility' the novel can envisage.

Yet it does not pass entirely without moral comment. *The Golden*

Bowl's occasional and understated ethical asides have a quite disarming, but also a disquieting, force. 'Dotty and Kitty supplied abundantly, for their situation, the oars or the sail' – in such incidentals does the cost of mutuality in this world register. So too does its frailty, its belated resistance to the constant encroachments of circumstance. Maggie assures herself that 'They *had* . . . each other', but she has already told Fanny that they are 'Lost to each other – father and I' (xxiv.vi.1, p. 333), and she must in the end sacrifice the unrepeatable privacy of her parental relation in order to maintain her marriage. The novel's conclusion here is again memorable and tragic: the narrator describes a world in which 'it doesn't always meet *all* contingencies to be right' (xxiii.ii.3, p. 167).

'Right' is of course an equivocal word here and will require clarification presently. It is equivocal because James blurs both its moral and its epistemological force. Being right – that is, accurate – about the inner worlds of others proves here to be extraordinarily difficult. No matter how intimate, knowledge is seen as always partial and its objects as seldom entirely predictable.[58] Being morally 'right' is no less complicated, since James sees just how subtle the constraints on 'the large freedoms only of others' can be. Morality and legality may overlap in many places, but *The Golden Bowl* insists that they are not identical. Like *Middlemarch*, *The Golden Bowl* conceives human relationships as intrinsically flawed and cracked. On this account James makes large accommodations, and his point is always that civilised society needs fiction, as well as legislation, to make its veiled intersubjective worlds intelligible.[59] And, indeed, to make them bearable. Dorothea Krook's reading of the novel as 'a great fable . . . of the redemption of man by the transforming power of human love'[60] surely understates the grimness of James's moral outlook. The description indeed better fits a George Eliot novel. As the 'foredoomed ingenuities' of Maggie's 'pity' suggests, James's understanding of altruism is as of a thing under siege, and in *The Golden Bowl* modernism makes of George Eliot's ethic an appalled, apprehensive and intensely strategic thing.

II

The formal correlative for this view is *The Golden Bowl*'s remote and indirect omniscient narrator. In place of the 'mere muffled majesty' of the social and moral historian of *Middlemarch* James fashions a persona who, like Adam Verver, seems to lack 'the general prerogative of presence' (xxiii.ii.4, p. 169). Here the convention of the limited narrator is carried to the edge of impersonality. Information, lavishly proffered in *Middlemarch*, dwindles to intimation: 'A dim explanation of phenomena once vivid must at all events for the moment suffice us' (xxiii.ii.1, p. 128). This gloss on Verver's motives holds out a promise that the narrator seldom finds himself able to honour. 'Our last possible analysis' (xxiii.ii.3, p. 167) is in *The Golden Bowl* never definitive or final.

Just how deep James's privileged fictional provisionalism goes is apparent in this description of Verver's eyes: 'Deeply and changeably blue, though not romantically large, they were yet youthfully, almost strangely beautiful, with their ambiguity of your scarce knowing if they most carried their possessor's vision out or most opened themselves to your own' (xxiii.ii.4, p. 170). This is the familiar Jamesian question about seeing and being: the odd impersonality of the aside in fact poses the fundamental post-Kantian epistemological problem: does mind produce and project meaning, or does it simply register it, 'open itself' to impressions? Verver's eyes are the icon of this uncertainty, and it is striking in this passage how far such uncertainty holds for the narrator whose 'creation' Verver ostensibly is: 'your scarce knowing' refers both to other people in Verver's life, and to the narrative perspective. Character and narration again collude in an opaque vision of human 'possibility'.

The byzantine Preface to the novel acknowledges the connection at length. James remarks upon a thoroughly characteristic feature of *The Golden Bowl*'s narrative structure: the 'marked inveteracy of a certain indirect and oblique view of my presented action'.[61] Then follows the portentous and memorable observation about 'mere muffled majesty':

> It's not that the muffled majesty of authorship doesn't here *ostensibly* reign; but I catch myself again shaking it off and disavowing the pretence of it while I get down into the arena and do my best to live and breathe and rub shoulders and converse with the persons engaged in the struggle. . . .[62]

James's point about 'authorship' is of course that it has been in writers such as George Eliot too anxiously responsible. Its self-consciousness has leached the fictional illusion; but, more than this, it has allegedly falsified the world of intersubjective relations by too insistently assimilating narration to knowing. James agrees with George Eliot on the centrality of personal relations. Indeed, he argues that 'all life comes back to the question of our relations with each other'.[63] However, he insists that narration ought more closely to observe the opaqueness we know in life. What he catches himself 'shaking off' is not an ultimate authority in the fiction – he rightly believed such impersonality to be impossible – but rather the appearance, and the expected coherence, of such authority. As is so often the case, his solution is to delegate vision to characters. The Preface celebrates 'the manner in which the whole thing remains subject to the register, ever so closely kept, of the consciousness of but two of the characters.'[64]

This is, of course, inaccurate: the narrative in fact revolves through the consciousnesses of all four protagonists at various times. However, James is quite right in suggesting that the teasing absence of definition in the narrative commentary is consistent with a highly subjectivised structure of report. This structure generates much of the syntax of uncertainty recently analysed in Ralf Norrman's *The Insecure World of Henry James's Fiction*;[65] it also leaves extraordinarily unclear the status and authority of the narrating voice. Leo Bersani argues that the 'psychological center of the drama in James's late novels is in the narrator's mind', and that 'the level of social reality is constantly being transformed into a level on which characters serve mainly allegorical functions'.[66] Whilst Bersani is correct in drawing attention to the ubiquitous presence of the narrating consciousness, he perhaps overstates the allegorical force of the characters. Indeed, character in *The Golden Bowl* is oddly enmeshed and yet independent of its source; it seems at once emblematically stylised and deeply private. This, perhaps the most recalcitrant formal feature of the novel, leads Peter Garrett to suggest that 'The narrator functions as a further level of consciousness, lying beyond and encompassing those of the characters, rendering them accessible and intelligible to the reader.'[67] The emphasis here on intelligibility is perhaps too great: the inner world of character in *The Golden Bowl* is surely less available than this; but Garrett's suggestion of levels of consciousness (a feature recognised by the Russian formalists as 'dialogic'[68]) does reflect the curious effect of displaced authority that James achieves. Perhaps Ian Watt's famous description of the narrative structure of the first paragraph of *The Ambassadors* also holds for this novel. Watt found 'a very idiosyncratic kind of multiple Impressionism: idiosyncratic because [of] the dual presence of Strether's consciousness and that of the narrator, who translates what he sees there into more general terms'.[69]

The idea of 'translation' might suggest to some a 'textual' decentring of the fictional self, a subsuming of individual consciousness by the discourse of the narrator. Technically, of course, this is the case; but in a peculiarly suggestive way, James's techniques for rendering consciousness produce a sense of difference as existing both within and beyond language, as if subjectivity were at once the source and the consequence of language. Mind in these novels is oddly recessive, despite its narrative stylisation. James seems to project a linguistic simulation of the extra-linguistic, a 'centredness' which is a shared condition of all minds in the book and, paradoxically, a guarantor of their opacity. As Paul Armstrong notes in his suggestive discussion of phenomenology and *The Golden Bowl*: 'language could not exist if solipsism prevailed. And, in fact, dialogue offers the best possibility of reducing the opacity and narrowing the gap that separates the self and the other.'[70] What needs to be added here is that opacity is in turn a property of otherness: the fundamental moral recognition that other people and the situations in which we meet them are complex and not wholly knowable must entail the assumption that other people are in some irreducible primitive sense 'real', not simply textual.

Here early forms of phenomenology perhaps have more to tell us about fictional humanism than their post-structural variants. Armstrong rightly draws parallels between the problematics of knowing in *The Golden Bowl* and the accounts of intersubjectivity offered in Husserl, Heidegger, Sartre and Merleau-Ponty. James, particularly in the late phase, does indeed reflect a crisis in epistemology for which works such as *Middlemarch* and 'The Lifted Veil' are clearly preparations. Like his brother William, Henry James wishes to rethink the subject–object dualism (Verver's eyes) and the ethical ramifications of holding that 'reality' is an intersubjective construct in which the individual has an overriding and inimitable say. In this sense *The Golden Bowl* looks

forward to the 'existential humanism' Sartre was to espouse in
Existentialism and Humanism.

However, James uses fictional structures to test rather than to
invest propositions with any final authority, and delegated
omniscient narration is his characteristic vehicle for doing so.
Thus *The Golden Bowl*'s narrator offers a partial report on the
subjectivity of his characters but disclaims ultimate authority.
Commentary demurs at overt Eliotean discussion or judgement;
the priority of sentient individual consciousness over a
synthesising omniscience is James's way of simulating situated
authority, and the limited omniscient structure he describes in the
Preface is its structural and epistemological equivalent in fiction.
Two qualifications are, however, important here. One is that *The
Golden Bowl* ultimately reads an individual-centred humanism
back into what at times looks like an existential account. The
other is that, as we have noted, James was not oblivious either to
the need for, or to the implications of, a narrating presence.
Indeed, he takes for granted just such a presence, and he knows
that impersonality, both in art and life, is an implausible and
ultimately destructive ambition.

Inevitably, *The Golden Bowl* evinces subtle but ineradicable
evidences of story-telling. As in any narrative, scenes and contexts
must be specified; likewise, a rhetorical relation between narrator
and reader must be established. This is sometimes done in the first
person, at others in the third. Thus will the narrator quietly but
insistently bridge the opaque world of individual intention and
the public one of manifest behaviour. Quizzically, he catches
himself doing it. Thus on the 'incalculable' Amerigo:
'What he had further said on the occasion of which we thus
represent him as catching the echoes from his own thought . . .'
(xxiii.i.1, pp. 10–11). On Maggie: 'Such were some of the reasons
for which Maggie suspected fundamentals, as I have called them'
(xxiv.iv.4, p. 78). Occasionally the reader's involvement is more
coercively encouraged, and never more so than during the
brilliant and uncharacteristically forward introduction of Verver
at the beginning of Book Second:

> We share this world, none the less, for the hour, with Mr.
> Verver; the very fact of his striking, as he would have said, for
> solitude, the fact of his quiet flight, almost on tiptoe, through
> tortuous corridors, investing him with an interest that makes

our attention – tender indeed almost to compassion – qualify his
achieved isolation.   (xxiii.ii.1, p. 125)

At times, too, a passing phrase can imply an intense kind of
involvement on the reader's part. Path imagery is used to chart
Maggie's experience ('the pathless wild of the right tone'), and in
a revealing moment it carries over to the process of reading itself:
the narrator refers to 'that appetite in Amerigo for the explanatory
which we have just found in our path' (xxiii.ii.3, p. 163). Reading
and personal revelation are alike hermeneutic activities, but, as
we shall see, James was not so besotted with Art as to think them
identical.

The narrator in *The Golden Bowl* is not so remote as entirely to
forgo what Leavis calls 'placing' commentary. There are
judgements in the book, though they are generally heavily implied
or ironic. One of the most overt occurs in the final scene. Amerigo
and Charlotte, 'high expressions of the kind of human furniture
required', sit amongst the 'pieces' in the room:

> The fusion of their presence with the decorative elements, their
> contribution to the triumph of selection, was complete and
> admirable; though to a lingering view, a view more penetrating
> than the occasion really demanded, they also might have
> figured as concrete attestations of a rare power of
> purchase.   (xxiv.vi.3, p. 360)

The subtle savagery of this indictment of American mercantilism
suggests that James had not entirely lost his 'moral grasp': the
'view more penetrating' is of course, his, and the conditional
'might' here is merely an urbane pretence of not having judged.
Similarly self-conscious are the narrator's occasional reflections
on his own narrative technique. On Maggie: 'might I so far
multiply my metaphors, I should compare her to the frightened
but clinging young mother of an unlawful child' (xxiv.iv.1, p. 7).

But the most significant traces of 'mere muffled majesty' are the
novel's rare narrative commonplaces. The Eliotean sublime has
here dwindled to whatever occasional asides the novel's
atmosphere of hushed insularity will permit. General
observations linking the world and the book are seldom
syntactically separated and almost never extended. The most
detailed concern Maggie: 'She had lived long enough to make out

for herself that any deep-seated passion has its pangs as well as its joys, and that we are made by its aches and its anxieties most richly conscious of it' (ibid.). More guarded still are: 'We have each our own way of making up for our unselfishness' (xxiv.iv.6, p. 101); and

> There reigned for her absolutely during these vertiginous moments [pondering the others involved] that fascination of the monstrous, that temptation of the horribly possible, which we so often trace by its breaking out suddenly, lest it should go further, in unexplained retreats and reactions.
>
> (xxiv.v.2, p. 233)

It is significant that Maggie should motivate what narrative generalising there is in the book, for its structure – closing with her point of view – also suggests a privileged position for her in the story. In James, as in other English masters of omniscience (Austen, Eliot, Lawrence and Hardy, for example), the formal distribution of narrative interest, especially of internal report, has a subtle but decisive moral force. Like Ursula Brangwen in *The Rainbow*, Maggie's inner world prevails at the close, and in either case it is the spiritual torment and tenuousness of the heroine that most arouses narrative comment and sympathy.

Like Lawrence, James, especially in the late phase, tends to privilege psychology over morality conventionally conceived. The existential quality of experience is more important to him than what society can say about it. Indeed, there are here foreshadowings of the existential rejection of the Kantian moral agent. Like Heidegger and Sartre, James envisions humanity in a condition of 'abandonment':[71] 'there can no longer be any good *a priori*';[72] 'man is condemned to be free',[73] at least in the sense that he must choose a certain kind of subjective alignment between self and the codes. Thus Amerigo finds himself condemned to 'gropings and fittings of his conscience and his experience' (xxiii.iii.6, p. 319), his 'experience' being of course complicated by the miscellany of national codes involved in marrying into an American family.

There are indeed many references to morality in *The Golden Bowl*; however, its uncertainty, rather than its authority, is generally at issue. Narrative commentary, such as it is, invests the novel's human situations with an arcane and highly provisional sense of moral expectation. The narrator's image of scales for Charlotte and Amerigo at Matcham is a striking example. He observes that

> hovering Judgement, the spirit with the scales, might perfectly have been imaged there as some rather snubbed and subdued but quite trained and tactful poor relation, of equal, of the properest, lineage, only of aspect a little dingy, doubtless from too limited a change of dress, for whose tacit and abstemious presence, never betrayed by a rattle of her rusty machine, a room in the attic and a plate at the side table were decently usual. (xxiii.iii.7, p. 331)

'Too limited a change of dress' signals the limits of moral authority in this opaque international world, but it by no means silences the questioners. Conversation turns with a kind of cautious casuistry on the problem of moral authority. Amerigo, who is sincerely troubled by the subtleties of the question, commends the indelicate Fanny on her 'rocket'-like American 'moral sense' (xxiii.i.2, p. 31). Fanny herself, a Jamesian study in hermeneutic hyperbole, inquires, 'what is morality but high intelligence?' (xxiii.i.4, p. 88) and tells Bob that 'the forms . . . are two thirds of conduct' (xxiii.iii.11, p. 390). Her general view is that morality is textual and intelligence a heightened sensitivity to signs. James has some sympathy with this perspective, yet, as we shall see, it finally excludes Fanny from the relational world that she so desperately wishes to penetrate. Here Amerigo is much shrewder. He knows that, bowl-like, human situations parade a 'moral paste' (xxiii.iii.5, p. 310), and that the glitter can conceal unsuspected flaws.

Mutuality's endemic moral relativism is evoked with extraordinary, controlled suggestiveness in *The Golden Bowl*. The world Fanny cannot enter is, for example, implied in the elusive moral ambience that subsists between Maggie and Verver. 'We want each other', he tells her;

> 'only wanting it, each time, *for* each other. That's what I call the happy spell; but it's also a little – possibly – the immorality.'
> ' "The immorality"?' she had pleasantly echoed.
> 'Well, we're tremendously moral for ourselves – that is for each other; and I won't pretend that I know exactly at whose

particular personal expense you and I for instance are happy. What it comes to, I dare say, is that there's something haunting – as if it were a bit uncanny – in such a consciousness of our general comfort and privilege'.   (xxiv.iv.5, pp. 91–2)

Being 'moral for ourselves' is 'haunting' precisely because the test of universalisability has been spurned. Like Charlotte and Amerigo, Maggie and Adam achieve at great cost an intersubjective accord, but it is glaringly, and knowingly, exclusive. James's first Notebook entry on *The Golden Bowl* envisions a 'vicious circle'[74] of devotion and deceit (a phrase echoed by Fanny – xxiii.iii.11, p. 394), and it is the condition of this circle that rightness is not right for all relations.

The post-Kantian problem of ethical universalisability eludes final formulations, in part because human subjectivity is too private and other to submit to comprehensive public description, but also because the hermeneutics of moral discourse are expressive rather than merely objective: people see moral situations and behaviour in strikingly divergent ways. Here, according to James, the creativity of human consciousness is both a blessing – since it can retrieve some order and beauty from the wreckage of mere contingency – and a blight. Maggie concludes on the terrace at Fawns that meaning or 'significance' can 'be no more after all than a matter of interpretation, differing always for a different interpreter' (xxiv.v.2, p. 244).

Yet the 'large freedoms' of 'others' must, the novel insists, be respected, and the narrator leaves to self-indict a kind of moral casuistry in which conscience capitulates to convenience. Thus does one of Fanny's elaborate efforts of rationalisation proceed 'touch by touch': 'Maggie's the great comfort. I'm getting hold of it. It will be *she* who'll see us through' (xxiii.iii.3, p. 280). But of course Maggie does not, and neither does the narrator. Though silent here, he holds Fanny's histrionics up to poignant derision. As is so often the case in *The Golden Bowl*, silence, innuendo, irony and the clinical precision of cumulative imagery imply narrative judgements about character that in a George Eliot novel would be less equivocal, a more robust and personalised assertion of moral authority.

III

Character in *The Golden Bowl* reflects James's moral reticence; indeed, James has here taken psychological narrative well beyond the realm of the moral naturalism which prompted Leavis to condemn James's failure openly to denounce Adam and Maggie's manipulative attitude to Amerigo.[75] *The Golden Bowl* spurns many of the traditional techniques of realist characterisation, but without collapsing character entirely into the allegorical functions Bersani finds in the novel. The novel's methods of characterisation are more complex and elusive than this.

Bersani is right to draw attention to a variety of counter-naturalistic techniques in the novel. The bowl which gives it its title is an obvious example. The shift from Eliotean metonymy to the economy and suggestiveness of metaphor is obvious here. Their fictional titles are also an interesting index of their outlooks. *Daniel Deronda* (and most of George Eliot's other novels) names a protagonist whose life confers upon the story a loose narrative unity. *Middlemarch* designates a place, a social organism within which people can be studied in context. *The Mill on the Floss* is poised somewhere between context and existential symbolism: *The Mill* is the scene of Maggie Tulliver's turbulent childhood, but also its symbol. The title *The Golden Bowl*, however, divests the novel of an individuating personal focus, but without implying a situational context. Rather, it refers eerily to each of the principal characters: the bowl's gloss is an icon of the general insincerity of the participants, of their constant and strategic resort to appearances; the flaw is a kind of relational notation reflecting the apparently intrinsic illogicality and inadequacy of human love; even the circumstances surrounding the object's acquisition are emblematic: the bowl is at once traditional and transactional, a treasure and a ruse for the unsuspecting Maggie. As so often in James, beauty, antiquity and duplicity fuse in the act of enchanted possession. That the bowl might have been a gift from Charlotte to Maggie, and chosen in Amerigo's presence, is the crowning irony: Charlotte's thwarted tribute stands metaphorically as an act of loving dissimulation, and it is this gift that Maggie eventually reciprocates through the 'foredoomed ingenuities of her pity' (xxiv.vi.1, p. 330). The symbol's air of appointed congruity with the principal participants is extraordinarily and chillingly suggestive. It implies extra-rational

but unconscious accords between characters, between characters
and their understanding of themselves, and between characters
and the superior but still partial knowledge of narrator and
reader. Moreover, it contributes powerfully to the sense that
consciousness is in this world strangely, yet incompletely, unitary.
The minds of characters seem to extend opaquely into one
another, and into the consciousness of the narrator. The Eliotean
divide between commentary and the individual consciousness is
subtly undermined at every turn.

In the Preface James terms this unitary quality the 'handsome
wholeness of effect',[76] and it involves a variety of techniques.
Dialogue, for instance, is in this novel less the source of
individualising self-signature than it is in George Eliot's fiction.
There are subtle differences in idiom but on the whole James
understates the idiomatic possibilities of having an international
cast. Speech, both verbal and mental, is richly and insistently
stylised; codes seem at once to constitute and to cross cultural
boundaries. James's obsession with national types also tends to
diffuse the naturalistic impression. To this extent Americanness is
an allegorical expression of manipulative innocence, and
Italianness a similarly stylised metaphor for the elusive
subtleties of aged and adept social usage. The patterns can seem
disconcertingly – and falsely – obvious.

However, the novel also contains powerful and persuasive
traces of naturalism that read personal specificity back into
stereotypes, self back into roles. No less than *Middlemarch*, *The
Golden Bowl* projects a premise of identity that links the novel with
extra-literary narrative assumptions and that serves as a basis for
differentiation that symbolism, allegory and stylisation seem to
deny. In its essentials this premise is not unlike George Eliot's.
Behind it lies the organicist ideal of a whole, integrated person.
Amerigo, who, like Isabel Archer, has been fragmented by
cultural discontinuity, has intimations of this when he is not
directly involved in the unfamiliarity of English life: 'it was much
more when he was alone or when he was with his own people – or
when he was, say, with Mrs. Verver and nobody else – that he
moved, that he talked, that he listened, that he felt, as a congruous
whole' (xxiii.iii.7, p. 328). Thus conceived, the self comprises the
forces of circumstance, choice and disposition. Choice is 'the
responsibility of freedom' (xxiv.iv.10, p. 186) that Maggie bears
as she seeks to manipulate her situation; the givenness of a certain

genetic make-up is suggested by observations like the one that describes Verver as 'so framed by nature as to be able to keep his inconveniences separate from his resentments' (xxiii.ii.1, p. 130); Adam possesses what may seem to be an Eliotean assimilation of thought and feeling, head and heart: 'The play of vision was at all events so rooted in him that he could receive impressions of sense even while positively thinking' (xxiii.ii.4, p. 188). Present and past are also assumed to be continuous in the evolution of selves. A certain amount is revealed about personal pasts: Adam's (xxiii.ii.1, pp. 140–3),[77] Fanny's (xxiii.i.1, p. 34) and Charlotte's (xxiii.i.3, p. 55), and Amerigo's 'sense of the past' – his urgent need that it inform and interpret his present – is one of the novel's central subjects: 'There were other marble terraces, sweeping more purple prospects, on which he would have known what to think' (xxiii.iii.9, p. 354). The expatriate burden of the present is relieved only when he revisits his personal past after Charlotte's arrival in London:

> The sense of the past revived for him nevertheless as it had n't yet done: it made that other time somehow meet the future close, interlocking with it, before his watching eyes, as in a long embrace of arms and lips, and so handling and hustling the present that this poor quantity scarce retained substance enough, scarce remained sufficiently *there*, to be wounded or shocked.   (xxiii.iii.4, pp. 297–8)

This completion of self through other, and of presence through mutual memory, is again reminiscent of George Eliot's fiction. Here, however, the thing is, as it so often is in James, illicit: self-completion goes on beyond the codes; adultery becomes a strange approximation to sincerity. Like the phenomenologists, James often sees a deep asymmetry in relationship: self and other are bound in a play of dependence, compassion, threat and resentment. 'Love' can have a part in this, but it is never George Eliot's wholesome emotion.

One reason for this is that mind in late James is a more fundamentally dissociated thing than it is in George Eliot. In her novels the radically dissociated consciousness – Hetty, Tito, Casaubon – simply perishes. It cannot meet her conditions of personhood. James, however, takes dissociation to be a condition of consciousness, and his great creations owe more to Gwendolen

Harleth and Princess Halm-Eberstein than they do to Dorothea
Brooke. Thus, although he too pictures consciousness as ranging
from conscious awareness to unconscious threat and horror, the
editorial mechanism between these realms is far more exacting.
The appalled vigilance of mind in James, its agonised and
unappeasable alertness, is a defence against the psychic life that
threatens to let intimations of the 'monstrous' both down into the
unmanageable opaqueness of the unconscious, and up into
consciousness where it might disrupt the individual's power to
interpret and manipulate human situations. As Ruth Bernard
Yeazell points out, this psychic configuration finds expression in
a certain circuitous 'syntax of knowing'[78] in the novels. It also
infuses symbolism and the techniques used to render the inner
lives of characters. In all these respects Maggie Verver is the
book's master creation. As we shall see, her famous pagoda vision
epitomises the symbolic logic of the Jamesian unconscious, and it
is she who, divided between the 'fear' and the 'fascination' of
knowledge, acts out of psychic discontinuities that George Eliot
would have thought fatal to the self.

IV

'Far down below the level of attention, in she could scarce have
said what sacred depths, Maggie's inspiration had come'
(xxiv.v.5,   pp. 315–16).   Maggie's   'inspiration'   compares
revealingly with Dorothea Brooke's 'ready understanding of high
experience'. George Eliot adds, 'Of lower experience such as plays
a great part in the world, poor Mrs Casaubon had a very blurred
shortsighted knowledge, little helped by her imagination' (iii.76,
p. 356). Dorothea of course gains some insight into 'lower
experience' through Casaubon's conduct and the political
machinations of Middlemarch, but she remains by Jamesian
standards an idealist at the end. Maggie Verver's 'long evolution
of feeling' (xxiv.iii.3, p. 58), however, makes her expert in orders
of 'experience' and 'knowledge' that are congenitally alien to
George Eliot's heroine. Maggie must meet 'the prescribed reach of
her hypocrisy' (xxiv.iv.8, p. 142) if she is to retrieve her position,
her dignity, and indeed that of the others involved in the marital
conundrum. Thus, while Dorothea's emergence from 'moral
stupidity' involves absolute straightness in relationships of

various kinds, Maggie embarks upon a nightmare of manipulative self-preservation.

In this sense Maggie lacks what James had termed Dorothea's 'indefinable moral elevation';[79] yet she is by no means merely a manipulator, for James has here given one of the great modernist accounts of the tragically conflicted complexion of many women's emotional lives. Maggie loves the Prince – that fairy-tale formulation disguises Maggie's extraordinary combination of devotion, disingenuousness and deceit within her marriage. As we shall see, James's familiar phrase for this is 'letting go': Maggie 'loves' Amerigo enough to wish him to be superlatively and freely himself; yet her love casts him in the constraining image of her own fantasy life. It also of course harbours the horror of loss, and it is when that horror begins obscurely to impinge that her 'inspiration' begins more deliberately to divert the energies of love into quiet but desperate acts of coercion. This is the 'multiplication of distractions and suppressions' (xxiv.iv.1, p. 10) that is the central concern of the second part of *The Golden Bowl*.

James had of course argued that Dorothea is insufficiently central in the dramatic structure of *Middlemarch*. She was 'too superb a heroine to be wasted'. But then *Middlemarch* seemed to him an 'indifferent whole', and he cherishes the belief that in *The Golden Bowl* he has achieved a 'handsome wholeness of effect'. In many respects this is so. The gradations between orders of character in *The Golden Bowl* are, at least among the main cast, more subtle than in *Middlemarch*, and Maggie's 'part' of the novel does indeed gain a curious recessive coherence by virtue of its being largely focused through her consciousness. This consciousness is an immensely complex thing. Maggie has 'no small self' (xxiv.iv.6, p. 101) when exposed to the initial hazards of her situation, yet it is a self that possesses a compelling sense of fictional completeness. James's desire to 'show as much' of her as 'coherent literary form will permit' is reflected in the range of information he gives about her. There are glimpses of her past (xxiii.ii.1, p. 142), and lavish attention to the Americanness that gives her an equivocal status as both an individual and a type. Her personal disposition is mentioned in passing, though here, as with Lydgate, the emphasis is existential: her mind is by natural tendency derivative: he has 'spots of commonness' at the deepest reaches of his romantic inclinations; she too is inauthentic in her responses to love and knowledge. She shares with Amerigo a 'boundless happy margin' that is a cheapened form of freedom: she enjoys the liberty of seeing 'other women reduced to the same passive pulp that had then begun, once for all, to constitute *her* substance' (XXIII.ii.3, pp. 164–5). This popular romantic conception of freedom is at root competitive and does not meet her deepest needs. Like those of the other characters, these needs are given as both conscious and unconscious – 'far down below the level of attention' – and her deepest need of all is to exercise 'the responsibility of freedom', her ethical will, in unifying her compartmentalised self. Thus pictured, Maggie reflects most of the features of *The Golden Bowl*'s premise of identity; however, James's method here is typically selective. Details are offered as hints and intimations; much more of the portrait is left to a moment-to-moment process of self-revelation than it is in a George Eliot novel. Like the other protagonists, Maggie seems to possess a privacy that the reader imaginatively charts and completes in reference to the general picture of personhood offered.

This privacy is as hypnotic as it is elusive. Interestingly, James chooses for Maggie a word George Eliot had adopted for the 'play' of Gwendolen Harleth's personality. Maggie's increasing subtlety and scepticism awakens her to the realities of 'iridescence', both in herself and in others: 'She was learning almost from minute to minute to be a mistress of shades – since always when there were possibilities enough of intimacy there were also by that fact, in intercourse, possibilities of iridescence' (XXIV.iv.8, p.142). The 'possibilities of iridescence' are the brutal but baffling realities of James's knowledge theme. One can be more or less transparent to others, more or less inquiring after their inner selves, but always there must be recourse to strategic necessities. No reading of *The Golden Bowl* can do Maggie justice that does not acknowledge the extent to which she becomes, by a necessity only partly self-induced, a 'mistress of shades'.

This process and its final outcome are charted with a largely unexplicated subtlety that James sought without satisfaction in George Eliot's novels. Maggie's 'long evolution of feeling' resembles Gwendolen Harleth's in that her mind, too, is made to 'ache with the pain of the process', but the process is opaque – even, James would have us believe, to the narrator.

It begins in American innocence, though it is an innocence of a disarmingly sophisticated kind. The Ververs seek to possess

Amerigo as they might one of Adam's priceless artifacts: 'Nothing perhaps might affect us as queerer, had we time to look into it, than this application of the same measure of value to such different pieces of property as old Persian carpets, say, and new human acquisitions . . .' (xxiii.ii.5, p. 196). The narrator's point about such 'acquisitions' is that, translated into 'human' terms, they rest on an effrontery of knowingness. Maggie relishes the romantic fascination of feeling that Amerigo is culturally and humanly other, unknown to her; yet she is all the while confident that he is in principle, if not in fact, knowable. Like Isabel Archer, Maggie makes the category mistake that is the perennial pitfall of the 'categories of the human appeal'. She tells Amerigo, 'you're so curious and eminent that there are very few others like you – you belong to a class about which everything is known' (xxiii.i.1, p. 12). This fantasy is of course profoundly ironic, since it conflates the categories and subjects of knowledge. *The Golden Bowl* insists that there is no special category of knowledge whose members are there by virtue of being entirely known. Being known is never so clearly the property of the object of knowledge and it is the 'very insolence of facility' (xxiii.ii.3, p. 166) to imagine that others will consent to live within such ingenuous imaginative confines. Indeed Amerigo, who in his turn finds the Ververs 'impenetrable' (xxiii.i.1, p. 22), tries to warn Maggie off the assumption that a demonstrable and documented personal past can be appropriated as if it were itself a demonstration. Amerigo insists that the codes do not reach down to the 'personal quantity' that is his 'single self'. As to knowing the Ververs, he jokingly claims, 'Ah love, I *began* with that. I know enough, I feel, never to be surprised.' But

'It's you yourselves meanwhile,' he continued, 'who really know nothing. There are two parts of me' – yes, he had been moved to go on. 'One is made up of history, the doings, the marriages, the crimes, the follies, the boundless *bêtises* of other people – especially of their famous waste of money that might have come to me. Those things are written – literally in rows of volumes, in libraries; are as public as they're abominable. Everybody can get at them, and you've both of you wonderfully looked them in the face. But there's another part, very much smaller doubtless, which, such as it is, represents my single self, the unknown, unimportant – unimportant save to *you* – personal quantity. About this you've found out nothing.'

'Luckily, my dear,' the girl had bravely said; 'for what then would become, please, of the promised occupation of my future?'   (xxiii.i.1, pp. 8–9)

Maggie's brave reply is tragically prophetic. Her 'promised occupation' is indeed to be a process of finding out, but it is destined to clash with her passionate, her erotic, her ethical and her self-protective need not to know. Like Isabel, she is drawn to precisely that which eludes the 'categories': Amerigo arouses her precisely because so much of her is touched in the effort of imagining his 'single self'. She is drawn, in an important phrase, to the 'unquenchable variety of his appeal to her interest' (xxiv.iv.2, p. 21).

Charlotte gives the expediently idealised view on Maggie's attitude to knowledge: 'if she loves . . . She lets it go' (xxiii.ii.5, p. 102). 'Letting it go' is *The Golden Bowl*'s version of the 'imagination of loving'. It means wishing genuine freedom upon those you love, and such 'moral elevation' as Maggie possesses resides in her sincerely feeling this way about Amerigo. She tells Adam that the finest love is exempt from jealousy:

My idea is this, that when you only love a little you're naturally not jealous – or are only jealous also a little, so that it does n't matter. But when you love in a deeper and intenser way, then you're in the very same proportion jealous; your jealousy has intensity and, no doubt, ferocity. When however you love in the most abysmal and unutterable way of all – why then you're beyond everything, and nothing can pull you down.   (xxiv.v.3, p. 262)

The magnificence of this ideal is, however, everywhere qualified in *The Golden Bowl*. Maggie is to learn not only that jealousy comes in close attendance on the intensest experiences of love, but in fact that jealousy and secrecy are themselves potent inducements to erotic appeal. Indeed, the extraordinary erotic intensity of the novel (written during what was almost certainly the most sexually active period of James's life) arises from a fusion of love, lust and distrust in relationship. Thus Amerigo's obscure submission to Maggie's knowledge of his secret moves her as the scented presence of a garden at night might move someone on a balcony taking air:

> Before *that* admiration she also meditated; consider as she might now she kept reading not less into what he omitted than into what he performed a beauty of intention that touched her fairly the more by being obscure. It was like hanging over a garden in the dark; nothing was to be made of the confusion of growing things, but one felt they were folded flowers and that their vague sweetness made the whole air their medium.   (xxiv.vi.4, p. 295)

The Golden Bowl does not dispel the agonised amalgam of feelings that possesses the enchanted and embattled Maggie. On the contrary, it conceives of love and knowledge as mutually dependent, yet deeply incompatible forces in a battle of wonderment, will and worldly wisdom.[80] As Paul Armstrong points out, James's image of relationships here often resembles Sartre's famous account in *Being and Nothingness*, and the resemblance surely reveals a good deal about James's underlying assumptions.

Sartre's vision of interpersonal relationships rests on the assumption that *'knowing . . . is a modality of having'*:[81] knowledge is, as in the case of the Ververs, inevitably a kind of possession of the other. But it is also a form of dependence, since the individual must seek self-knowledge and self-completion through others. Sartre in fact pictures relationships as veering between extremes of masochism and sadism, as participants seek either to subsume themselves in the Other, or to assert a callous detachment. Both the lover and the loved are 'held captive' by what Sartre calls 'alienated freedom':[82] relationship sets limits on the individual's freedom to be and each becomes alienated from a potential self in the experience of involvement. The precise status of this destructive dynamic of love is hard to ascertain. At one stage Sartre in fact explicitly links it to Kantian liberalism, arguing that the ideal of the Other as an end-in-itself must inevitably lead to objectification and so alienation of self.[83] The implication thus seems to be that such patterns of relation are culturally engendered rather than in any sense endemic, and Sartre's existential solution seems to lie in a more self-conscious and intense personal assertion of freedom that will deliver consciousness as 'for-itself' from the compromise of self-otherness.

Sartre asserts, 'Consciousness is in fact a project of founding itself; that is, of attaining to the dignity of the in-itself-for-itself or in-itself-as-self cause.'[84] Yet the specifics of such a 'project' are not detailed with any concreteness, and *Being and Nothingness* concludes with a series of portentous questions in a brief section entitled 'Ethical Implications'.

Sartre's subsequent departure from this kind of existential analysis suggests that the conflicted logic of love and knowledge outlined in *Being and Nothingness* was not to be resolved through a commitment to existential self-assertion, nor even able to be diagnosed from the standpoint of an existential psychoanalysis. Sartre turned to Marxism. James was of course notoriously unsympathetic with materialist accounts of mind and history,[85] but his own image of love, knowledge and human context remained tortured to the end. It also remained elusive. Thus, though he consistently reworks the torments of relationships as a kind of enchanted, capitalistic act of mutual appropriation, he seldom permits acquisitive symbolism to be more than menacingly symbolic: the Verver ethos is typical in being an indictment of certain capitalistic values rather than of capitalism itself.

In fact, James seems to have believed that the dreadful and often sadistic dynamics of relationships were structurally ineradicable. His late fiction depicts a crisis in humanist ethics but, in so far as its social philosophy can be abstracted, it urges shifts in attitude rather than social organisation. Maggie embarks on such shifts through 'the slim rigour of her attitude' (xxiv.iv.3, p. 60). Torn between loving reticence and manipulative insecurity towards Amerigo she experiences the 'terror of her endless power of surrender' (xxiv.vi.2, p. 352). 'Terror' and 'monstrous' are common words in *The Golden Bowl* – Maggie comes to know the 'fascination of the monstrous' (xxiv.v.2, p. 233) – and they reflect the kind of conflicted, psychic desperation that Sartre finds at the heart of love.

If Sartre's solution is to deobjectify the self-as-known, Maggie's is subtly to undermine the economy of secrecy, love and suspicion upon which the adulterous understanding that threatens her marriage rests. This she does by infusing others' understanding with her own uncertainty, and with a mounting uncertainty about her. In this, one of her most potent weapons is her need and ability to delay 'the outbreak of the definite' (xxiv.iv.9, p. 169). The unsaid is, as Charlotte discovers at Fawns, immensely powerful. In the great balcony scene late in the novel, the anguished Charlotte bids Maggie to satisfy 'My natural desire to know. You've done that for so long little justice' (xxiv.v.2, p. 248). Maggie's refusal to divulge the extent of her knowledge is enigmatic but conclusive: 'You must take it from me' (p. 251) is her repeated phrase of denial – Charlotte must accept because it is within Maggie's power to withhold. Maggie exploits the silence Charlotte has created.

Maggie of course uses a similar tactic with Amerigo. Having fantasised him variously as knowable, expendable and properly entrusted to others like a 'lamb tied up with pink ribbon' (xxiii.ii.2, p. 161), she gradually confesses to herself that she is 'jealous' (xxiv.iv.6, p. 110) and that she wants sexual and psychological possession of her husband. Some of the great scenes in *The Golden Bowl* depict Maggie eschewing intimacy in her need for an ingenuity that will recover the socially appointed congruity of passion and possession. One such is again extraordinary in its erotic force. Amerigo's return from Matcham prompts in his wife 'the sense of possession'. After dressing,

> Her husband had reappeared – he stood before her refreshed, almost radiant, quite reassuring. Dressed, anointed, fragrant, ready above all for his dinner, he smiled at her over the end of their delay. It was as if her opportunity had depended on his look – and now she saw that it was good. There was still for the instant something in suspense, but it passed more quickly than on his previous entrance. He was already holding out his arms.
>
> It was for hours and hours later on as if she had somehow been lifted aloft, were floated and carried on some warm high tide beneath which stumbling-blocks had sunk out of sight. This came from her being again for the time in the enjoyment of confidence, from her knowing, as she believed, what to do. All the next day and all the next she appeared to herself to know it. She had a plan, and she rejoiced in her plan: this consisted of the light that, suddenly breaking into her restless reverie, had marked the climax of that vigil.   (xxiv.iv.2, pp. 24–5)

The passage characteristically fuses a sense of being and of being sure, of knowing and thereby feeling at liberty to let go. Its discordant imagery of anointment and orgasm casts Maggie as a kind of Mary Magdalene, rather than an Eliotean Theresa: she is sainted and sinning, committed to a strategic solicitude that threatens constantly to collapse into a despairing and desperate emotional dependence. For his part, Amerigo is trapped by Maggie's manipulative reticence. Having displaced commitment from Maggie to Charlotte, he cannot now call upon its trust, though he must eventually repose in its forgiveness. *Middlemarch* will not settle for Casaubon's ethos of 'hidden alienation and suspicion' of secrecy, but *The Golden Bowl* seems to take the 'crudities of mutual resistance' (xxiv.iv.3, p. 61) between the couple for granted as a condition of relationship.

In the end, of course, Maggie wins out. Yet the novel's conclusion is too equivocal to be clear as to the nature of her victory. Amerigo has perforce exchanged his 'pink ribbon' for the 'steel hoop of intimacy': this is the love that does not let go.

> Here it was then, the moment, the golden fruit that had shone from afar; only what *were* these things in the fact, for the hand and for the lips, when tested, when tasted – what were they as a reward? Closer than she had ever been to the measure of her course and the full face of her act, she had an instant of the terror that, when there has been suspense, always precedes, on the part of the creature to be paid, the certification of the amount. Amerigo knew it, the amount; he still held it, and the delay in his return, making her heart beat too fast to go on, was like a sudden blinding light on a wild speculation. She had thrown the dice, but his hand was over her cast.
>
> He opened the door however at last – he had n't been away ten minutes; and then with her sight of him renewed to intensity she seemed to have a view of the number. His presence alone, as he paused to look at her, somehow made it the highest, and even before he had spoken she had begun to be paid in full. With that consciousness in fact an extraordinary thing occurred; the assurance of her safety so making her terror drop that already within the minute it had been changed to concern for his own anxiety, for everything that was deep in his being and everything that was fair in his face. So far as seeing that she was 'paid' went he might have been holding out the money-bag for her to come and take it. But what instantly rose for her between the act and her acceptance was the sense that she must strike him as waiting for a confession. This in turn charged her with a

new horror: if *that* was her proper payment she would go without money. His acknowledgement hung there, too monstrously, at the expense of Charlotte, before whose mastery of the greater style she had just been standing dazzled. All she now knew accordingly was that she should be ashamed to listen to the uttered word; all, that is, but that she might dispose of it on the spot for ever.

'Is n't she too splendid?' she simply said, offering it to explain and to finish.

'Oh splendid.' With which he came over to her.

'That's our help, you see,' she added – to point further her moral.

It kept him before her therefore, taking in – or trying to – what she so wonderfully gave. He tried, too clearly, to please her – to meet her in her own way; but with the result only that, close to her, her face kept before him, his hands holding her shoulders, his whole act enclosing her, he presently echoed: "She"? I see nothing but *you*.' And the truth of it had with this force after a moment so strangely lighted his eyes that as for pity and dread of them she buried her own in his breast.

(xxiv.vi.3, pp. 367–9)

The dazzling oscillations of Maggie's consciousness pose the familiar problem of interpretation. Are these the 'limits' of knowledge, worldy or other? How deep and pure is her disinclination to have him confess? Having already decided that 'she did not want his pain' (xxiv.iv.10, p. 182), what is the ease she now desires for him? Dorothea Krook reads in this scene a Christian fable of 'redemption'; Philip Weinstein is one of many readers to feel that, on the contrary, it reinforces the book's insistence on 'the enormous contrivance and manipulation of human relationships'.[86] The truth is, perhaps, that we cannot be sure. James's point is not that we make such a circumstantial judgement; rather that the oscillations of the mind to which his form has committed us bring home the opaque complexity of human interaction. Maggie's mind darts from the familiar to the consolation of an exclusive love: ' "See"? I see nothing but *you*.' James charts its momentary movements – 'within the minute', 'instantly', 'this in turn' – and its passionate yearning for rest and dissolution: 'that she might dispose of it on the spot for ever'. It is both in 'pity' and in 'dread' that she finally buries her head in his breast, the 'truth' of his reassurance being as always a thing she must uncertainly know 'in his eyes'. Though it hints at a 'moral', this extraordinary scene ventures only indirect and highly generalised attitudes. Maggie's long struggle is for the moment at least circumstantially over, yet that distinctively female pattern of dread, need and capitulation infuses this last moment of awareness. It is far from certain what kind of an emotional being she has or will become; indeed, even Isabel Archer is at the end of her narrative less of an enigma. James has so intermingled the salving power of passion and the stench of stratagem that his 'appeal to incalculability' is magnificently, but bafflingly, suggestive.

One reason for this is no doubt that James is so selective in interpreting the challenge to 'reveal as much of character as a coherent literary form will allow'. In fact the 'coherence' of this novel is more an atmospheric than an encyclopaedic thing: questions and impressions loom and disperse, character drifts in and out of focus. In fact what we know of Maggie, Amerigo and the rest is a kind of localised, momentary consciousness, a series of elaborately expanded instants of dread, registration, reflexion and calculation. In this, indeed, the various characters all share, though Charlotte's consciousness is significantly – and tactically – withheld for most of the narrative. Again, *The Golden Bowl* largely eschews the continuum of incident and information that marks the naturalistic plot, preferring its strangely specialised windows in on private worlds. 'What is character but the determination of incident; what is incident but the determination of character?' the young James had inquired. By the late phase, 'character' has become predominant but also indeterminate: the problematics of knowing all but absorb the intricacies of plot as George Eliot and other Victorians had conceived it. The problematics, of course, bridge all participants in the fiction: character and character; character and reader; character, reader and narrator. That James's reticent narrator does not intercede with any decisive imputation at the end seems entirely consistent with the novel's strange translucency, and an epilogue such as concludes *Middlemarch* would seem even more arbitrary than it does in George Eliot's novel. Typically, James here prefers exhibition to explanation and lets the concluding facts suggest what they will to the individual reader.

V

The facts themselves are intimated through highly specialised techniques of character and narration. Some of these – flashbacks, typecasting, occasional commentary – do not require further discussion, but two others that reveal much about the late method of James warrant closer analysis. One is his method of interior report. Here his craft is more homogeneous than in an earlier novel such as *The Portrait* and very much more so than in George Eliot's novels. Readers sometimes gain an impression that James's late characters are presented through a stream-of-consciousness technique, but in fact his most prominent method is a highly controlled form of psychonarration that in turn reflects the enormous efforts of control the characters require of themselves. Here is an instance of Maggie in meditation:

> It may be said of her that during these passages she plucked her sensations by the way, detaching nervously the small wild blossoms of her dim forest, so that she could smile over them at least with the spacious appearance, for her companions, for her husband above all, of bravely, of altogether frivolously, going a-maying. She had her intense, her smothered excitements, some of which were almost inspirations; she had in particular the extravagant, positively at moments the amused, sense of *using* her friend to the topmost notch, accompanied with the high luxury of not having to explain. Never, no never should she have to explain to Fanny Assingham again – who, poor woman, on her own side, would be charged, it might be for ever, with that privilege of the higher ingenuity. . . . It all fell in beautifully moreover; so that, as hard at this time, in spite of her fever, as a little pointed diamond, the Princess showed something of the glitter of consciously possessing the constructive, the creative hand. She had but to have the fancy of presenting herself, of presenting her husband, in a certain high and convenient manner, to make it natural they should go about with their gentleman and their lady. To what else but this exactly had Charlotte during so many weeks of the earlier season worked her up? – herself assuming and discharging, so far as might be, the character and office of one of these revolving subordinate presences that float in the wake of greatness. (xxiv.iv.8, pp. 144–5)

The passage envinces the 'dual presence' of narrator and character to which Watt refers. 'It may be said' is a narrative aside in the narrative 'voice', yet 'To what else but this exactly had Charlotte during so many weeks of the earlier season worked her up?' is closer to narrated monologue, the question mark suggesting Maggie's perspective, perhaps even her idiom. What disrupts the impression, however, is the oddity of the syntactical ordering: 'To what else but this exactly' and 'so many weeks of the earlier season' both suggest narrative intervention, a filtering of consciousness through an anonymous creative perspective. The effect is remarkable in that it does not undermine the impression of deeply recessive privacy that is so typical of the Maggie narrative. The 'constructive, the creative hand' appears to be hers, though the passage is intricately and in a sense obviously orchestrated. The ethical co-ordinates of the exhibition are also typical. The 'high luxury of not having to explain' is conceded as a necessary aspect of the deadly knowledge game in which Maggie is involved, but the narrator does not so readily overlook her 'blameless egoism', her deeply exigent attitude to others. Indeed, he anatomises just such an attitude, revealing it to be measured, calculated and controlled, almost in proportion as it is appalled and horrified. The mind here presented is again insistently edited ('her intense, her smothered excitements') and agonisingly alert. Only in the psychological notation that threads its way through images of blossoms, and in the tense compression of the prose, does narration here begin to probe the murderous depths upon which James's gorgeous dishonesty so clearly rests.

Similar techniques are evident, though in different measure, in the famous pagoda passage at the beginning of the fourth book. The reader is introduced to Maggie's consciousness thus:

> Yet these instinctive postponements of reflexion were the fruit, positively, of recognitions and perceptions already active; of the sense above all that she made at a particular hour, made by the mere touch of her hand, a difference in the situation so long present to her as practically unattackable. This situation had been occupying for months and months the very centre of the garden of her life, but it had reared itself there like some strange tall tower of ivory, or perhaps rather some wonderful beautiful but outlandish pagoda, a structure plated with hard bright porcelain, coloured and figured and adorned at the

overhanging eaves with silver bells that tinkled ever so charmingly when stirred by chance airs. She had walked round and round it – that was what she felt; she had carried on her existence in the space left her for circulation, a space that sometimes seemed ample and sometimes narrow: looking up all the while at the fair structure that spread itself so amply and rose so high, but never quite making out as yet where she might have entered had she wished. . . . The great decorated surface had remained consistently impenetrable and inscrutable. At present however, to her considering mind, it was as if she had ceased merely to circle and to scan the elevation, ceased so vaguely, so quite helplessly to stare and wonder: she had caught herself distinctly in the act of pausing, then in that of lingering, and finally in that of stepping unprecedentedly near. The thing might have been, by the distance at which it kept her, a Mahometan mosque, with which no base heretic could take a liberty; there so hung about it the vision of one's putting off one's shoes to enter and even verily of one's paying with one's life if found there as an interloper. She had n't certainly arrived at the conception of paying with her life for anything she might do. . . .   (xxiv.iv.1, pp. 3–4)

This is worth quoting at length for the characteristic hypnotic precision with which the movements of mind are articulated through extended simile and meditative accretion. Perhaps the most striking thing about the passage is the sense in which the pagoda metaphor seems paradoxically a private yet shared property of character and narrator. The description in fact omits conditionals: there is no 'as if' about the structure having 'reared itself there like some strange tower of ivory'. Metaphor is here oddly liberal: the narrator and his character seem agreed that in an important sense the pagoda *is* Maggie's situation. This, after all, is how she thinks through and around her position, and in this highly subjective world mind threatens constantly to annex or establish its own actuality. This kind of metaphor is present in George Eliot, but never in so extended a form, nor with this power of dramatic contraction. Maggie at her mosque is in a sense all the Maggies we come to know. She is by turns cautious, fearful, inquisitive, passive, tactful and assertive. Her personality unfolds as if by anticipation with the description.

The effect is remarkably suggestive, not least because metaphor here displaces the encumbrances of action that would so manifestly occupy a more conventional plot. James had denounced plot as 'nefarious',[87] and his preference is for an intimation of many possible courses of action that does not commit the reader to the finality of any one. The power of mind is as always his primary interest. But also (and here his fiction is intriguing to psychoanalysis) its *patterns*. Maggie's 'instinctive postponements of reflexion' are 'the fruit, positively, of recognitions and perceptions already active'. She is as it were unconsciously aware, and the syntax of delay, qualification and recognition simulate the psychic economy of knowledge and strategic ignorance. Thus, 'The thing might have been, by the distance at which it kept her, a Mahometan mosque' promotes confusions that are both temporal ('might have been') and spatial ('the distance at which it kept her') before disclosing the object of the sentence after a delaying qualifying clause. The mosque is established as a thing contingent on perception and thereby, however falsely, a thing subject to the control of mind. But ironically, of course, it all the while elucidates mind, and the narrator is so using it with an open and still teasing deliberation.

No doubt the combination of detachment and a certain colloquial ease in the tone contributes to the strange sensation of managed impersonality in the passage; but it is again the enigmatic quality of James's psychonarration that produces much of the impression of lucid surface and impenetrable depth. Interestingly, though George Eliot uses narrated monologue more prominently for Dorothea than James does for Maggie, *The Golden Bowl*'s hushed, associative logic of image and symbol can seem more powerfully suggestive of the private person and of understanding's eerie indirections.

In a sense James's narrator seems more deeply implicated in the limitations of knowledge than his counterpart in *Middlemarch*. He surrounds Maggie with an approving but provisional understanding and is often evasive when dramatic exhibition calls for omniscient analysis. Yet the orchestrating hand of art is here extraordinarily adept. Like Maggie, the narrator resorts to the 'foredoomed ingenuities' of pity and makes of knowing a deeply strategic source of generosity and control. He purports to share his limitations with his heroine and to chart her experience.

VI

The character of Maggie is in its own way as deep a threat to received modes of fictional humanism as is George Eliot's mysticism in *Daniel Deronda*. Maggie's 'fantastic flight[s] of divination' themselves constitute a kind of ecumenical mysticism. Yet in a George Eliot novel they would be counted a travesty of fundamental personal entitlements. James's late humanism takes the Eliotean premise of an opaque other knowable through love to a point of crisis. *The Golden Bowl* is a study in moral apocalypse. It asks what form sympathetic consciousness can possibly take without placing constraints on the inward and interminable varieties of others. This of course is precisely Sartre's question about liberal humanism. In his view it pictures the self as a thing that must inevitably injure and be injured in relationship. But James seems also to be asking how else the self can be conceived. At this point he backs off from a fully developed phenomenology. *The Golden Bowl* insists on the 'horror', the 'monstrosity' and the 'terror' of a situation – a 'vicious circle' – in which so few of the codes of commonality obtain that knowledge becomes a kind of nightmare. However luxuriant James finds the subjective response, however central he makes it in his aesthetic 'experiments', he fears a complete collapse of consensus and the resultant loss of intersubjective accord. It is this loss, rather than a loss of innocence, Americanness or Italianness *per se*, that torments the protagonists in James's last finished novel. Yet he does not overtly denounce it: it is too much a part of his own isolated, expatriate experience. *The Golden Bowl* reflects a situation James accepts rather than commends, and the tension in his outlook registers in the novel's interplay between form and theme. Though the narrator makes few Eliotean claims to wisdom, he centres his account on the damage done to the inner person by an effete criminalising of intersubjective codes. The novel enters an appeal on behalf of the substantial self, whose need to know and be known is in tragic proportion to its capacity to suffer the agonies of exclusion. Maggie at least strikes a new and efficacious accord between knowledge, ignorance and mastery. But some gain nothing but exclusion in the process. One such is Charlotte: needy, dignified and poignantly tragic. Another is one of those faintly absurd compulsive knowers that people James's fiction, Fanny Assingham.

It is Fanny's appalling fate to be a compulsive and intrusive knower in an unmanageably opaque world. Indeed, the portrait of this 'suggestive woman' (XXIII.i.5, p. 203) is a particularly interesting version of James's knowledge theme. She is, in the first instance, something of an aesthetic anomaly: poised between farce and tragedy, she lacks the haunting naturalistic presence of the other main characters. Here James's 'handsome wholeness of effect' begins to break down. However, she does reflect his determination to 'reveal as much' as 'coherent literary form' will allow of individual character, and her pathetic and derivative prurience is given a lavish attention that is quite out of proportion with her prominence in the plot.

It is interesting that some of the descriptions of Fanny echo James on another compulsive knower, the novelist. James's allusion in the Preface of *What Maisie Knew* to 'the author's irrepressible and insatiable, his extravagant and immoral, interest in personal character' is here repeated in Charlotte's reference to Fanny's 'irrepressible interest in other lives' (XXIII.iii.1, p. 254), and Fanny herself admits after seeing the gravity of her miscalculations that she had 'fallen in love with the beautiful symmetry of [her] plan' (XXIII.iii.11, p. 389). The phrase is again familiar in the Prefaces and the implication is reminiscent of 'The Lifted Veil': narration, like intersubjective knowledge, is a worryingly strategic form of solicitude. Fanny, too, is an imaginatively stunted version of the novelist.

In fact she describes herself as 'a woman of imagination' (XXIV.iv.6, p. 114) who, like Latimer, is prone to misapply the faculties of understanding and interpretation. George Eliot's antithetical vocabulary of attention and intrusion is strikingly prominent here. Fanny is said to have a power of manipulative mastery that fuses 'sympathy' and 'curiosity': 'sympathy and curiosity could render their objects practically filial' (XXIII.i.2, p. 35); also, with Bob, to possess a 'little fortune of curiosity and alarm' (XXIII.i.4, p. 68). This 'alarm', like Maggie's, can, however, quickly escalate to 'terror', and what sets Fanny apart from Latimer is that knowledge is for her ultimately and humiliatingly limited. The horror of his situation is by contrast to know everything.

Not surprisingly, critics disagree over this novelist-like character's role in the novel. James's friend Edith Wharton thought that the Assinghams are 'forced into [the story] for the

sole purpose of acting as spies and eaves'-droppers',[88] while Ora
Segal argues that Fanny is a character who 'expresses some of the
novel's most important *aperçus*, both diagnostic and prognostic,
who gives expression to some of its most crucial generalizations,
who illuminates obscure points, and who fulfills a variety of
expository, explanatory, and anticipatory functions'.[89] Nicola
Bradbury suggests that Fanny acts as an exemplar for the reader
of the requisite 'immersion in the novel process'.[90] Segal and
Bradbury are surely right to see Fanny as more than a mere
convenience; however, she is also very clearly set at a distance
from the narrator and his ethical norms. Her strangely and
derisively histrionic introduction establishes the tone: 'She looked
as if her most active effort might be to take up, as she lay back, her
mandolin, or to share a sugared fruit with a pet gazelle' (xxiii.i.2,
p. 34). Scarcely more flattering are some blunt references to her
intrusive character, especially to the 'admitted grossness of her
avidity' to know (xxiv.iv.7, p. 121), but Fanny's 'anxiety of
intelligence' (xxiii.iii.1, p. 256) is too great not to run to
self-consciousness, and she does in fact pronounce herself 'a most
dreadful person' (xxiii.iii.10. p. 372).

Just how deep this self-deprecation reaches is hard to say, but
James leaves the reader in no doubt as to the misery Fanny's sense
of failure and exclusion in the knowledge game causes her. Her
excuse for having so involved herself in other lives is that the
persons concerned didn't know how to live them: ' "One was no
doubt a meddlesome fool; one always *is*, to think one sees people's
lives for them better than they see them for themselves. But one's
excuse here," she insisted, "was that these people clearly *did n't* see
them for themselves – did n't see them at all" ' (xxiii.iii.11,
p. 388). Again, the sincerity of this is hard to gauge, but the
propriety is not: like many of Fanny's moments of self-indictment,
this one registers the limits of proper intrusion in the affairs of
others. Her punishment, however, goes beyond self-accusation or
narrative disapproval. Fanny's fate is finally to suffer exclusion
from the charmed and opaque world of mutuality that she tries so
desperately to manipulate. The possessors of the lives she so
wishes to penetrate spit her out with a quite horrific callousness.
'Fanny Assingham does n't matter' (xxiii.iii.5, p. 309), insists
Charlotte. Even Maggie, late in the novel, accords her 'a severely
simplified function' (xxiv.v.1, p. 208); and Amerigo comes to see
her in 'her objective absurdity' (xxiv.vi.8, p. 338). His defection is

indeed the most chilling of all, and in charting it James gives one of the great fictional descriptions of the rationalised rejection of one human being by another. Amerigo concedes that the 'theory of their relation' as 'pupil and kind instructress' has rested on his acute need for enlightenment: 'it had been he, no doubt, who had most put it forward, since his need of knowledge fairly exceeded her mild pretension'. Having assured Fanny of her efficaciousness in this office, however, he has begun to share Charlotte's less charitable view:

> It had never indeed, before that evening, come up as during the passage at the official party, and he had for the first time at those moments, a little disappointedly, got the impression of a certain failure, on the dear woman's part, of something he was aware of having always rather freely taken for granted in her. Of what exactly the failure consisted he would still perhaps have felt it a little harsh to try to say; and if she had in fact, as by Charlotte's observation, 'broken down,' the details of the collapse would be comparatively unimportant. They came to the same thing, all such collapses – the failure of courage, the failure of friendship, or the failure just simply of tact; for did n't any one of them by itself amount really to the failure of wit? – which was the last thing he had expected of her and which would be but another name for the triumph of stupidity.   (xxiii.iii.6, pp. 313–14)

The appalling thing here is the Prince's indiscriminateness. Not bothering to distinguish between orders of 'failure' and frailty, Amerigo levels at Fanny the most devastating charge of which he, given his immensely subtle understanding of the exigencies of survival, can conceive: 'stupidity' is all but irredeemable in this intensely alert world. The Prince's meditation then proceeds to what is called the 'romantic tradition'. Of the Assinghams he thinks, 'He might vulgarly have put it that one had never to plot or lie for them; he might humorously have put it that one had never, as by the higher conformity, to lie in wait with the dagger or to prepare insidiously the cup' (xxiii.iii.6, pp. 314–15). The pathetic couple lack the glamour that an older and more idiosyncratic tradition of feeling leads Amerigo to require. The 'higher conformity' is ruthless in its adherence to this tradition and, however appealing James too may have found it, *The Golden Bowl* singles its effete ruthlessness out for condemnation.

For her own part, Fanny, who has perpetrated merely a less cultured form of ruthlessness, is generally left to self-indict. She has as great a need to have and proffer knowledge as her younger charges, and the intense scenes given over to her machinations leave pointedly uncorrected a kind of casuistic structure in which she too attempts to rationalise her part in the politics of knowing. One such scene finds her sharing her mounting apprehensions with her conjugal functionary, Bob:

For what she was most immediately feeling was that she *had* in the past been active for these people to ends that were now bearing fruit and that might yet bear a larger crop. She but brooded at first in her corner of the carriage: it was like burying her exposed face, a face too helplessly exposed, in the cool lap of the common indifference, of the dispeopled streets, of the closed shops and darkened houses seen through the window of the brougham, a world mercifully unconscious and unreproachful. It would n't, like the world she had just left, know sooner or later what she had done, or would know it only if the final consequence should be some quite overwhelming publicity. She fixed this possibility itself so hard, however, for a few moments, that the misery of her fear produced the next minute a reaction; and when the carriage happened, while it grazed a turn, to catch the straight shaft from the lamp of a policeman in the act of playing his inquisitive flash over an opposite house-front, she let herself wince at being thus incriminated only that she might protest, not less quickly, against mere blind terror. It had become, for the occasion preposterously terror – of which she must shake herself free before she could properly measure her ground. The perception of this necessity had in truth soon aided her; since she found on trying that, lurid as her prospect might hover there, she could none the less give it no name. The sense of seeing was strong in her, but she clutched at the comfort of not being sure of what she saw. Not to know what it would represent on a longer view was a help, in turn, to not making out that her hands were embrued; since if she had stood in the position of a producing cause she should surely be less vague about what she had produced. This, further, in its way, was a step toward reflecting that when one's connexion with any matter was too indirect to be traced it might be described also as too slight to be deplored. By the time they were nearing Cadogan Place she had in fact recognised that she could n't be so curious as she desired without arriving at some conviction of her being as innocent. But there had been a moment in the dim desert of Eaton Square when she broke into speech.   (xxiii.iii.3, pp. 276–7)

If the spectral vigilance of the policeman is a characteristically blatant piece of symbolism, it contributes luridly enough to the reader's sense of the peculiar 'terror' Fanny here experiences. It is of course the terror at once of the known and the unknown. Her appalling suspiciousness tells her that the world at large will 'know sooner or later' about her cupidity and her crudeness; indeed, her conviction is so overpowering that she tries desperately to edit it out: 'The sense of seeing was strong in her, but she clutched at the comfort of not being sure of what she saw.' But this is a part of a larger attempt to deny responsibility that calls into question the very notion of moral agency. Fanny hopes that by attempting 'not to know' she can blur or obscure her role as 'cause'; further, that by indulging in an agony of uncertainty she can demonstrate a detachment that belongs to innocence. The word 'curious' comes up again: 'she had in fact recognised that she could n't be so curious as she desired without arriving at some conviction of her being as innocent'. 'In fact' is of course brutally ironic. This is mere casuistry on Fanny's part. She cannot conceal that it is a condition of moral agency, as of moral responsibility, that in some way, however opaque, one *does* 'know'; and the disingenuous questions she frames are themselves testimony to the fact that she does indeed 'know'. She cannot conceal the damning fact of her conscience from herself, from the reader, or from the narrator who here simulates an individual inner world.

What Fanny 'knows', however, is the nature of her own involvement. That of others remains for much of the novel a mystery to her. But in the perverse and rather precious marital relationship James fashions for her the quantities are redistributed. The 'small crisis' she shares with the long-suffering Bob begins in his wondering at the extent of the involvement:

He might have been trying to guess what she had really done, to what extent, beyond his knowledge or his conception, in the affairs of these people, she *could* have committed herself. But to hear her cry and yet do her best not to was quickly enough too much for him; he had known her at other times quite not make the repressive effort, and that had n't been so bad. He went to her and put his arm round her; he drew her head to his breast, where, while she gasped, she let it stay a little – all with a patience that presently stilled her. Yet the effect of this small crisis, oddly enough, was not to close their colloquy, with the natural result of sending them to bed: what was between them had opened out further, had somehow, through the sharp show of her feeling, taken a positive stride, had entered, as it were, without more words, the region of the understood, shutting the door after it and bringing them so still more nearly face to face. They remained for some minutes looking at it through the dim window which opened upon the world of human trouble in general and which let the vague light play here and there upon gilt and crystal and colour, the florid features, looming dimly, of Fanny's drawing-room. And the beauty of what thus passed between them, passed with her cry of pain, with her burst of tears, with his wonderment and his kindness and his comfort, with the moments of their silence, above all, which might have represented their sinking together, hand in hand for a time, into the mystic lake where he had begun, as we have hinted, by seeing her paddle alone – the beauty of it was that they now could really talk better than before, because the basis had at last once for all defined itself.   (xxiii.iii.10, pp. 377–8)

Here the mutual horror of not knowing becomes a 'basis' for a new mutuality. It is not that Fanny's 'sharp show' of 'feeling' has been in any ordinary way 'straight'; rather that her humiliating failure is so familiar and so intense that it elicits unqualified sympathy in Bob – a sympathy, indeed, far less exacting than the one she has intrusively exerted in other lives. For all its exorbitant subtlety, this scene does oddly open out 'upon the world of human trouble in general' as the great moments in late James can. After all, Fanny's humiliation, her exclusion from the endlessly alluring world of other-knowledge, is extraordinarily, embarrassingly, common. The 'mystic lake' into which husband and wife rather absurdly 'sink' is that of common frailty and failures of insight; and 'what was between them' is a personification of much the same thing. It becomes eerily a third party to the scene, embodying a 'general' sense – the reader's, the narrator's, everyone's – of tormenting confusion. The 'region of the understood' is James's ironic metaphor for the universal and benighted predicament that makes his knowledge theme the urgent thing it is; and the metaphor is oddly consonant with the scene: Fanny's room becomes just such a 'region', until, like Maggie at the end of the novel, she capitulates to a primitive need for consolation.

Yet her respite is temporary. What the couple 'bring up from the depths' proves to be merely a more mutual form of curiosity and calculation: 'What was the basis, which Fanny absolutely exacted, but that Charlotte and the Prince must be saved?' (xxiii.iii.10, p. 378). Typically, a moment of subtle promise modulates into further promiscuities of curiosity and manipulation. This curve of feeling is as central to *The Golden Bowl* as it is anathema to *Middlemarch*, where George Eliot wishes above all to commend candour above 'the alienation of secrecy and suspicion'. Thus do the Bulstrodes share their sense of humiliation:

> It was eight o'clock in the evening before the door opened and his wife entered. He dared not look up at her. He sat with his eyes bent down, and as she went towards him she thought he looked smaller – he seemed so withered and shrunken. A movement of new compassion and old tenderness went through her like a great wave, and putting one hand on his which rested on the arm of the chair, and the other on his shoulder, she said, solemnly but kindly –
> 'Look up, Nicholas.'
> He raised his eyes with a little start and looked at her half amazed for a moment: her pale face, her changed, mourning dress, the trembling about her mouth, all said, 'I know;' and her hands and eyes rested gently on him. He burst out crying and they cried together, she sitting at his side.   (iii.74, pp. 334–5)

'I know' is here not only more frank, but also more complete, than it is in James. Mrs Bulstrode knows enough to sense the depths of her husband's frailty and this in turn is enough to release him from the torment of secrecy. It is typical of George Eliot that a loss of control – crying – should attend the dissolution of the boundaries that duplicity has created. That, for her, is a new beginning. But

Fanny's tears are, like her confidences, infinitely more controlled, and correspondingly less childlike, in their simplicity. They create a 'basis' that to George Eliot would signal more tragic waste. And so, ultimately, do they signal this in James. Fanny does not possess Maggie's 'flight[s] of divination'. Though a 'woman of imagination', her imaginative construction of others somehow leaves their essences out of count. Thus does she misread, mislead and misunderstand. Maggie, by contrast, strikes a balance between love, manipulation and knowledge that secures, however tenuously, an intense mutuality Fanny cannot know. This much does *The Golden Bowl*, steeped as it is in the ethos of cultured convenience, concede to a benighted humanism.

5 Morality: *Romola* and *The Wings of the Dove*

ROMOLA

I

George Eliot's historical novel *Romola* reflects in a particularly obvious way her use of fiction as a means to test the powers and possibilities of various forms of humanism. Set in fifteenth-century Florence, this 'experiment' poses in dramatic form many of the issues that have dominated ethics since the Greeks. However, as always, it was George Eliot's intention that the novel's depiction of ethical situations be more than merely diagrammatic. As she explained in a famous letter, she sought to present a 'picture', not a 'diagram'.[1] The 'aesthetic' teacher aspired to what she considered the highest office of art: the arousing and guidance of sympathy. Thus 'the most effective writer is not he who announces a particular discovery, who convinces men of a particular conclusion, who demonstrates that this measure is right and that measure wrong; but he who rouses in others the activity that must issue in discovery'.[2] Strictly didactic writing could not, she believed, move the reader to intelligent reflection: 'Art is art, and tells its own story.'[3]

Henry James, who thought George Eliot's fiction the 'last word of a philosophy endeavouring to teach by example', did not of course find her insistence on the 'aesthetic' convincing; and, as we shall see, he was sceptical in just this respect about *Romola*. George Eliot's feelings about the novel are interesting. She conceded that the novel was too 'ideal'[4] and that it placed too heavy an emphasis upon setting,[5] yet she esteemed it more than many of her critics have done. Having read through the Cheap Edition, she writes that 'there is no book of mine about which I more thoroughly feel that I could swear by every sentence as having been written with my best blood, such as it is, and with the most ardent care for veracity of which my nature is capable'.[6] 'Veracity' was of course central to her conception of fiction. In 'Leaves from a Note-Book' she calls for 'something different from the schemed picturesqueness of ordinary historical fiction'. And she continues, 'I want brief, severely conscientious reproductions, in their concrete incidents, of pregnant moments in the past'.[7] Such 'reproductions' must, as she writes in another letter, reconstruct character in context: 'It is the habit of my imagination to strive after as full a vision of the medium in which a character moves as of the character itself'.[8]

As Chapter 2's account of George Eliot's theory of fiction indicates, she developed an organicist theory of representation in order to rationalise the realism that was her central tenet as a novelist. However, the novels themselves repeatedly test the power and status of representation, inquiring after the forms that knowledge, be it personal or historical, take. *Romola* is particularly suggestive here, because, like 'The Lifted Veil' and *Daniel Deronda*, it explores the claims of extra-rational – especially 'visionary' – experience. Yet it ultimately concedes less to the visionary than do these works and is in most respects closer to the quasi-positivist *Middlemarch* in its undertaking to depict 'character' within its historical 'medium'.

Romola is also distinctive in its narrative technique. Though George Eliot here retains a commenting narrator, narrative commentary is less expansive than it is in the other novels. Her intention seems to have been to give a less mediated and edited account of Renaissance Florence than the other novels give of nineteenth-century England; to let a distant epoch exhibit itself without unduly anxious orchestration. For all this, however, *Romola* remains, in George Eliot's own word, 'conscientious', more impressive for its 'ardent care' in reconstructing the past than for its living 'veracity'.

George Eliot's choice of Renaissance Florence is momentous, not least because it focuses attention so directly on certain varieties of humanism. Thus the classical humanism of Bardo is set against the Christian asceticism of Savonarola on the one hand, and the Machiavellian politics of expediency on the other. Moreover, the novel seeks to assess the Renaissance achievement more generally: to explore its relationship to the Middle Ages and, importantly, its parallels with nineteenth-century England. Thus might a contemporary reader of *Romola* have associated the Florence of Savonarola with the England of Newman and the religious revivalists, and the Florentine rationalists with Mill, Comte and other exponents of nineteenth-century positivism.

In a more general sense George Eliot uses Florentine society to ask fundamental questions about political life. How far, and in what ways, does radical social change impact itself upon individuals? How specific are forms of social life to particular cultures? What forms of interdependence exist between individual and society? And, after Kant, to what extent do moral and social imperatives overlap with personal ones?

Though Romola herself is a fascinating study in female passivity, strength and conscience, Tito Melema is perhaps the novel's most audacious and revealing piece of moral portraiture. Tito, an outsider to the Florentine city state, enables George Eliot to pose the question of ethical universality that has marked political discussion since the Sophists: are the norms of a particular city state properly or plausibly applicable to someone not raised within them? Tito, who is Greek in origin, is by no means of course entirely an outsider – indeed, much of his appeal in Florence arises from his Greek antecedence and from his seeming an incarnation of the classical revival – but neither is he a bearer of continuity. On the contrary, he is psychologically and culturally dissociated, a creature of expedience who is uncommitted to any settled version of the past. The novel's resounding organicism – historical, social, psychological – symbolises this discrimination through Tito's repudiation of his stepfather. Significantly, Machiavelli, who figures in the novel, had written in *The Prince* that the prince 'should abstain from taking the property of others; because men sooner forget the death of their own father than the loss of their patrimony'.[9] Tito is thus a test case for the new ethics set within a progressive Comtean historical schema.[10] Unlike Deronda, who is reunited with a paternalistic medieval world, Tito is the unsentimental man of the future.

Many readers have found this lack of sentiment, and indeed Tito's moral collapse more generally, implausible.[11] And so ultimately it is. Yet, as Baruch Hochman's interesting discussion of the crisis of paternity and origin in George Eliot suggests,[12] this pattern links Tito with some of George Eliot's most powerful and impressively conflicted creations, for complexity as she understands it is frequently bound up with this kind of crisis. Seldom, however, does Tito get free of the 'conscientious' pastoral techniques that George Eliot uses to fashion him. In Tito she tries to depict a quality about which she is unable to write with conviction – unmotivated malice. As we shall see in *The Wings of the Dove*, this is quintessentially a Jamesian emotion.

II

Tito is used to illustrate a moral argument and its terms are familiar enough in George Eliot. Having massively researched the period, she does not find overriding dissimilarities between it and her own. On the contrary, her emphasis is as always universalist. The novel's Proem alludes to 'the broad sameness of the human lot' (I, p. 2), and the human psychology offered is essentially that of the other novels: self exists on a continuum bridging the extremes of egoism and empathy; some individuals develop, others stagnate or wither. 'It is in the nature of all human passion, the lowest as well as the highest, that there is a point where it ceases to be properly egoistic, and is like a fire kindled within our being to which everything else in us is mere fuel' (I.30, p. 413). 'All human passion' crosses cultural and historical boundaries: we can, she believes, make sense of the present only because it is deeply continuous with the past. This applies, too, to human relationships. In an important passage late in the novel the narrator argues that 'in strictness there is no replacing of relations: the presence of the new does not nullify the failure and breach of the old' (II.69, p. 414). Here, as elsewhere, 'relations' is a slippery word: while it suggests an interpersonal structure that might be emulated by the individual at another stage of life, its force is in fact more restrictively organicist: you cannot break with the past, even by repeating it. No doubt George Eliot's immense anguish about her own past generates much of this guilty determinism, but it is more emphatic in some novels than in others. In *Romola* it is ultimately stultifying and unacceptable, especially as it is a novel that wants, like the others, to penetrate some of the shifting subtleties of human relationships. Like them, it insists upon 'the complicated play of human feelings' (I.11, p. 176), 'the many-twisted conditions of life' (II.69, p. 414), and the resultant   agonising   uncertainties   of   relationships.

Significantly, however, the narrator dismisses the thoughts of an exposé of marital life as disloyal and cheap, an unacceptable lifting of a veil: 'She who willingly lifts up the veil of her married life has profaned it from a sanctuary to a vulgar place' (I.31 p. 428). Yet the novel must lift this veil precisely because relationships, entailing as they do an inevitably flawed attempt at self-completion through other, are so unstable and so fragile. Like *Middlemarch* and *The Golden Bowl*, *Romola* images relationships as a flawed vessel. Between Romola and Tito there arises 'a terrible flaw in the trust: she was afraid of any hasty movement, as men are who hold something precious and want to believe it is not broken' (I.29, p. 394). Further, in another distant foreshadowing of James, Romola's betrayed innocence is likened to a wounded bird. As it becomes apparent that Tito does not return 'the deeper sympathies that belong to young love and trust', 'the larger possibilities' of Romola's 'nature' lie 'folded and crushed like embryonic wings' (I.27, p. 376), and, as she drifts 'orphaned' upon the lake after her flight from Florence, the narrator reflects that 'Memories hung upon her like the weight of broken wings that could never be lifted' (II.61, p. 326). In this as in other ways, *Romola* looks forward to James's late study of innocence, temptation and betrayal, *The Wings of the Dove*.

A clear connection here is the knowledge theme. Like so much else in *Romola*, this is ostensibly complex, yet disconcertingly lucid in exposition. The familiar ideal of solicitousness and unintrusiveness is revealed early when Bardo refrains from further questions about Tito's past: 'Bardo sank backward again too delicate to ask another question that might probe a sorrow which he divined to be recent' (I.6, p. 93). Romola, too, possesses this kind of delicacy, but her powers of divination are less developed than those of her benighted father. Like Dorothea and other Eliot heroines, she fills in what blanks Tito's appealing shallowness presents, constructing – in this case weaving – the inner man: 'A girl of eighteen imagines the feelings behind the face that has moved her with its sympathetic youth, as easily as primitive people imagined the humours of the gods in fair weather: what is she to believe in, if not in this vision woven from within?' (p. 104).

Steadily this 'vision' betrays her. The couple's 'undisturbed mutual consciousness' dwindles to a 'double solitude' (I.27 p. 378), thence to the familiar 'dread' (I.6, p. 108) of the Eliot heroine, and ultimately to absolute alienation. In charting the demise of Romola's trust, love and knowledge, the novel is intriguingly uncertain. Her early and anxious efforts at marital accommodation are commended: 'Romola was labouring, as a loving woman must, to subdue her nature to her husband's' (I.27, p. 379), yet Tito's announcement that he is to visit San Gaggio elicits a response that indicates that the 'sweet clinging instinct, stronger than all judgments' (II.36, p. 42) is not properly to be depended upon in his wife. Romola possesses compassion, nobility and integrity, and the combination is to cause them both anguish. But the novel insists that such anguish is in fact a very general thing, virtually a condition of mutuality. At times, indeed, it describes relationships in terms that look forward to Sartre: 'Love does not aim simply at the conscious good of the beloved object: it is not satisfied without perfect loyalty of heart; it aims at its own completeness' (I.28, p. 389). According to Eliot's universal dynamic of love, such 'completeness' is simply not attainable; yet Romola deeply desires it and her need for what Sartre calls 'self-transcendence' seems often to be commended. This dual emphasis on self-assertion and limitation is, of course, typical: George Eliot insists that the self is free to choose, change and grow, but an unyielding determinism threatens constantly to deny it. One of many obvious examples is the assertion that 'our deeds are like children that are born to us; they live and act apart from our own will' (I.16, p. 248). 'Will' is here so far displaced from the moral agent that the past becomes a script for later life.

The novel's difficulty in envisaging the moral agent also bedevils its account of the individual's relation to society. *Romola* wishes to connect the problem of power in personal relationships – like Grandcourt and Osmond, Tito has the 'husband's determination to mastery' (II.48, p. 184) – with politics, but it founders on the Kantian dilemma of ethical agency and answerability. Like Kant's Kingdom of Ends, George Eliot's fictional societies are essentially organicist: individual selves constitute them as social by means of a shared commitment to universalisable moral choices. But, notoriously, Kant's kingdom is vulnerable precisely because such choices *are* individual: moral authority is thus conceived as coming from within and Kant seriously understates the threat this poses to polity. If individuals feel that forms of anti-social behaviour are consistent with the exhortation to 'act only on that maxim through which you can at the same time will that it should become a universal law',[13] then social life collapses into individual self-assertion. *Romola* is of course set in a period in which the underlying assumptions of social life are changing rapidly and dramatically: oligarchy, democracy and theocracy compete as alternative forms of political organisation, and the community is riven by profound disagreements over political and religious belief and tradition. Thus the narrator observes of Savonarola that 'no preacher ever had more heterogeneous materials to work upon' (I.25, p. 358). It is against this background that George Eliot tries to envisage certain stable features of moral and political life.

Again, the underlying assumptions are organicist. The self is a narrative unity that can maintain moral coherence only if it is continuous with its past. Tito's first great crime is to refuse 'the backward vista of his remembered life' (I.9, pp. 151–2), a propensity that gradually hardens into a matter of policy. Thus he tells Romola, who is incapable of such dissociation, that 'my Ariadne must never look backward now' (I.20, p. 309). An important passage links the novel's belief in the self's narrative intelligibility with the cognate conception of society as historically evolving and continuous: 'Our lives make a moral tradition for our individual selves, as the life of mankind at large makes a moral tradition for the race' (II.39, p. 88). And another well-known organicist metaphor proposes a deep interdependence between society and self:

> Since that Easter a great change had come over the prospects of Florence; and as in the tree that bears a myriad of blossoms, each single bud with its fruit is dependent on the primary circulation of the sap, so the fortunes of Tito and Romola were dependent on certain grand political and social conditions which made an epoch in the history of Italy.   (I.21, p. 313)

Thus too, of course, in *Felix Holt*: 'there is no private life which has not been determined by a wider public life' (Ch. 3, p. 45).

The most problematic word here is 'determined', for, as we have seen, George Eliot's conception of the self is not as fatalistic as such pronouncements may suggest. When Romola sets herself adrift on the lake of moral abnegation she yearns 'To be freed from the burden of choice when all motive was bruised, to commit herself, sleeping, to destiny' (II.61, p. 325). But she can no more do this than George Eliot's other heroines: social life does visit a

Kantian 'burden of choice' upon the individual, and Romola may not, eventually does not, repose in 'destiny'. The novel suggests that there are at least two powerful reasons for this. One is that passivity is socially and politically dangerous. The narrator remarks caustically upon the 'long-established' Florentine 'conviction that there could be no moral sifting of political agents' (II.45, p. 152). Without such 'sifting', and without active intervention against crude political expediency, society cannot hope to be rational or just. A second reason is related and again reflects the novel's thoroughgoing organicism. It is necessary both to understand and to exercise moral choices if the individual is to live responsibly. The familiar organicist metaphor of the web is used in *Romola* to discourage facile assumptions about moral life. Good motives and ill, it insists, often intermingle, with self-interest and sophistry shading one into the other. Thus it is on a 'calculation of his own possible need' that Tito initially leaves Tessa under the illusion that she is married to him; but George Eliot's logic of Nemesis insists that his bad faith must inevitably compound and perpetuate itself: 'the web had gone on spinning itself in spite of him, like a growth over which he had no power'. And the narrator observes, 'The elements of kindness and self-indulgence are hard to distinguish in a soft nature like Tito's' (II.34, p. 15). Yet the novel insists that the distinction can and must be made: Tito's loss of volition and the 'power' of spiritual self-determination imperils others; they – in this case, Romola – must be strong and discerning in proportion as he is weak. Knowledge in *Romola* is, then, above all a matter of understanding and exerting moral agency, but the asymmetries of vice and virtue render such understanding extraordinarily difficult. Whilst urging that psychological processes are in a sense universal, the novel offers in the portrait of Tito an image of unmotivated moral degeneration which is radically dissimilar from 'the presence of noble womanhood' (I.9, p. 144) it depicts in Romola. Herein lies a problem. George Eliot has Machiavelli argue that 'veracity is a plant of paradise' (II.45, p. 160), but it is not a sentiment she can really accept.

In fact the novel's moral argument tries to counter cynicism by reopening two central problems in Western ethics. It asks how far and in what ways other persons can be conceived as individual, and how great a part in their formation is played by nature and culture. On nature and culture *Romola*'s thrust is again

universalist. Tito's decision about the jewels – a fictional
reworking of Machiavelli on paternity and possession – takes the
form of a casuistical contrast between 'ordinary affairs', a
'radically natural view' and 'the sentiment of society':

> Certainly the gems and therefore the florins were, in a sense,
> Baldassarre's: in the narrow sense by which the right of
> possession is determined in ordinary affairs; but in that large
> and more radically natural view by which the world belongs to
> youth and strength, they were rather his who could extract the
> most pleasure out of them. That, he was conscious, was not the
> sentiment which the complicated play of human feelings had
> engendered in society. The men around him would expect that
> he should immediately apply those florins to his benefactor's
> rescue. But what was the sentiment of society? – a mere tangle of
> anomalous traditions and opinions, which no wise man would
> take as a guide, except so far as his own comfort was concerned.
> Not that he cared for the florins save perhaps for Romola's sake:
> he would give up his florins readily enough. It was the joy that
> was due to him and was close to his lips, which he felt he was not
> bound to thrust away from him and so travel on, thirsting. Any
> maxims that required a man to fling away the good that was
> needed to make existence sweet, were only the lining of human
> selfishness turned outward: they were made by men who
> wanted others to sacrifice themselves for their sake. He would
> rather that Baldassarre should not suffer: he liked no one to
> suffer; but could any philosophy prove to him that he was
> bound to care for another's suffering more than for his own? To
> do so he must have loved Baldassarre devotedly, and he did *not*
> love him: was that his own fault? Gratitude! seen closely, it
> made no valid claim: his father's life would have been dreary
> without him: are we convinced of a debt to men for the pleasure
> they give themselves?   (i.9, pp. 175–6)

This is one of many occasions in the novel in which George Eliot
uses omniscient narration to unmask a process that corrupts
something like the Aristotelian practical syllogism into self-deceit.
Tito tries to deny the universal force of 'ordinary affairs' – a
situation subsisting in various societies – by appeal to a 'natural'
view; but 'natural' is here a synonym for selfishness, and George
Eliot's conception of the natural man is much closer to that of her

beloved Rousseau than to Hobbes or Machiavelli. She believes that natural man has strong sympathetic and social tendencies and that social life can nurture and organise these. What Tito calls 'the sentiments of society' have, therefore, a doubly binding authority. His tactic for evading authority is to appeal to the arbiter Kant discourages – feelings. According to Kant, 'love out of inclination cannot be commanded'; 'practical love' is a love 'residing in the will and not in the propensions of feeling'.[14] The passions are too capricious to guide moral choices reliably. Thus does George Eliot condemn Tito's appeal to 'love'. His overriding concern ought to be duty.

Yet the novel is uncertain here and like the others it implicitly tests the adequacy of the Kantian position on duty. It is, after all, the tragically flawed Savonarola who voices the Kantian injunction to Romola when she first seeks to leave Florence. The novel asks whether the individual can in fact choose which duties he or she is to obey. Savonarola insists, 'You wish your true name and your true place in life to be hidden, that you may choose for yourself a new name and a new place, and have no rule but your own will. And I have a command to call you back' (II.40, p. 100). And again: 'But can man or woman choose duties? No more than they can choose their birthplace or their father and mother' (p. 102). Like passages cited earlier from *Daniel Deronda* and *The Portrait of a Lady*, these propose limits – genetic and social – to the power of individual choice. Savonarola claims a transcendental authority in urging particular social and ethical constraints upon Romola. He argues that, since she has been socialised and shaped by Florentine society, she must meet her destiny there. She cannot, therefore, 'choose' her 'duties'. This view of duty, resting as it does on a claim of visionary authority, of course introduces elements not present in the Kantian perspective, and Romola must decide how far she can accept such claims. Ultimately she cannot, and the novel tries – surely unsuccessfully – to reformulate the problem of moral choice in relation to forms of non-transcendental obligation.

Here the status of the individual is central, for the novel must rest its case for a secular ethics on a persuasive account of the various and intricate accommodations that the self makes to social life. Hence the description cited above of the conflicted Savonarola:

The mysteries of human character have seldom been presented
in a way more fitted to check the judgments of facile
knowingness than in Girolamo Savonarola; but we can give him
a reverence that needs no shutting of the eyes to fact, if we
regard his life as a drama in which there were great inward
modifications accompanying the outward changes.

(1.25, p. 359)

And, again, of Tito's impure feelings for Romola. His 'love' for her
is disturbingly enmeshed with his lust for power. It is a love 'which
formed one web with all his worldly hopes, with the ambitions and
pleasures that must make the solid part of his days – the love that
was identified with his larger self – was not to be banished from his
consciousness' (1.14, p. 232). In both Savonarola and Tito this
'larger self' is ultimately eclipsed by worldliness, and, despite the
narrator's caution against 'facile knowingness', she will often
insist that such personal failures can and must be charted: 'A
course of action which is in strictness a slowly-prepared
outgrowth of the entire character, is yet almost always traceable to
a single impression as its point of apparent origin' (11.35, p. 34).
Not surprisingly, the novel cannot sustain this claim, but it does
try to reconstruct the process by which the varied, conflicted and
impressionable inner person internalises cultural systems –
aesthetic, ethical, political.

As is generally the case in George Eliot, the inner person is
assumed to have an existence prior to and beyond the social codes
that surround it. Thus the narrator speaks of the 'sentiment which
the complicated play of human feelings had engendered in society'
(1.11, p. 176). Just how codes are internalised and modified by the
individuals is not specified in any detail; however, the description
of Romola removing her betrothal ring indicates the assumption
upon which characterisation in this novel rests:

But that force of outward symbols by which our active life is knit
together so as to make an inexorable external identity for us, not
to be shaken by our wavering consciousness, gave a strange
effect to this simple movement towards taking off her ring – a
movement which was but a small sequence of her energetic
resolution.   (11.36, p. 46)

The self, then, draws on a stock of social symbols and designations in order to formulate a conscious 'identity'. Self and system are mutually entailed. Moreover, this identity solidifies at a certain stage to an extent that permits it to survive a great deal of upheaval and change. The word 'inexorable' does not here imply a static personality – though it is again suggestive of determinism – but rather implies one that is sufficiently coherent to absorb and undergo change without surrendering its hard-won sense of selfhood.

Yet upheaval can be traumatic and it is indeed a feature of a coherent personality in George Eliot that pain cannot be pigeonholed or displaced: the whole person suffers, and a kind of gestalt shift sends shock waves through the individual's sense of past, present and future. This is the 'heart-cutting comparison of the present with the past' (p. 49) to which Tito drives Romola. During these crises not only the achieved sense of self is shaken, but so too are the structures by which self has appropriated information and symbolism from without, and the self-as-moral-agent is especially vulnerable. In *Romola* this takes the form of an acute revulsion against a narrowly authoritarian sense of duty. Romola ultimately rejects Savonarola's counsel about choice and duty and leaves Florence for a second time.

This choice is carefully prepared for in narrative commentary and dialogue. The narrator refers to 'those lawless moments which come to us all if we have no guide but desire' (i.13, p. 209), and to a form of moral 'dread which has been erroneously decried as if it were nothing higher than a man's animal care for his own skin' (i.11, p. 177). Later, but in the same vein, she argues that 'There is no kind of conscious obedience that is not an advance on lawlessness' (ii.49, p. 199). Eventually, however, the novel offers its radical qualifications to this rule. There are, it seems, moments at which the urgings of the inner person are and must be sovereign over social norms. Romola reaches such a moment as she contemplates seeking a separation from Tito: 'She was thrown back again on the conflict between the demands of an outward law, which she recognised as a widely-ramifying obligation, and the demands of inner moral facts which were becoming more and more peremptory' (ii.56, p. 272). These 'inner moral facts' lie at the very heart of George Eliot's moral realism, and, though she acknowledges that particular social languages and codes render them formulable, she also insists that they are a kind of species characteristic, a feature of human society that is so general as to be present in all manifestations of social life. This in part is what she means by 'the broad sameness of the human lot'.

One of the immense difficulties with this position is, of course, that it displaces moral authority to a realm of private legislation. Kant had tried to make this realm structurally continuous with social norms by characterising it as rational, but George Eliot knows that the distortions of sentiment and expediency can easily neutralise rational appraisal. Tito's bad faith in rationalising his choice not to retain the proceeds from the sale of his jewels is seen in just this light. The narrator notes that 'he had avowed to himself a choice which he would have been ashamed to avow to others' and continues,

> But the inward shame, the reflex of that outward law which the great heart of mankind makes for every individual man, a reflex which will exist even in the absence of the sympathetic impulses that need no law, but rush to the deed of fidelity and pity as inevitably as the brute mother shields her young from the attack of the hereditary enemy – that inward shame was showing its blushes in Tito's determined assertion to himself that his father was dead, or that at least search was hopeless.   (i.9, p. 154)

The natural analogy suggests that moral impulses are a kind of automatic species response that cross cultural boundaries. The 'great heart of mankind' is universal and expresses itself typically in certain forms of 'outward law'. Yet these do not prevent Tito's slide into depravity. He is here an inverted Telemachus, deserting his own father and suffering nothing more than a transient sense of guilt. The novel's avowed social and psychological organicism cannot concede threateningly idiosyncratic orders of feeling. Yet it is a fact of the history that the novel documents that socially enshrined orders of feeling do not always suffice: social change causes shifting and conflicting assumptions and some social expectations are simply incompatible with authentic moral action. *Romola* is ultimately unable to resolve the problems involved here and, like *The Mill on the Floss*, it resorts in the end to the symbolic simplifications of fable. The classical humanist Bardo is literally blinded and forfeits much of the legacy he has wished to bequeath. His son repudiates him and becomes a visionary ascetic; his son-in-law Tito sells his library and attempts to expunge Romola's devotion to him. But Tito is in his turn quite literally claimed by the past he has sought to repudiate. Having almost suffered the familiar Eliotean punishment by drowning, he is throttled by his vengeful stepfather. Romola, however, lives on, one of the most curious and equivocal of the many Eliotean heroines who survive to forge a new accord with society. At the close she has rejected the visionary asceticism of Savonarola and the Machiavellianism of Tito and has assumed the status of a religious humanistic madonna, a role most potently symbolised by her abiding loyalty to her father and by her holding a Jewish baby in the plague-ridden community towards which her drifting takes her. Interestingly, she does not re-enter the world of male geneticism and power after the demise of Tito. Dorothea remarries; Gwendolen is left alone but with an image of the shining Deronda. Romola settles with Tessa, the 'other wife' of this novel's other wife theme. Having managed, like Gwendolen and Dorothea, not to grant her husband biological continuity by bearing him children, she assumes an oddly privileged status. As Sally Shuttleworth notes, she 'becomes the object of her own cult',[15] a figure of potent mystical significance in a society which she now in many ways transcends. The myth of Romola thus holds in suspension the self as an end-in-itself and the ideal of social and ethical integration. Romola does not resolve the conflict between 'the sacredness of obedience' and 'the sacredness of rebellion' (II.56, p. 273), but George Eliot was to return creatively to this conflict in later novels. *Middlemarch* and *Daniel Deronda* pose the same set of questions, but with a less schematic sense both of history and of narrative.

III

The comparative reticence of the narrator in *Romola* is one of its most significant formal features and no doubt reflects George Eliot's desire to avoid the 'schemed picturesqueness of ordinary historical fiction'. Yet it by no means entails a reticence about the novel's moral issues. On these, needless to say, the narrator is open and indeed often assertive. One of many examples typifies the rhetorical use of commentary to involve the reader in a 'broad sameness' that applies equally to Renaissance Florence and Victorian England: 'All who remember their childhood remember the strange vague sense, when some new experience

came, that everything else was going to be changed, and that there
would be no lapse into the old monotony' (i.10, p. 169). Thus is
the reader also encouraged to conceive of his or her life as a
narrative unity, to which change must constitute a form of
disruption. Reading, even of remote historical eras, becomes an
appeal to continuity. Another example concerns Romola's loss of
faith in Savonarola:

> No one who has ever known what it is thus to lose faith in a
> fellow-man whom he has profoundly loved and reverenced, will
> lightly say that the shock can leave the faith in the Invisible
> Goodness unshaken. With the sinking of high human trust, the
> dignity of life sinks too; we cease to believe in our own better
> self, since that also is part of the common nature which is
> degraded in our thought; and all the finer impulses of the soul
> are dulled.   (ii.61, p. 323)

A sense of the 'better self' is what the idealising energies of an Eliot
novel attempt to restore to the reader. This passage is in fact part
of one of the more extended pieces of commentary in the novel
and, like the one quoted in the previous section, it is notable for its
poetic restraint. Little of the commentary in *Romola* possesses the
'luminous' meditative range that marks narration in the other
novels. The narrator offers herself more as a transparent medium
for historical recollection than as a self-dramatising persona
whose personality interacts powerfully, as it does elsewhere, with
the characters. Her style here is typically simple and uninflected
and does not attract undue attention to the narrative voice.
Neither does it enlist a diverting or suggestive pattern of image
and metaphor in order to suggest opaque depths in character.
Where it does work more by implication – as in the references to
the Ariadne and Telemachus myths, the various allusions to
Greek political and philosophical life – it is generally within a
clearly defined range of specification. The same is true of the use of
art as an index of the inner life. Chapter 18, entitled 'The Portrait',
raises the familiar Jamesian contrast between iconic and realistic
functions in art. How far can an image penetrate and project an
individual world? The answer here is that it can say a lot not only
about that world but also about the patterns of power,
appropriation and relationship in which it seeks definition.
Romola's and Tito's 'imaged selves' (i.20, p. 305) are a tribute to

the authenticity of art and an almost diagrammatic piece of exposition for the reader. It is, by an irony none too subtle, the characters pictured who fail to heed the deeper meanings.

As we shall see, this kind of technique is part of a more general refusal of creative and psychic 'lawlessness' in the novel. *Romola* is too much intent upon dramatising the social costs of rampant romantic individualism, and too remote from the society it depicts, to concede much to the 'unmapped country' of characters' minds. Its process is rather one of referring both social and psychological phenomena to a clear scheme of narrative values whose terms – 'love', 'truth', 'trust' – are often too reductive for the complex purposes George Eliot has in mind. However much she may appeal to a sense of complexity, this narrator is intriguingly loath to evoke it.

One of the narrator's first acts is, of course, to displace authority from her Victorian self to that of an anonymous Florentine citizen. The Proem hands the narrative over to the Spirit of a citizen who is permitted imaginatively to revisit his old city. Here again the technique is far from subtle. The Spirit at times reflects in ponderous direct speech: ' "Surely", he thinks, "Florence can still ring her bells with the solemn hammer-sound that used to beat on the hearts of her citizens and strike out the fire there . . ." ' (I, p.4). This patent falsity of tone haunts the novel throughout, though the device of displaced narrative authority is more successfully used in other novels – *The Mill on the Floss*, *Felix Holt* – where the effort of historical reconstruction is not so immense. In this instance, the narrator reclaims her authority from the Spirit even while repeatedly suggesting that it is really history – the final arbiter and authority – that is speaking. But this places intolerable strain upon George Eliot's psychological realism: *Romola*'s heroic effort of exemplification ultimately reduces its cast to a transparency that it was everywhere George Eliot's intention to avoid.

IV

The novel's 'patterned picturesqueness' holds for all its characters. Unlike *Middlemarch* or *Daniel Deronda*, this narrative does not evince powerfully discordant orders of character. Indeed, the cameos of Florentine life are in this sense oddly consistent with the depth portraits offered of the main cast.

Perhaps the most revealing example here is Tito, for his alienness to Florence is one of the novel's chief concerns. He is not of course the only alien in the work (one of the first questions he is asked in Florence is, 'You're not a Hebrew, eh?' – I.1, p. 20), but, unlike the Jews who have been expelled from Portugal and are ravaged by the plague outside society's margins, Tito adapts to a new human environment and becomes more expert in working the system than many of the Florentine natives. In this view he is of course aided by the politics of exigency, already embodied in – and later to be formulated by – Machiavelli, and by racial factors that make him appealing to the Florentines he cultivates.

The novel also repeatedly suggests that Tito is much aided by what ultimately destroys him – his given 'nature': 'his nature was one of those most remote from defiance or impudence' (I.31, p. 423). Yet the argument does not rest smugly with nature, for the novel has to explain Tito's slide into 'defiance', 'impudence' and moral barbarism. Here George Eliot encounters a set of difficulties familiar in ethical discussion. *Romola* wishes cautiously to endorse the doctrine of the goodness of man: we are born egoists but with strong social propensities. However, it depicts a man whose 'nature' is too shallow to reflect such propensities and who does not respond to certain features of his adopted social code, features which George Eliot often holds to be universal. Tito's spiritual suicide is thus explained in two often incompatible ways: it is the result of historical contingency – being displaced, adopting a new place that is politically and ethically unstable and fragmented, being influenced by an ambience of ruthless expediency – but it is also the consequence of an irreversibly flawed nature. Like Grandcourt and Raffles, Tito possesses a propensity for unmotivated evil that George Eliot has great difficulty either in explaining or depicting. Similarly, we are able to believe that Baldassarre is driven by the sheer callousness of Tito's behaviour to a state of obsessive malignity that has no gradations and ambiguities of motives in the usual Eliotean sense: 'Baldassarre felt the indestructible independent force of a supreme emotion, which knows no terror, and asks for no motive, which is itself an ever-burning motive, consuming all other desire' (II.38, p. 70). Elsewhere the narrator suggests that such a state is latent in everyone, circumstances permitting: 'It is in the nature of all human passion, the lowest as well as the highest, that there is a point where it ceases to be properly egoistic, and is like a fire kindled within our being to which everything else is mere fuel' (I.30, p. 413). Precisely why the Casaubons, Grandcourts, Baldassarres and Titos of this world become so alienated while others change and grow is ultimately unexplained in George Eliot; however, her general premise is that an explanation must be reconstructed from a combination of circumstantial, historical and psychological factors. As she asserts in *Middlemarch*, 'A human being in this aged nation of ours is a very wonderful whole, the slow creation of long interchanging influences' (II.4, p. 206).

But one further factor features decisively in *Romola*'s conception of the self, and this is the question of choice. In *Romola*, as in *Adam Bede*, the famous Nemesis theme which asserts the ineluctable consequences of bad faith is required to shoulder too much of the burden of explanation. After Tito encounters Baldassarre in Florence for the first time, the narrator world-wearily observes that 'Tito was experiencing that inexorable law of human souls, that we prepare ourselves for sudden deeds by the reiterated choice of good or evil which gradually determines character' (I.23, p. 340). It is the same 'inexorable law' that ordains that Tito will pay the ultimate cost for his sins. This could come from *Adam Bede*: 'But our deeds are like children that are born to us; they live and act apart from our will. Nay, children may be strangled, but deeds never: they have an indestructible life both in and out of our consciousness . . .' (I.16, p. 248). As many a sceptical reader of George Eliot has been moved to reflect, this is simply not the case in anything like the proportion of circumstances she suggests. Countless tawdry and malicious lives go, now, as in her time, unpunished either from without or from within; the ungrateful adopted child is not generally throttled by a step-parent. To this extent the portrait of Tito is an intellectual as well as an aesthetic failure, though, as always, there is a subtle interplay between these levels of the text.

The tone of careful comment and appraisal that accompanies Tito throughout the narrative is aptly reflected in the narrator's assurance (early in Chapter 34) that 'This, in brief, had been the history of Tito's relation to Tessa up to a very recent date' (II.34, p. 17). The same faintly fastidious tone infuses even descriptions of intense emotion. Having inferred from Tessa that she has met Baldassarre the reader is told: 'Tito was quite unconscious of her movements – unconscious of his own attitude: he was in that wrapt state in which a man will grasp painful roughness, and press and press it closer, and never feel it' (p. 24). Of all George Eliot's novels, *Romola* is surely the least successful in capturing a sense of a hidden 'unconscious' life. It may talk about the pressure of 'hidden anxieties' (i.26, p. 365), about the great complexity of human motivation, but the great effort of historical deliberation and typification inhibits Eliot's powers of empathetic creation.

No doubt the centrality of so blatantly an evil man as Tito in the plot also presented problems.[16] In no other George Eliot novel does unredeemed and ultimately criminal egoism occupy so much narrative attention, and the commentary charts the young man's demise with undisguised deliberation. There are a series of crises – selling the jewels, deciding what to do with the proceeds, seeing and meeting Baldassarre, conflicts with Romola and others – and each is given its due moral significance. The commentary traces Tito's decline from an innocence which entails a prior choice to evade responsibility, to the 'tacit falsity' (i.11, p. 175) of particular acts of bad faith, thence to a kind of self-consciousness George Eliot, usually so much a votary of self-consciousness, feared above all: 'the self-conscious adoption of a part in life' (i.22, p. 329) which somehow sunders social roles and the inner man. Here Tito with his 'double consciousness' (ii.39, p. 95) is a distant relative of Leonora, Latimer and other Eliotean figures who come to enact their own characters. Beyond this point, however, the portrait is one of the least interesting pieces of psychopathology in any Eliot novel and there is little profit in looking closely at the machinations that mark Tito's Machiavellian political involvements.

An earlier moment in the novel, in which Tito has 'after-thoughts' after first encountering Baldassarre in Florence, reflects the peculiarly interesting but unsatisfactory quality of George Eliot's portrait of Renaissance villainy:

> There was still one resource open to Tito. He might have turned back, sought Baldassarre again, confessed everything to him – to Romola – to all the world. But he never thought of that. The repentance which cuts off all moorings to evil, demands something more than selfish fear. He had no sense that there was strength and safety in truth; the only strength he trusted to lay in his ingenuity and his dissimulation. Now that the first

shock, which had called up the traitorous signs of fear, was well past, he hoped to be prepared for all emergencies by cool deceit – and defensive armour.

It was a characteristic fact in Tito's experience at this crisis, that no direct measures for ridding himself of Baldassarre ever occurred to him. All other possibilities passed through his mind, even to his own flight from Florence; but he never thought of any scheme for removing his enemy. His dread generated no active malignity, and he would still have been glad not to give pain to any mortal. He had simply chosen to make life easy to himself – to carry his human lot, if possible, in such a way that it should pinch him nowhere; and the choice had, at various times, landed him in unexpected positions. The question now was, not whether he should divide the common pressure of destiny with his suffering fellow-men; it was whether all the resources of lying would save him from being crushed by the consequences of that habitual choice.   (1.23, pp. 341–2)

The passage reads like a blueprint for a better George Eliot novel. The familiar emphasis upon 'choice' – its quality and consequences – is there (he has elsewhere come to think of life as 'a game in which there was an agreeable mingling of skill and chance' – II.35, p. 35) but without the usual dramatic power. Technique will account in part for this. The presence of the typifying narrator is obvious in the assurance that the response depicted is a 'characteristic fact in Tito's experience' and in the abrupt transitions from a stilted attempt at narrated monologue ('confessed everything to him – to Romola – to all the world') to sober narrative reflection: 'But he never thought of that. The repentance which cuts off all moorings to evil, demands something more than selfish fear.' The description implies an urgency and an impetuosity of mind ('All other possibilities passed through his mind') but is too inhibited to evoke it. The prose is lifeless: George Eliot here uses the verbal phrase 'cut off' where she would often choose the stronger 'sundered' or 'severed'. Typically, the account of Tito's motives is unsatisfactory: 'His dread generated no active malignity, and he would still have been glad not to give pain to any mortal.' But of course Tito does knowingly give immense pain, and George Eliot seems disinclined to acknowledge the ruthless criminality already present in his self-justification.

Tito remains interesting as a study in much that George Eliot feared, not least the chilling and unsociable quality she calls 'reticence' (I.9, p. 143). Occasionally her aversion to what she is here depicting infuses the portrait with unintended interest; but it remains on the whole a diagrammatic instance of what Barbara Hardy calls the Eliotean 'correcting study of the downward path',[17] its argumentative stolidness quite unequal to the murderousness that was to be a great Jamesian theme.

JAMES ON *ROMOLA* AND MORALITY IN FICTION

Romola is in many respects the sociological novel *par excellence*. It seeks to give both a causal and a qualitative account of a particular form of social life and it asks an impressive range of moral, philosophical and pragmatic questions. How do rank, work and religious allegiance shape individual lives? What forms of consciousness and self-expression does this society permit or compel? In particular, how do its moral concepts and vocabularies reflect and regulate ethical experience? On all these matters *Romola* remains an immensely interesting failure in creative social analysis. What it lacks, superficially at least, is a certain imaginative assurance and inwardness; more fundamentally, however, it suffers from a divided philosophical allegiance: whilst asserting the 'broad sameness' of human affairs, it also reposes great confidence in a progressive Comtean sense of history. Its findings can as a consequence seem strained and conflicting.

Henry James also, of course, reposed great confidence in the past, but a comparison of *Romola* and *The Wings of the Dove* reveals just how different the two senses of history were. With exceptions such as the unfinished novel *The Sense of the Past*, in which time is surreally dislocated, James does not generally set his major works as far back in time as did the nineteenth-century historical novelists. Moreover, the past does not in James possess the power to explain the present that it has in such a novel as *Romola*. It is a more elusive, though of course a subtly decisive, thing. The Jamesian attitude is aptly encapsulated in a phrase in *The Wings of the Dove*: he alludes to 'the many-coloured stream of history' (XIX.v.7, p. 287), a phenomenon, which, like any other, must be creatively constructed from impressions.

James's responses to *Romola* are revealing and reflect his sense not only of history, but also of positivism and didacticism in fiction more generally. It will be recalled that he had asserted in an early review that 'there have been no great didactic novelists'. But of course he did not dismiss the moral element from fiction entirely. On the contrary, he argues that 'to count out the moral element in one's appreciation of an artistic total is exactly as sane as it would be (if the total were a poem) to eliminate all the words in three syllables, or to consider only such portions of it as had been written by candle-light'.[18] The question, then, is how best to cultivate such 'appreciation', and James's answer is to minimise extrinsic commentary, 'To make the presented occasion tell all its story itself'.[19] By so doing the novelist can at once maintain the intensity of the fictional illusion and keep the reader's moral sense in play; indeed, he argues in an important passage that to ensure the illusion (realism) is in itself a moral achievement in fiction: 'Every out-and-out realist who provokes serious meditation may claim that he is a moralist for that, after all, is the most that the moralists can do for us.'[20] To 'provoke meditation' – the James of the final phase seldom seeks to do more than this.

In theory, of course, George Eliot is basically in agreement here. Art can only arouse and organise moral sentiment and, she insists, 'Art is art, and tells its own story'. Yet in practice the approaches were very different. Hence the famous passage about moral fiction in James's review of the Cross *Life*. A jotting of George Eliot's about *Le Père Goriot* 'illuminates the author's general attitude with regard to the novel, which, for her, was not primarily a picture of life, capable of deriving a high value from its form, but a moralised fable, the last word of a philosophy endeavouring to teach by example'.[21] Her recourse to 'direct exhortation'[22] and extended commentary threatens the persuasiveness of the fictional illusion, and so the moral power the work may possess. James esteems George Eliot's sense of the 'moral ideal'[23] but thinks it an imposition upon much of her art.

Not surprisingly, James does not consider *Romola* a 'masterpiece': it lacked, he thought, the necessary 'simplicity'.[24] Yet his final assessment is flattering. The novel was 'on the whole the finest thing she wrote'.[25] He admired it as a 'great placed and timed prose fiction';[26] and, interestingly, he thought highly of the character of Tito Melema. Like some of George Eliot's other successful figures – Hetty Sorrel, for example – Tito seemed almost to be his work's hero by default. Of *Romola* he notes that 'the technical hero has been eclipsed by the real one',[27] and he sees in Tito 'the firm and elaborate delineation of individual character'[28] that such a creation as Adam Bede lacks. Indeed, in a typically equivocal appraisal in the Cross *Life* review, he claims that, 'except in the person of Tito Melema, it [*Romola*] does not seem positively to live.'[29] In the now famous phrase, it lacks 'free aesthetic life',[30] and is too 'deeply studied'.[31] Memorably, 'It carries to a maximum the in-door quality'[32] – a quality not, of course, unfamiliar in James's own work.

On *Romola* as a historical novel James concludes that it is 'pre-eminently a study of the human conscience in an historical setting'[33] and that as such it strikes the reader 'less as a work of art than as a work of morals'.[34] This is consistent with what James takes to be George Eliot's creative method more generally: 'More than any of her novels it was evolved, as I have said, from her moral consciousness – a moral consciousness encircled by a prodigious amount of literary research'.[35] The result is that 'the excellence both of the spirit and of the execution of the book is emphatically an obvious excellence'. Few have profoundly questioned this judgement, and one of James's explanations for the obviousness of *Romola* seems to hold: the novel's particular formal and thematic features 'make no demand upon the imagination of the reader'.[36] This is James's familiar charge against the rhetorical structure of George Eliot's fiction. The great novelist 'makes the reader' as he 'makes his characters'; thus does the reader do 'half the labor'.[37] Reading *Romola* seemed to James a passive exercise in moral exemplification. As such, the novel falls short of the 'perfection' that was his aesthetic ideal.[38]

Like many of James's other strictures upon George Eliot's art, this one raises fundamental questions about the novel as a form of representation and appraisal and about developments in fiction since the Victorians. It is generally acknowledged that one such development involves a shift in attitudes towards fictional rhetoric, and it is here of course that James's criticism concentrates. So too has much of the literary criticism written in its wake. Whether in the manifestos of modernists (Joyce, Woolf, Conrad, Ford and many others) or in recent discussion of the 'poetics' of fiction, the recurrent question has been: what kind of authority can fictional rhetoric plausibly lay claim to?

FICTIONAL RHETORIC AND A COMPARISON OF *ROMOLA* AND *THE WINGS OF THE DOVE*

One influential answer has come from Wayne C. Booth's *The Rhetoric of Fiction*, a work that insists on the decisive influence of the narrator's moral outlook in a fiction. Booth states his position thus: 'The emotions and judgments of the implied author are, as I hope to show, the very stuff out of which great fiction is made.'[39] According to Booth, fiction cannot but evaluate what it presents; moreover, it cannot even communicate until this evaluative outlook has impressed itself upon the reader. Booth's notion of fictional 'rhetoric' entails believing that 'any story will be unintelligible unless it includes, however subtly, the amount of telling necessary not only to make us aware of the value system which gives it its meaning but, more important, to make us willing to accept that value system, at least temporarily'.[40] As Booth has subsequently conceded, this is an exacting and not altogether clear requirement. How subtle may the communication of the novel's 'value system' be? At times Booth seems disinclined to set any limits to indirection. After all, in any narrative structure 'the author's voice is never really silenced'.[41] Yet the weight of the demonstration reflects Booth's desire to correct the influence of James, to 'restore telling to critical respect'.[42]

> Perhaps it is too much to expect that my readers will at this point incorporate into their view of the rhetoric of fiction their experience with the best analyses of impersonal works. But I have more than enough to do if I am to discuss here the uses of authorial silence and, in the remaining chapters, the new problems that this silence presents to authors and readers.[43]

Various facts are urged against 'authorial silence': symbolism, so often a substitute for commentary, may be just as obtrusive as the old-fashioned narrator; intrusive narrators may be as moving and interesting as characters themselves; commentary can mediate authorial indulgences; it can integrate disparate aspects of a fiction; and, above all, it can highlight, explain and morally appraise characters in a fashion unavailable to the impersonal narrator.[44] In general, then, Booth's view privileges the Eliotean novel over the Jamesian one on the grounds that the intrusive narrator is the more potent, prudent and persuasive moral authority. But of course Booth is too subtle a reader to propose this as an absolute evaluative standard, and, in a case such as this comparative reading of *Romola* and *The Wings of the Dove*, it clearly cannot be. James's novel, which implicitly proposes itself as a 'work of art' first and a 'work of morals' only in a secondary and subliminal way, achieves a subtlety of psychological and ethical report far beyond that of George Eliot's historical pastoral. The comparison, then, needs to be handled with care, not least because *The Wings of the Dove* is a consummate late novel and *Romola* one written before George Eliot's own great final creative phase.

Certain broad parallels are, however, clear enough. Both plots turn on temptation: Romola tempts Tito to righteousness; Kate Croy tempts Merton Densher to just about the ultimate depravity: making up to a dying heiress. In either case, many of the most difficult ethical questions are focused through the male protagonists. Merton's ultimate renunciation of Kate's plan is a kind of inversion of the *Romola* plot, in which Tito, unresponsive alike to Romola's nobility and to the universalist ethical perspective that infuses George Eliot's fiction, slides into sophistry and treachery. Each novel also, of course, has a somewhat idealised and ambiguous female protagonist. Both Romola and Milly Theale come to represent an ideal order of value in brutally exigent worlds, yet each is at the close oddly poised at a remove from the historical community depicted. Romola is something of an anachronism, a moral and spiritual order unto herself; Milly has died but is in a sense more powerfully present than ever. That both novels evoke historical communities is also significant. For George Eliot's Florence we have in *The Wings of the Dove* Victorian England and James's Venice. His sense of place is typically far less sociological than hers; yet the savagery of *The Wings of the Dove*'s social criticism is not to be understated. It is indeed an aspect of an unemphatic, yet surely influential, moral argument.

THE WINGS OF THE DOVE

I

In its less 'obvious' way, *The Wings of the Dove* centres its moral argument on the Kantian question that so preoccupies *Romola*. As Lionel Croy's early injunction to Kate indicates, this too is a novel about love and duty. The degenerate father tells his daughter,

> 'I'm not talking only of what you might, with the right feeling, do *for* me, but of what you might – it's what I call your opportunity – do *with* me. Unless indeed,' he the next moment imperturbably threw off, 'they come a good deal to the same thing. Your duty as well as your chance, if you're capable of seeing it, is to use me. Show family feeling by seeing what I'm good for. . . .'   (xix.i.1, p. 18)

That the novel should begin (and indeed end) on such a tawdry Dickensian note is central to the argument. Though much of the brutal manipulative suavity of the world it depicts is in James's view a manifestation of general human propensities, this novel quite clearly lays specific moral and social blame at the door of the English class system. Life may in a famous Jamesian phrase be 'ferocious and sinister',[45] but it is peculiarly so at Lancaster Gate, where the ethos of making means of others – of 'working' them – has been elevated to a thing as subtle, if not as solicitous, as a form of art. As Kate explains to Milly,

> every one who had anything to give – it was true they were the fewest – made the sharpest possible bargain for it, got at least its value in return. The strangest thing furthermore was that this might be in cases a happy understanding. The worker in one connexion was the worked in another; it was as broad as it was long – with the wheels of the system, as might be seen, wonderfully oiled. People could quite like each other in the midst of it, as Aunt Maud, by every appearance, quite liked Lord Mark, and as Lord Mark, it was to be hoped, liked Mrs. Lowder, since if he did n't he was a greater brute than one could believe.   (xix.iv.2, p. 179)

The ethos is nakedly transactional and utilitarian[46] and its emotional ambience is a calculating compromise of 'love': 'quite liked' is the novel's catch phrase for the savagery of English reserve.

No one is more sensitive to the menace of this environment than Densher, himself a psychological and social outsider. Waiting for

Aunt Maud at Lancaster Gate, he thinks of its oppressively imperial 'British' quality as 'cruel' (xix.ii.2, p. 78). And of course it is Densher who is to be subtly and severely tested by its ethos. It is this, through the machinations of Aunt Maud and Kate, that coerces him into making up to Milly. Thus does Milly herself also become a victim, though not a totally unsuspecting one. She is aware of the mutual exclusiveness of 'an hierarchical, an aristocratic order' (xix.iv.3, p. 191) and from the outset tries to disentangle the 'human' from the 'English' at Lancaster Gate: 'It was n't a question, in short, of the people the compatriot was after; it was the human, the English picture itself' (xix.iii.2, p. 135).

Like the other late international novels, *The Wings of the Dove* opens out with extraordinary subtlety the problems of nationality, 'humanity' and morality. As James notes in the Preface to the novel, its formal pattern may suggest a 'scheme of clearness', but the work is in no sense 'a simple statement'.[47] The 'scheme' may at times appear Manichean – Milly yearns for 'the pleasant human way', not the 'depths of darkness' (xx.vii.4, p. 151) – yet the confrontation between New World innocence and the usages of the British élite is not so 'obvious' as some critics have suggested.[48] *The Wings of the Dove* in fact envisages everyone as being omnivorously anxious to know, to control and to triumph. It is in this sense a novel about a transcultural (though, of course, historically kindred) 'human predicament' (xix.iii.1, p. 125) that one may meet in England and America, and about the ways in which specific cultural environments mediate and shape responses to this predicament.

At its heart is the familiar Jamesian question of perception. Is the world a fabrication of individual consciousness or an irrefusable reality to which, like a dying girl, we must submit? *The Wings of the Dove* entertains both of these propositions and, as we shall see, it dwells especially upon their implications for human relationships. The knowledge theme is again paramount and the international situation an all-embracing metaphor for the problems of intersubjective understanding. Is England, the novel seems to ask, so quintessentially 'English' that an American mind cannot fathom it; or are there orders of wisdom and intuition that make out the inner world of others, no matter how opaque or overlaid with convention?

All of the main characters are implicated in these questions. Indeed, the extraordinary sinister and suspicious 'moral air' (xx.viii.2, p. 193) of the work reflects a deeper cultural and epistemological uncertainty. Here again James inquires after the implications of a phenomenological emphasis on the creativity of perception. Thus does the by-no-means naïve Milly inquire after her perception of Kate:

> Kate had for her new friend's eyes the extraordinary and attaching property of appearing at a given moment to show as a beautiful stranger, to cut her connexions and lose her identity, letting the imagination for the time make what it would of them – make her merely a person striking from afar, more and more pleasing as one watched, but who was above all a subject for curiosity.   (xix.v.1, pp. 211–12)

The word 'curiosity' will by now suggest a dual problem. There is the epistemological one as to how far Milly's image of Kate actually conforms to some 'truth' about her. Clearly, *The Wings of the Dove* does not entirely refuse the existence of 'pure historic truth' (xx.viii.2, p. 195). The second problem is ethical. Milly's curiosity renders Kate 'a figure conditioned only by the great facts of aspect, a figure to be waited for, named and fitted' (xix.iv.1, p. 212). *The Wings of the Dove*, too, is a novel about the 'categories of the human appeal' and the imaginative injustices that can be done in 'fitting' others into established typologies. As usual in James, 'curiosity' is thus seen as a potential threat.

But it is not, of course, nearly so dangerous as naïvety or moral lassitude, for this world is such that, if one refuses its actualities, others will fictionalise to their own advantage. Here, indeed, *The Wings of the Dove*'s treatment of the knowledge theme is perhaps the most sinister in all of James's major fiction. It teems with fictionalisers who would make of Milly whatever is required to meet the requirements of their grasping imaginations. The most benign fictionaliser in the novel is Susan Stringham, herself a minor romantic novelist. Like Madame Merle, Susan is 'The woman in the world least formed by nature' (xix.iii.1, p. 104). She is that person so paradoxical to James – an American who seems entirely spoken for by culture. In many respects, in fact, she has more in common with the less appalling Fanny Assingham. Here is the narrator's account of the nature of Milly's initial appeal to her imagination. Milly was alone, she was stricken, she was rich, and in particular was strange – a combination in itself of a nature to engage Mrs. Stringham's attention. But it was the strangeness that most determined our good lady's sympathy, convinced as she had to be that it was greater than anyone else – anyone but the sole Susan Stringham – supposed.   (p. 106)

Susan's 'sympathy' is at this stage, then, essentially curious, a faintly indecent fascination. That this is novelist-like is in fact asserted by the narrator. Significantly, Susan's creativity ceases in the presence of the life to which her imagination aspires. Milly the American princess routs her fictional categories: 'but all categories failed her – they ceased at least to signify – as soon as she found herself in the presence of the real thing, the romantic life itself' (p. 107). As the appalling reality of Milly's fate comes home to her, Susan's 'sympathy' softens and she is humanised by the suffering she sees, a suffering horrifically compounded by a kind of fictionalising far beyond her ingenuous American variety.

One practitioner of this darker form is of course Susan's friend, Aunt Maud. Susan in fact expends some of her 'psychological instincts' (xix.iv.2, p. 169) in trying to define Maud's attitude to moral life and, by implication, the differences between the American and the English mind. Thus, the American lady muses, 'The joy, for her, was to know *why* she acted – the reason was half the business; whereas with Mrs. Lowder there might have been no reason: "why" was the trivial seasoning-substance, the vanilla or the nutmeg, omittable from the nutritive pudding without spoiling it' (ibid.). The gustatory metaphor may be disarming but the implication is grim: there is a hollowed-out, ossified quality about moral life at Lancaster Gate; moral behaviour tends to be a ritual enactment of hierarchical power relationships rather than a recognition of personal desire and entitlement. Feelings and the forms fuse in an ambience of ruthless calculation; reality becomes a fixed and expedient fiction. Thus does Densher, ensnared by the coercive Kate, feel 'with a strange mixed passion the mastery of her mere way of putting things' (xx.viii.2, p. 196).

In important ways, of course, both Kate and Densher are outsiders at Lancaster Gate and it is an indication of the potency of the Maud ethos that it should so envelop social aspirants such as this young couple. But envelop them it does, and the 'mixed passion' and 'mastery' of their relationship constitutes one of

James's most disturbing versions of the knowledge theme. In depicting the relationship James emphasises the way in which the erotic, the empathetic and the imaginative may conspire to transform a situation into a kind of enchanted moral convenience. Here is one of many descriptions of the tactical 'intimacy' Kate and Densher enjoy:

> It had come to be definite between them at a primary stage that, if they could have no other straight way, the realm of thought at least was open to them. They could think whatever they liked about whatever they would – in other words they could say it. Saying it for each other, for each other alone, only of course added to the taste. The implication was thereby constant that what they said when not together had no taste for them at all, and nothing could have served more to launch them, at special hours, on their small floating island than such an assumption that they were only making believe everywhere else. Our young man, it must be added, was conscious enough that it was Kate who profited most by this particular play of the fact of intimacy.   (XIX.ii.1, pp. 65–6)

The 'realm of thought' is a euphemism for ruthless ambition: it is that image of fulfilment that the couple oppose to the given state of things in their quest for mutual and social satisfaction. 'Making believe' is like Kate's 'way of putting things': it reconceives the world as the place they want it to be, and it calls where necessary on apparently limitless reserves of sophistry and evasion. The 'straight way' is one of *The Wings of the Dove*'s countless terms of effete moral evasion. It means in this instance, like many others, making up new rules and disfiguring the old; manipulating situations through scheming, subtle misrepresentation and omission. Well might the vulnerable Milly fear a thing seldom conceded in George Eliot: 'the machinations of sympathy' (XIX.v.5, p. 261).

The telepathic treachery of Kate and Densher is yet another Jamesian indictment of cheapened and exigent knowledge. Their 'deep and free interchanges' (XIX.ii.2, p. 90) are so according only to the laws of their own self-interest, and their 'compact' (p. 95) is a more gruesome form of the one that unites the Assinghams in *The Golden Bowl*. There the 'basis' for mutuality is Maggie's situation; here it is Milly's (XX.vi.2, p. 24). Moreover, this novel's deep scepticism about relationships finds expression, as it does in both *The Golden Bowl* and *Romola*, in the metaphor of a 'flaw' in mutuality: Milly suspects one (xix.iv.2, p. 176) but, drawn to Densher, she permits 'the smash of her great question' (xix.v.7, p. 300); Kate and Densher 'each had the beauty, the physical felicity, the personal virtue, love and desire of the other', we are told, 'without a flaw' (xx.vi.4, pp. 54–5).

The 'flaws' here go well beyond adultery. 'Making up' to a dying girl is a kind of murder by default. It apparently hastens Milly's death and it all but destroys Densher as a moral being: 'I *am* dead' (xx.x.3, p. 272), he tells Susan with more than a hint of self-despair. Yet – and this no doubt explains much of the critical disagreement about the novel – *The Wings of the Dove* does not indulge in wholesale denunciation. As we shall see, this is in part because it does not need to; but also because it is more concerned to open its situation out in all its ominous ambiguity than to precipitate uninquiring judgement. This entails seeing that, in the first instance, there are subtle degrees of culpability in any situation: Kate acts under the duress of a crippling and dehumanising set of social alternatives; Densher out of weakness, need and sheer erotic compulsion. It also means unmasking the mechanisms of moral suppression and evasion, so far as an undogmatic narrative form will permit. In this respect James's belief that a moralist is best advised to prompt 'meditation' on moral matters finds artistic expression in this late reworking of the problems of motivation, code and interpretation.

The 'appetite for motive' (xix.iv.3, p. 201) is pervasive in the novel, though, as Susan's reflections upon Maud suggest, some have a more highly inquisitive attitude to the inner world of moral intention than others. James, however, is well aware that such a world is not *merely* inner: it is to a significant degree shaped by social coding and assumption, much of it deeply embedded. Thus Milly, discussing Maud with Lord Mark, has 'on the spot, with her first plunge into the obscure depths of a society constituted from far back, encountered the interesting phenomenon of complicated, of possibly sinister motive' (xix.iv.1, p. 154). A society 'constituted' this 'far back' is difficult to interpret and may possess its own savage means of self-preservation. Milly of course fails to acknowledge how 'sinister' its motives can be. In part this is because she so pathetically needs Densher and the realm of experience he can belatedly open out to her; but it is also because selves – especially English ones – are enmeshed in tacit codes and unspoken habits of description. There is much here, as in *The Golden Bowl*, about the 'incalculable' quality of other persons. This is Milly's word for Kate (xix.iv.1, p. 150). But it is also a quality that Milly possesses for Kate and Densher. Kate prides herself on their (or rather her) possessing intelligence (xix.ii.1, p.72) and imagination (xix.ii.2, p. 87), and Densher likes to feel that there is something 'determinant' (p. 94) between them. Yet Milly is never quite 'determinant' for them; she is too much bound up in their desire to transform their situation, to have a kind of reality that is ultimately unavailable to them. As Kate muses in an important passage, 'There was no such misfortune . . . as to be formed at once for being and for seeing. You always saw, in this case something else than what you were, and you got in consequence none of the peace of your condition' (xix.i.2, pp. 33–4). The familiar Jamesian conflict between 'being' and 'seeing' here means either settling for an obdurate and unpalatable given social reality or denaturing that reality in accordance with the dictates of desire, of deeply subjective fulfilment. In the case of such a woman as Maud, who is so much the incarnation of stupefying social norms, the problem is related but different. Densher speaks of her as representing 'the great public mind that we meet at every turn and that we must keep setting up "codes" with' (xix.ii.2, p. 91). He speaks here as a journalist, but this is in turn a metaphor for the problem of codes more generally: because they tend to be self-perpetuating, closed and ritualistic, those desiring social acceptance have in effect to invent their own modes of complexity and exclusion (Kate and Densher's 'language of exaggeration' – xix.ii.1, p. 65) and tactically to insinuate these into existing usages.

All of this is – and James does not pretend otherwise – potentially amoral and predatory. Yet even those not so embroiled face problems in understanding the motives and manners of others. As Milly talks evasively to Susan about her sense of her predicament, the narrator wonders, through an invented auditor, 'to what inner thought of her own the good lady was trying to fit the speech' (xix.iv.3, p. 186) in question. This 'fit' is seldom the lovingly empathetic thing in *The Wings of the Dove* that it can be, for instance, in *Romola*: motives are often too 'sinister' for innocent reconstruction. Yet the final phase of the novel, in which Densher's conscience forbids him to carry out the plan that Kate has largely fashioned, is in a sense a tribute to something like an Eliotean belief in the power of humanistic redemption. Milly in fact redeems Densher as Romola cannot redeem Tito. Here is an interesting, and perhaps surprising, reversal of outlook between the novelists. The moral argument of *The Wings of the Dove* seems ultimately to be that people possess in the love of others the power to change. The critical debate as to whether such power is in Milly's case 'transcendental'[49] or merely richly human is probably insoluble – and also quite probably secondary. The narrator's wish is more to chart and depict change than conclusively to define its deepest sources.

II

The narrator in *The Wings of the Dove* is still more impersonal than his reticent counterpart in *Romola*; yet the subliminal traces and techniques of story-telling are everywhere apparent. One such is pragmatic and is, as James often insisted, inevitable: the story has at a rudimentary level to be orchestrated and stage-managed. Thus we are told that Milly's attributes 'feed Mrs. Stringham's flame' as that lady awaits her charge near the Alpine cliff in Book Third. And the narrator locates those attributes within the unfolding context of the narrative and hints at their significance: 'They are things that will more distinctly appear for us, and they are meanwhile briefly represented by the enthusiasm that was stronger on our friend's part than any doubt' (xix.iii.1, p. 126). The necessities of placing and pacing the story are similarly apparent when the narrator notes, with reference to Milly's confidences with Susan, that, 'All the same, it should with much less delay than this have been mentioned, she had n't yet – had n't, that is, at the end of six days – produced any news for her comrade' (xix.iv.3, p. 183).

Less pragmatic, and less pronounced than in *Romola*, are the novel's generalising narrative commonplaces. The scarcity and brevity of these in *The Wings of the Dove* partially accounts, as it does in *The Golden Bowl*, for the novel's impression of charmed insularity; but they are there none the less. It is interesting that a high proportion of these in the major phase concern passion. Thus one at the beginning of Book Sixth expresses an awareness, as do others, of passion's ambiguity of pain and exultation. Had Kate agreed to accompany Densher to his house, 'there would probably enough have occurred for them, at the foot of his steps, one of those strange instants between man and woman that blow upon the red spark, the spark of conflict, ever latent in the depths of passion' (xx.vi.1, p. 6). Significantly, the first scene of the novel includes a commonplace which serves to establish an ethical perspective. Kate reflects upon the irritations of her father's conniving diplomacy, and the narrator comments, 'The inconvenience – as always happens in such cases – was not that you minded what was false, but that you missed what was true' (xix.i.1, p. 7). That moral terms are used is significant: the ethical issues are, however obliquely, conjured into focus.

The narrator is similarly oblique in his description of particular characters. George Eliot, of course, highlights individual figures with challenging directness and intensity; here the narrator may refer to Milly as 'the young lady in whom we are interested' (xix.iii.1, p. 104) or, again in reference to Milly, recommend 'the charms of our subject' (xix,iv.1, p. 157). Late in the novel he even notes of Densher's decision not to call on Sir Luke Strett that 'We should have known, walking by his side', what the decision had been (xx.x.3, p. 352). The reader is thus cast as an anonymous onlooker for whom character is at once close and closed, compelling and resistant. Again, it is when Maud is trying to penetrate Milly's thoughts that the narrator remarks that 'another person present at such times might have wondered to what inner thought of her own the good lady was trying to fit the speech' (xix.iv.3, p. 186).

Such gestures at narrative accompaniment seldom, however, convey explicit moral or attitudinal biases. Occasionally the narrator permits himself a 'poor Milly' (xix.v.6, p. 283) or a 'poor Densher' (xx.vi.3, p. 37); elsewhere he alludes to the 'strangest fact' (xx.ix.2, p. 255) of one of Densher's rationalisations, thus hinting obliquely at an ethical emphasis. But for the most part he presents himself merely as an observer. Sometimes he appears confident in this capacity: the 'effect' of Kate's impression on Milly – her appearance of complicity with Densher – prompts the remark that 'It produced in fact more than one [effect], and we take them in their order' (xix.v.4, p. 257). Elsewhere, though, there is less confidence and a suggestion that certain limitations are keenly felt. Life seems more complex than his account of it. Milly, musing on Kate's good fortune, for instance occasions the admission that 'These things, for Milly, inwardly danced their dance; but the vibration produced and the dust kicked up had lasted less than our account of them' (p. 258). Such reticence contributes to what Nicola Bradbury rightly terms the novel's 'mood of hypothesis':[50] much of the discussion and questioning is left to the characters. However, as Wayne C. Booth will concede, James has other means for opening out his moral concerns. One of course is symbolism. As *The Golden Bowl*'s symbol alludes to Ecclesiastes, so *The Wings of the Dove* echoes Psalm 55:4–6: 'My heart is sore pained within me: and the terrors of death are fallen upon me. Fearfulness and trembling are come upon me, and horror hath over-whelmed me. And I said, Oh that I had wings like a dove! then would I fly away, and be at rest.' Typically James does not limit the symbol to a prescribed field of reference. What is important about the 'dove' image is the way it is used to place, appropriate and characterise Milly by a variety of parties. It is Kate who provides it (xix.v.6, p. 283), Maud, Densher, and even Milly herself who take it up. In this sense Maud's final announcement that Milly's 'wings' have spread 'wider' – 'for a flight, I trust, to some happiness greater' (xx.x.3, p. 356) – is the brutally ironic culmination of a process of destructive imaginative collusion. Yet the novel does not rest with this grim conclusion, for it is just this act that reveals to Densher the necessary limits of imaginative manipulation. Understanding what it really means to be dove-like entails behaving towards the person so designated with a proper reverence. Thus does symbolism become heuristic, a means finally for 'seeing things as they were' (xix.v.6, p. 278) all along. And this in turn offers the possibility of some kind of personal redemption.

Symbolism in *The Wings of the Dove* may in a sense supplant commentary but it does not thereby defuse moral intensity; moreover, the novel uses other techniques to promote a sense of ethical concern in the reader. One is its use of moral diction. Like the other two late-phase novels, this one holds up for analysis a highly specialised language of moral convenience and evasion. As Ruth Bernard Yeazell so admirably demonstrates,[51] talking in late James is often a matter of bending the rules and emptying moral precepts of their ethical force. Both dialogue and passages of narrated monologue teem with examples. Some are very familiar in James: phrases such as 'made it smooth' (xx.vi.4, p. 64), which are used to appease compromised consciences; or disingenuous abstractions such as 'straightness' (xx.viii.3, p. 204), which test or deny the limits of propriety. Key moral words such as 'ought' (xx.viii.3, p. 203), 'conscience' (xx.x.1, p. 326), 'sincerity' (xx.x.2, p. 336) and 'fidelity' (xx.ix.1, p. 238) are similarly tested. Indeed, one of the great achievements of James's late fiction is to simulate moral situations and the ways in which ethical vocabularies can be applied or misapplied in and to them; to see how far received ethical terms will in fact elucidate the situations we meet and how far we creatively constitute moral language by using it in context. There is no pretence in the novel that ethical words or imperatives can in any abstract way redeem a sordid intention, or that a suave moral style will substitute for substance. Motives, as a famous confession of Kate's makes clear, get revised at a deeper level than this. Kate says of the grim game they are playing with Milly, 'I don't like it, but I'm a person, thank goodness, who can do what I don't like' (xx.viii.3, p. 226). However opaque its medium, narration in *The Wings of the Dove* establishes a hazy divide between the high brutality of such bad intentions and the sort of consciousness over which 'scruple' (xx.ix.1, p. 246) will eventually assert its claim.

III

The character who possesses such consciousness is of course Densher, arguably the one who, like Tito Melema in *Romola*, is the 'real hero' in the novel.[52] Indeed, it is James's judgement in the Preface to the work that *The Wings of the Dove* suffers from a 'displaced centre'. The 'latter half' seems to him 'deformed' and inadequately to resolve the 'difficulties' the first has established. Milly of course dies before the conclusion, and the focus rests with Kate and Densher. Critics have disagreed about what status this ultimately confers upon Milly. Again, the question cannot be definitively settled, but it is clear that the latter half devotes lavish attention to Densher's crisis of 'conscience' and that something like a moral sensibility in recoil from treachery is opened out to the reader.

The stages of this process are too intricate to paraphrase here, and there are of course many occasions, not least those which are either omitted or eluded in conversation, in which Densher's true motives are impossible to ascertain. But the general trend of his development is surely clear enough. It is one that James had sought to reveal in as much detail as coherent narrative form would permit. He speaks in the Preface of his desire to achieve 'amplitude'[53] in this piece of characterisation. And he continues, 'The young man's situation . . . was to have been so decanted for us that we should get all the taste'.[54] However, much of the fabric of his consciousness has alas remained 'entwined upon the reel'.[55] James in fact concludes that 'the hand of generosity' – that is, of the novelist of character – 'has been cautioned and stayed'.[56] Densher seems to him unclear and incomplete.

It may be argued that what Densher lacks in obviousness and completeness he gains in suggestiveness. James had of course insisted in an early review of George Eliot's novels that a character must have the 'capacity to be tempted' if he is to be 'interesting'. Densher, who is a more powerful and interesting creation in this respect than Tito Melema, is in fact initially described as being an 'interesting mixture' (xix.ii.1, p. 49) of a man. Like Tito he is something of an outsider. He has returned from various corners of the Empire (and indeed from Cambridge) a 'Briton', but also, in some obscure and embryonic way, a dove: 'But brave enough though his descent to English earth, he had passed, by the way, through zones of air that had left their ruffle on his wings – he had been exposed to initiations indelible' (xix.ii.2, p. 93). The phrasing here is no doubt somewhat pompous but the image is prophetic: Densher is ultimately to come out on Milly's side, despite corrupting social pressures, a compulsive attraction to Kate and the 'general plasticity' (xx.viii.1, p. 182) of temperament that he shares with Tito. James's narrative method for presenting this circuitous and subtle process is, however, a great advance upon George Eliot's evocation of temptation and choice. Here is Densher's 'case of conscience' upon first visiting Milly in England:

> Odd enough was it certainly that the question originally before him, the question placed there by Kate, should so of a sudden find itself quite dislodged by another. This other, it was easy to see, came straight up with the fact of her beautiful delusion and her wasted charity; the whole thing preparing for him as pretty a case of conscience as he could have desired, and one at the prospect of which he was already wincing. If he was interesting it was because he was unhappy; and if he was unhappy it was

because his passion for Kate had spent itself in vain; and if Kate was indifferent, inexorable, it was because she had left Milly in no doubt of it. That above all was what came up for him – how clear an impression of this attitude, how definite an account of his own failure, Kate must have given her friend. His immediate quarter of an hour there with the girl lighted up for him almost luridly such an inference; it was almost as if the other party to their remarkable understanding had been with them as they talked, had been hovering about, had dropped in to look after her work. The value of the work affected him as different from the moment he saw it so expressed in poor Milly. Since it was false that he was n't loved, so his right was quite quenched to figure on that ground as important; and if he did n't look out he should find himself appreciating in a way quite at odds with straightness the good faith of Milly's benevolence. *There* was the place for scruples; there the need absolutely to mind what he was about. If it was n't proper for him to enjoy consideration on a perfectly false footing, where was the guarantee that, if he kept on, he might n't soon himself pretend to the grievance in order not to miss the sweet? Consideration – from a charming girl – was soothing on whatever theory; and it did n't take him far to remember that he had himself as yet done nothing deceptive. It was Kate's description of him, his defeated state, it was none of his own; his responsibility would begin, as he might say, only with acting it out. The sharp point was, however, in the difference between acting and not acting; this difference in fact it was that made the case of conscience. He saw it with a certain alarm rise before him that everything was acting that was not speaking the particular word. 'If you like me because you think *she* does n't, it is n't a bit true; she *does* like me awfully!' – that would have been the particular word; which there were at the same time but too palpably such difficulties about his uttering. Would n't it be virtually as indelicate to challenge her as to leave her deluded? – and this quite apart from the exposure, so to speak, of Kate, as to whom it would constitute a kind of betrayal. Kate's design was something so extraordinarily special to Kate that he felt himself shrink from the complications involved in judging it. Not to give away the woman one loved, but to back her up in her mistakes – once they had gone a certain length – that was perhaps chief among the inevitabilities of the abjection of love. Loyalty was of course

supremely prescribed in presence of any design on her part,
however roundabout, to do one nothing but good.

(xx.vi.5, pp. 75–7)

In such passages James seems to take the ethics of liberal
humanism in fiction to the brink. Densher uses the familiar
language of bogus moral syllogism ('Since it was false') and of
elusive moral abstraction ('straightness', 'as pretty a case of
conscience') to rationalise the reverse of the 'good faith' he
imputes to Milly. In so doing, however, he finds himself in a
double bind. At one level this is emotional. Like so many of the
triangular relationships in *The Wings of the Dove*, the one between
Densher, Milly and Kate entails such dissimilar moral worlds
that ostensibly universal ethical words such as 'love' and 'loyalty'
seem not to be transposable from one situation to the next.
Loyalty to the 'extraordinary' plan Kate has fashioned is also
loyalty to an inimitable one. It entails treachery to Milly. At
another level the dilemma is both emotional and, as it were,
theoretical. The passage uses Densher to inquire after the moral
content of words and actions. The 'difference between acting and
not acting' is precisely what the users in this intensely
calculating world wish to appeal to. Milly can be duped by verbal
impression. Both Kate and Densher know this, and he comes
ultimately to recognise that what one means, what one says and
what one does are part of a moral continuum. Many situations
are, after all, verbal constructions; moreover, language is
intrinsically intentional: we use it to formulate, to explore and to
express the intentions we have.

This much James can reveal without undue recourse to
intrusive narration. The horror of making up to a sick girl is, after
all, what George Eliot calls 'a moral sentiment already in
activity'.[57] James knows he does not have to preach. He prefers to
depict bad faith and let it self-indict. The highly stylised energy of
Densher's ingenuity is oddly but powerfully effective here. The
formality of syntax and argumentative transition suggests a mind
already under highly conscious scrutiny – its own – whilst the
occasional lapse into awkward qualification ('once they had gone
a certain length') keeps the reader close to the character's field of
vision. Out of this slightly precious privacy, indeed, the reader
reconstructs a moral agent. He does much of the work. This agent
is powerfully poised between the 'sweet universality' (xix.v.7,

pp. 300–1) of human things that claims the exquisite Milly and something much more specific to time and place. The Venice in which Milly dies is an emblematic place of mercantilism, moods and romance. It is much more a symbol than George Eliot's Florence. Yet James does not deny the facts of history. His Venice, like George Eliot's Florence, is reimagined in order to picture recurrent moral situations in context, and to lend them the coherence that the reader brings from his own historically situated and shifting sense of time and place.

Conclusion

The various strands of this essay require that it conclude with a review of several themes.

In reading character in Eliot and James I have argued that we must concede the power of imaginative literature to extend and even produce authoritative images of human personality, and that some of the more persuasive images available retain an emphasis upon the centred, morally active and partially private individual person. The blur at the centre of my account no doubt concerns the individual so conceived: I cannot pronounce with any certainty upon the questions of essence, privacy and agency that remain recalcitrant problems to the philosophers, the social scientists and the psychologists. I do, however, believe that the innerness imputed to selves in an Eliot or James novel is a thing to be respected and that in formulating theories of the self we must query models which, either by a reordering of descriptive priorities, or an aggressive anti-humanism, serve to marginalise or deny it. If our theories cannot accommodate the complexities of selves, it is the theories that must be reconsidered. Anti-humanist attacks upon the substantial individual entail real dangers.

I have argued that Eliot's and James's fictional 'experiments' are a means of reconsidering available images of self, of asking what follows if we imaginatively explore various assumptions about choice, intersubjective knowledge and moral judgements. Both novelists use the novel to test the powers of an image of human individuality that we would now think of as (roughly) liberal-humanist. With this image they are essentially in sympathy; however, in probing it they invoke alternative premises that we would now associate with existentialism and phenomenology. What happens, they inquire, if we emphasise the decisiveness of individual choices, the subjectivity of individual perception and knowledge (even within personal relationships), and the ultimate sovereignty of the individual moral agent? George Eliot's answer is that we lose moral, social and psychological coherence. James, I believe, ultimately agrees; but his fictional flirtation with phenomenology is more daring, more sanguine and less apologetic than hers. His middle-phase novel *The Portrait of a Lady* subjectivises and so problematicises individual choice further than does George Eliot's final novel, *Daniel Deronda*, and his late fiction again extends the phenomenological premises further than she was prepared to do: *The Golden Bowl* acknowledges a more radical process of fictionalising in intersubjective relationships than does *Middlemarch*, and *The Wings of the Dove* concedes more to the isolated moral sovereignty of the individual than does *Romola*.

This drift towards phenomenology is surely typical of the English novel's evolution from Victorian modes to modernism,[1] and I have suggested that the transition from Eliot to James encapsulates this evolution in this respect, as in others. However, since the wider literary context is not a central concern here, readers will need to read this essay in conjunction with studies that take the broader view: Hardy's *The Appropriate Form*, Hochman's *The Test of Character*, Garrett's *Scene and Symbol from George Eliot to James Joyce*, Sergio Perosa's *Henry James and the Experimental Novel*, Patrick Swinden's *Unofficial Selves*,[2] and others. It must also be borne in mind that the particular pairings offered here, especially that of *The Portrait* and *Daniel Deronda*, to some extent distort the chronology to which historical surveys rightly appeal. Such, no doubt, are the liabilities of my method.

The method has, however, been chosen in order to point up philosophical and aesthetic correspondences and contrasts between Eliot and James. Their fiction, like their theories of the novel, reflects wide areas of agreement, but also significant deviations on James's part. In defining his creative individuality against Eliot's he proposes a less intrusive narrative persona in fiction, a greater dependence upon metaphor and symbolism as modes of characterisation, a more unified aesthetic structure for novels, and a more reticent moral emphasis.

Why should such revisions of our understanding of novels be so important? My suggestion here is that novels are a particularly complex and revealing form of narrative report upon the social, psychological and spiritual lives of individuals and that we can learn much about our varied potentialities if we are aware of the ways in which narrative structures express, mediate and report upon our experience. It may be, indeed, that the greatest novels are those which make us most richly and variously aware in just these ways, but without refusing our need for imaginative involvement. An Eliot or James novel has this capacity. It might of course be objected that the aesthetic and philosophical tensions I adduce in Eliot's and James's fiction in fact signal the failure of humanism, rather than its capacity to inform further and more satisfactory theories of the self; but I have tried to suggest that this is not a necessary implication.

Appendix: An Eliot and James Chronology

The following chronology gives only dates directly relevant to this study. Unless otherwise stated, James's writings on George Eliot are reprinted in Haight's *A Century of George Eliot Criticism*.

1819	George Eliot (Mary Anne Evans) born, 22 November.
1843	Henry James born, 15 April.
1846	Eliot translates Strauss's *Life of Jesus*.
1854	Eliot translates Feuerbach's *The Essence of Christianity*.
1856	Completes translation of Spinoza's *Ethics* (not published until 1981).
1857	Eliot publishes her first important work of fiction, *Scenes of Clerical Life*, in *Blackwood's Edinburgh Magazine*.
1859	*Adam Bede*.
	'The Lifted Veil' published in *Blackwood's* in July.
1860	*The Mill on the Floss*.
1861	*Silas Marner*.
1862–3	*Romola* appears in serial form in the *Cornhill Magazine*.
1863	*Romola* published.
1864	James publishes his first story in February.
1866	*Felix Holt the Radical*.
	James reviews *Felix Holt* in the *Nation* (16 Aug).
	James publishes an article, 'The Novels of George Eliot', surveying her fiction up to and including *Felix Holt*, in the *Atlantic Monthly* (Oct).
1868	'The Spanish Gypsy'.
	James reviews 'The Spanish Gypsy' in the *Nation*, VII (2 July) pp. 12–14.
	James again reviews 'The Spanish Gypsy' in the *North American Review* (Oct).
1869	First meeting between George Eliot and Henry James, 9 May.
1871	James's first novel, *Watch and Ward*, serialised August–December.
	Publication of *Middlemarch* commences in December; concludes in December 1872.
1873	James reviews *Middlemarch* in the *Galaxy* (Mar).
1874	'The Legend of Jubal and Other Poems'.
	James reviews 'The Legend of Jubal' in the *North American Review* (Oct).
1875	*A Passionate Pilgrim*, *Transatlantic Sketches* and James's first important novel, *Roderick Hudson*.

1876 *Daniel Deronda* appears in three parts, February–September.

James reviews first part of *Daniel Deronda* in the *Nation* (24 Feb).

The American commences serial publication in June; concludes in May 1877.

'*Daniel Deronda*: A Conversation', published in the *Atlantic Monthly* (Dec). (Repr. with revisions in *Partial Portraits*.)

1878 *French Poets and Novelists*.

Eliot and James meet for a second time, on 10 April.

A further meeting between Eliot and James on 21 April.

James reviews 'The Lifted Veil' and 'Brother Jacob' in the *Nation* (25 Apr).

The Europeans published in book form in England on 18 September.

Final meeting between Eliot and James, 1 November.

1878–80 The Cabinet Edition of *The Works of George Eliot*.

1879 James's biography of Hawthorne.

1880 *Washington Square*.

Impressions of Theophrastus Such.

The Portrait of a Lady commences serial publication in October; concludes in November 1881.

George Eliot dies, 22 December.

1881 *The Portrait of a Lady* published in book form.

1884 'The Art of Fiction'.

1885 James reviews Cross's *Life of George Eliot* in the *Atlantic Monthly* (May). (Repr. in *Partial Portraits*.)

The Bostonians.

The Princess Casamassima.

1888 *Partial Portraits*.

1893 *Essays in London and Elsewhere*.

1897 *What Maisie Knew*.

1898 *In the Cage*.

1901 *The Sacred Fount*.

1902 *The Wings of the Dove*.

1903 *The Ambassadors*.

1904 *The Golden Bowl*.

1905 *The Question of our Speech*.

1907–9 The New York Edition of The Novels and Tales of Henry James.

1911–14 James at work on autobiographical volumes. *The Middle Years*, containing his final recollections of George Eliot, published posthumously in 1917.

1914 *Notes on Novelists*.

1916 Henry James dies in London, 28 February.

Notes

The following abbreviations are used throughout:

GEL *The George Eliot Letters*, ed. G. S. Haight, 9 vols (New Haven, Conn.: Yale University Press, 1954–78).

HJL *Henry James Letters*, ed. Leon Edel, 4 vols (London: Macmillan, 1974–84).

INTRODUCTION

1 *HJL*, I, pp. 116–17.
2 *HJL*, II, p. 172.

CHAPTER 1. CHARACTER, NARRATION AND THE NOVEL

1 Henry James, 'The Art of Fiction', in *Partial Portraits* (London: Macmillan, 1888), intro. Leon Edel (Ann Arbor: University of Michigan Press, 1970) p. 392.
2 *GEL*, VI, p. 216.
3 *HJL*, II, p. 193.
4 Anne Jefferson and David Robey (eds), *Modern Literary Theory: A Comparative Introduction* (London: Batsford, 1982) p. 97.
5 Fredric Jameson, *The Prison-House of Language: A Critical Account of Structuralism and Russian Formalism* (Princeton, NJ: Princeton University Press, 1972) p. vii.
6 Ibid., p. 140.
7 Roger Fowler, *Linguistics and the Novel* (London: Methuen, 1977) p. 35.
8 Jameson, *The Prison-House of Language*, p. 139. See, however, his attack on humanism in *The Political Unconscious: Narrative as a Socially Symbolic Act* (London: Methuen, 1981) ch. 1.
9 See, for example, Jacques Derrida on speech and 'the myth of consciousness' in *Of Grammatology*, tr. Gayatri Chakravorty Spivak (Baltimore: Johns Hopkins University Press, 1976) p. 166, and Lacan on 'ex-centricity' in *Écrits*, tr. Alan Sheridan (London: Tavistock, 1977) p. 171.
10 See, for example, *Of Grammatology*, p. 65.
11 See, for example, Roland Barthes's (post-structural) discussion of the semic code in *S/Z*, tr. Richard Miller (New York: Hill and Wang, 1975).
12 Raymond Williams, *Marxism and Literature* (Oxford: Oxford University Press, 1977) p. 168.

13 Ludwig Wittgenstein, *Philosophical Investigations*, tr. G. E. M. Anscombe (Oxford: Basil Blackwell, 1968).

14 Ibid., p. 11e. See Martin Price, *Forms of Life: Character and Moral Imagination in the Novel* (New Haven, Conn.: Yale University Press, 1983).

15 Roland Barthes, *Writing Degree Zero*, tr. Annette Lavers and Colin Smith (New York: Hill and Wang, 1967) pp. 67–8.

16 Charles Altieri, *Act and Quality: A Theory of Literary Meaning and Humanistic Understanding* (Amherst: University of Massachusetts Press, 1981) p. 25.

17 Ibid., p. 127.

18 Ibid., see esp. ch. 3.

19 Ibid., p. 47.

20 Ibid., p. 130.

21 Ibid., p. 131.

22 Ibid., p. 10.

23 G. J. Warnock, *The Object of Morality* (London: Methuen, 1971) p. 15.

24 C. B. Macpherson, *Democratic Theory: Essays in Retrieval* (Oxford: Clarendon, 1973) p. 53.

25 Ibid.

26 Jameson, *The Political Unconscious*, p. 152.

27 See Terry Eagleton's account of Adorno, Althusser, Macherey and Benjamin in *Marxism and Literary Criticism* (London: Methuen, 1976). Mikhail Bakhtin's *Problems of Dostoevsky's Poetics*, tr. Caryl Emerson (Minneapolis: Univ. of Minnesota Press, 1984) is especially relevant to this study of character.

28 Terry Eagleton, *Criticism and Ideology: A Study in Marxist Literary Theory* (London: New Left Books, 1976) p. 101.

29 See references to Alisdair MacIntyre's moral theory below.

30 Others who have been described as 'liberal' or 'neo-liberal' critics include Barbara Hardy, W. J. Harvey, Patrick Swinden, John Bayley and Lionel Trilling. These critics are 'theoretical' in varying and quite often dissimilar ways. The most remarkable critical appreciations to have emerged from this group are perhaps Bayley's writings on Shakespeare, Tolstoy, Pushkin and others, where he argues for a literature of loving indeterminacy centred on character.

31 Iris Murdoch, 'Against Dryness', in Malcolm Bradbury (ed.), *The Novel Today* (London: Fontana, 1977) p. 29.

32 Ibid.

33 Ibid., p. 30.

34 Ibid.

35 See Barthes on 'the Book (of culture, of life, of life as culture)', *S/Z*, p. 21.

36 Alasdair MacIntyre, *After Virtue: A Study in Moral Theory* (London: Duckworth, 1981) p. 57.

37 See MacIntyre's postscript to the 2nd ed.

38 MacIntyre, *After Virtue*, p. 26.

39 Ibid., pp. 150–1.

40 Ibid., p. 30.

41 Ibid., p. 31.

42 Terry Eagleton, *Literary Theory: An Introduction* (Oxford: Basil Blackwell, 1983) pp. 112–13.

43 MacIntyre, *After Virtue*, p. 203. See also Barbara Hardy's more specifically literary account, *Tellers and Listeners: The Narrative Imagination* (London: Athlone Press, 1975).

44 See Alasdair MacIntyre's volume on the concept of the unconscious: *The Unconscious: A Conceptual Analysis* (London: Routledge and Kegan Paul, 1958).

45 Iris Murdoch, *The Sovereignty of Good* (London: Routledge and Kegan Paul, 1970).

46 Ibid., p. 2.

47 Ibid., p. 42

48 Ibid., p. 20.

49 Ibid., p. 44.

50 Ibid., p. 14.

51 Ibid., p. 33.

52 Jameson, *The Prison-House of Language*, pp. 109–110.

53 Jacques Lacan, 'The Mirror Stage as Formative of the Function of the I as Revealed in Psychoanalytic Experience', in *Écrits*, ch. 1, is perhaps the clearest discussion.

54 MacIntyre, *After Virtue*, p. 203.

55 Murdoch, *The Sovereignty of Good*, p. 29.

56 Immanuel Kant, *Groundwork of the Metaphysic of Morals*, tr. H. J. Paton (New York: Harper and Row, 1964) p. 100.

57 Thomas Docherty, *Reading (Absent) Character: Towards a Theory of Characterization in Fiction* (Oxford: Clarendon Press, 1983).

58 See two other important studies by C. B. Macpherson: *The Political Theory of Possessive Individualism* (London: Oxford University Press, 1962) and *The Life and Times of Liberal Democracy* (London: Oxford University Press, 1977).

59 See John Goode's Marxist attack on the Kantian liberalism of W. J. Harvey's *Character and the Novel* (London: Chatto and Windus, 1965): 'Character and Henry James', *New Left Review*, Nov–Dec 1966, pp. 55–75.

CHAPTER 2. TWO VIEWS OF THE NOVEL: ELIOT AND JAMES ON THE NOVEL, JAMES ON GEORGE ELIOT

1 *The Letters of Henry James*, ed. P. Lubbock, 2 vols (London: Macmillan, 1920) II, p. 102.

2 For surveys see Richard Stang, *The Theory of the Novel in England, 1850–1870* (London: Routledge and Kegan Paul, 1959); and Kenneth Graham, *English Criticism of the Novel 1865–1900* (London: Oxford University Press, 1966).

3 See Stang, *Theory of the Novel in England*, pt i, ch. 7; and W. J. Harvey, *The Art of George Eliot* (London: Chatto and Windus, 1961) ch. 2.

4 M. H. Abrams, *The Mirror and the Lamp: Romantic Theory and the Critical Tradition* (London: Oxford University Press, 1953).

5 Samuel Taylor Coleridge, *Biographia Literaria*, ed. George Watson (London: Dent, 1975) p. 91.

6 Sally Shuttleworth, *George Eliot and Nineteenth-Century Science: The Make-Believe of a Beginning* (Cambridge: Cambridge University Press, 1984).

7 On romantic and realist elements in George Eliot's fiction see U. C. Knoepflmacher, *George Eliot's Early Novels: The Limits of Realism* (Berkeley, Calif., and Los Angeles: University of California Press, 1968).

8 See one of George Eliot's most detailed comments on Kant's epistemology in *Essays of George Eliot*, ed. Thomas Pinney (New York: Columbia University Press, 1963) pp. 150–1.

9 Raymond Williams considers this problem in relation to George Eliot's fiction in *The City and the Country* (Frogmore, Herts: Paladin, 1975) ch. 16.

10 See Williams's discussion of the relationships between social convention and narrative structure in *Marxism and Literature*, pp. 173–9.

11 See Jonathan Culler, *Structuralist Poetics: Structuralism, Linguistics and the Study of Literature* (London: Routledge and Kegan Paul, 1975) ch. 7.

12 Dorrit Cohn, *Transparent Minds: Narrative Modes for Presenting Consciousness in Fiction* (Princeton, NJ: Princeton University Press, 1978).

13 See the comparative discussions of George Eliot and James in Peter Garrett, *Scene and Symbol from George Eliot to James Joyce: Studies in Changing Fictional Mode* (New Haven, Conn.: Yale University Press, 1969); Barbara Hardy, *The Appropriate Form: An Essay on the Novel* (London: Athlone Press, 1971) chs 1 and 2; and Harvey, *The Art of George Eliot*, ch. 1.

14 For detailed studies of narrative point of view and its implications see Wayne C. Booth, *The Rhetoric of Fiction* (Chicago: University of Chicago Press, 1961); and Boris Uspensky, *A Poetics of Composition: The Structure of the Artistic Text and Typology of a Compositional Form*, tr. Valentina Zavarin and Susan Wittig (Berkeley, Calif., and Los Angeles: University of California Press, 1973).

15 *Essays of George Eliot*, p. 367.

16 *GEL*, IV, p. 49.

17 *Essays of George Eliot*, p. 325.

18 Ibid., p. 270.

19 Ibid., p. 262.

20 Ibid., p. 444.

21 Ibid., p. 270.

22 K. M. Newton, *George Eliot: Romantic Humanist. A Study of the Philosophical Structure of her Novels* (London: Macmillan, 1981) p. 55.

23 *Essays of George Eliot*, p. 451.

24 Ibid., p. 270.

25 Ibid., p. 288.

26 Ibid., p. 433.

27 Ibid.

28 Ibid.

29 Ibid., p. 270.

30 Ibid., pp. 272–3.

31 *GEL*, IV, p. 472.

32 *Essays of George Eliot*, p. 382. In *The Sovereignty of Good* Murdoch argues that 'Love is knowledge of the individual' (p. 28).

33 *Essays of George Eliot*, p. 271.

34 See Chapter 3's discussion of deconstruction and textual disunity; also John Bayley's study *The Uses of Division: Unity and Disharmony in Literature* (London: Chatto and Windus, 1976); and David Lodge, *The Modes of Modern*

Writing: Metaphor, Metonymy, and the Typology of Modern Literature (London: Edward Arnold, 1977).

35 See Barbara Hardy's excellent account in *The Novels of George Eliot: A Study in Form* (London: Athlone Press, 1963) ch. 8.

36 *GEL*, v, p. 459.

37 *Essays of George Eliot*, p. 446.

38 By metonymy I mean a rhetorical figure whereby the term for one thing is applied to another with which it has become closely associated in experience. The implications of the term for nineteenth century and modernist fictional modes is explored in Lodge's *The Modes of Modern Writing*. Metonymic modes of characterisation will tend towards inclusiveness and realism.

39 See Ruby V. Redinger's discussion of androgyny and narration in *George Eliot: The Emergent Self* (London: Bodley Head, 1976) ch. 1.

40 *Essays of George Eliot*, p. 445.

41 Ibid., p. 362.

42 Ibid., p. 287.

43 *GEL*, iv, p. 97.

44 Ibid., p. 300.

45 On beginnings: 'Men can do nothing without the make-believe of a beginning' (*Daniel Deronda*, i.1, p. 3); on endings: 'Every limit is a beginning as well as an ending' (*Middlemarch*, iii, p. 455; and *GEL*, ii, p. 324).

46 See Barbara Hardy, *The Novels of George Eliot*, ch. 2.

47 *Essays of George Eliot*, p. 264.

48 *GEL*, vi, p. 216.

49 Henry James, *Autobiography*, ed. Frederick W. Dupee (Princeton, NJ: Princeton University Press, 1956) p. 574.

50 Repr. in G. S. Haight (ed.), *A Century of George Eliot Criticism* (London: Methuen, 1966) p. 87.

51 See Harold Bloom: *The Anxiety of Influence: A Theory of Poetry* (New York: Oxford University Press, 1973); *A Map of Misreading* (New York: Oxford University Press, 1975); *The Breaking of the Vessels* (Chicago: University of Chicago Press, 1982); *Poetry and Repression* (New Haven, Conn.: Yale University Press, 1976).

52 James, *Autobiography*, p. 574. All subsequent references to the *Autobiography* relate to pp. 573–85, i.e. ch. 5 of *The Middle Years*.

53 See Leon Edel's biography, *Henry James*, 5 vols (London: Rupert Hart-Davis, 1953–72) ii: *The Conquest of London*, pp. 370–3. Also G. S. Haight's *George Eliot: A Biography* (London: Oxford University Press, 1968) pp. 416–17 and 513–14.

54 *HJL*, i, pp. 116–17.

55 Not all feminists agree on the inadequacy of Bloom's theory. In *The Madwoman in the Attic* (New Haven, Conn.: Yale University Press, 1979), Sandra Gilbert and Susan Gubar endorse Bloom's theory on the grounds that 'literary history *is* overwhelmingly male' (p. 47).

56 James, *Partial Portraits*, p. 81.

57 Paul B. Armstrong, *The Phenomenology of Henry James* (Chapel Hill: University of North Carolina Press, 1983).

58 For introductions to phenomenology, see Robert R. Magliola, *Phenomenology*

and Literature: An Introduction (West Lafayette, Ind.: Purdue University Press, 1977) and Mary Warnock, *Existentialism* (London: Oxford University Press, 1970).

59 *HJL*, ii, p. 424.
60 James, *Partial Portraits*, p. 49.
61 Henry James, *The House of Fiction*, ed. Leon Edel (London: Mercury Books, 1962) p. 259.
62 Ibid., p. 266.
63 James, *Partial Portraits*, p. 51.
64 Ibid., p. 50.
65 Ibid., p. 46.
66 Haight (ed.), *A Century of George Eliot Criticism*, p. 93.
67 Ibid., p. 89.
68 Ibid., p. 57.
69 Ibid., p. 48.
70 James, *Partial Portraits*, p. 91.
71 See '*Daniel Deronda*: A Conversation', ibid., ch. 3.
72 James, *The House of Fiction*, p. 264.
73 See esp. the discussion in his Preface to *The Portrait of a Lady* in *The Art of the Novel: Critical Prefaces*, ed. R. P. Blackmur (New York: Charles Scribner's Sons, 1934).
74 James, *Partial Portraits*, p. 50.
75 Ibid., p. 51.
76 Haight (ed.) *A Century of George Eliot Criticism*, p. 39.
78 See Warnock, *Existentialism*.
79 Henry James, *Essays in London and Elsewhere* (London: Osgood, McIlvaine, 1893) p. 158.
80 Two more detailed accounts are Sarah B. Daugherty, *The Literary Criticism of Henry James* (Columbus, Ohio: Ohio University Press, 1981), and 'Henry James' in René Wellek, *A History of Modern Criticism 1750–1950*, 4 vols (Cambridge: Cambridge University Press, 1955–65) iv, pp. 213–37.
81 James, *Partial Portraits*, pp. 257–8.
82 Ibid., pp. 78–9.
83 Ibid., p. 228.
84 Henry James, *The Question of our Speech* [*and*] *The Lesson of Balzac* (Boston, Mass., and New York: Houghton Mifflin, 1905) p. 80.
85 James, *Partial Portraits*, p. 390.
86 James, *The House of Fiction*, p. 246.
87 James, *Partial Portraits*, p. 217.
88 *HJL*, iv, p. 770.
89 James, *The Art of the Novel*, p. 149.
90 Ibid., p. 120.
91 Ibid., p. 29.
92 *The Letters of Henry James*, ed. Lubbock, ii, p. 11.
93 See the discussion of romance in the Preface to *The American*, in *The Art of the Novel*.
94 James, *Partial Portraits*, p. 406.
95 Ibid., p. 388.

96 Martin Heidegger, *Being and Time*, tr. John Macquarrie and Edward Robinson (Oxford: Basil Blackwell, 1962).
97 James, *The Art of the Novel*, pp. 46–7.
98 Armstrong, *The Phenomenology of Henry James*, ch. 1.
99 James, *Essays in London and Elsewhere*, p. 149.
100 See among James's various discussions of Turgenev the essay in *French Poets and Novelists* (London: Macmillan, 1878) pp. 269–320.
101 See James's review of *The Temptation of St Anthony* in *Literary Reviews and Essays*, ed. Albert Modell (New York: Grove Press, 1957) p. 146.
102 Henry James, *Hawthorne*, ed. Tony Tanner (London: Macmillan, 1967) p. 64.
103 Henry James, *Notes on Novelists, with Some Other Notes* (London: Dent, 1914) p. 225.
104 James, *Partial Portraits*, p. 392.
105 James, *The Art of the Novel*, p. 53.
106 Ibid., p. 55.
107 Ibid., p. 118.
108 *HJL*, IV, p. 619.
109 James, *The Art of the Novel*, p. 84.
110 John Bayley, *Tolstoy and the Novel* (London: Chatto and Windus, 1966).
111 James, *Partial Portraits*, p. 378.
112 Henry James, *Notes and Reviews*, ed. Pierre de Chaignon la Rose (Cambridge, Mass.: Dunster House, 1921) p. 18.
113 James, *Partial Portraits*, p. 140.
114 Iris Murdoch, *Sartre: Romantic Rationalist* (London: Collins, 1967) p. 9. (First published 1953.)
115 James, *Partial Portraits*, p. 389; see Armstrong's discussion of 'the teleology of the impression', in *The Phenomenology of Henry James*, pp. 40–9.
116 Ibid., p. 59.
117 Ibid., p. 40.
118 James, *The Art of the Novel*, p. 328.
119 Henry James, 'Dallas Galbraith', *Nation*, VII (22 Oct 1868) p. 331.
120 James, *The Art of the Novel*, p. 329.
121 James, *Notes on Novelists*, p. 275.
122 James, *Partial Portraits*, p. 116.
123 *HJL*, IV, p. 513.
124 James, *French Poets and Novelists*, p. 256.
125 Ibid., p. 81.
126 James, *Partial Portraits*, p. 256.
127 Ibid., p. 106.
128 Ibid., p. 402.
129 See, for instance, on 'lucid reflector[s]', James, *Notes on Novelists*, p. 322, and *The Art of the Novel*, pp. 300–1; on '*ficelles*', ibid., pp. 55, 322.
130 Ibid., p. 111.
131 James, *Hawthorne*, p. 120.
132 James, *Partial Portraits*, pp. 317–18.
133 Ibid., p. 72.
134 James, *French Poets and Novelists*, p. 123.

135 James, *Partial Portraits*, p. 105.
136 James, *The Question of our Speech* [*and*] *The Lesson of Balzac*, p. 97.
137 James, *The Art of the Novel*, p. 62.
138 James, *Hawthorne*, p. 61.

CHAPTER 3. CHOICE: *DANIEL DERONDA* AND *THE PORTRAIT OF A LADY*

 1 Martin Buber, *I and Thou*, tr. Walter Kaufmann (Edinburgh: T. and T. Clark, 1970) p. 54.
 2 *GEL*, VI, p. 304.
 3 In George Eliot, *The Impressions of Theophrastus Such*, pp. 257–93.
 4 See Graham Martin's essay '*Daniel Deronda*: George Eliot and Political Change', in Barbara Hardy (ed.), *Critical Essays on George Eliot* (London: Routledge and Kegan Paul, 1970) pp. 133–150.
 5 William Baker, *George Eliot and Judaism* (Salzburg: Universität Salzburg, 1975). My own sketchy account is much indebted to Baker's detailed work. See also Graham Handley, Introduction to the Clarendon Edition of *Daniel Deronda*.
 6 *GEL*, VI, p. 196.
 7 Gillian Beer, *Darwin's Plots: Evolutionary Narrative in Darwin, George Eliot and Nineteenth-Century Fiction* (London: Routledge and Kegan Paul, 1983).
 8 *GEL*, II, p. 153.
 9 Ludwig Feuerbach, *The Essence of Christianity*, tr. Marian Evans [George Eliot], 2nd edn (London: Trübner, 1881) p. 112.
10 *GEL*, I, pp. 246–7.
11 See Julius Carlebach's account of attitudes to Judaism in Feuerbach, Strauss, Marx and others in *Karl Marx and the Radical Critique of Judaism* (London: Routledge and Kegan Paul, 1978).
12 See Baker, *George Eliot and Judaism*, ch. 6; and Handley, Introduction to Clarendon Edition of *Daniel Deronda*, p. xiii.
13 Cecil Roth, *A History of the Jews* (New York: Schocken, 1970) ch. 29.
14 See ibid., book V; and, on earlier developments, Michael A. Meyer, *The Origins of the Modern Jew: Jewish Identity and European Culture in Germany, 1749–1824* (Detroit: Wayne State University Press, 1967).
15 Jean-Paul Sartre, *Anti-Semite and Jew*, tr. George J. Becker (New York: Schocken, 1965) pp. 78–9.
16 Ibid., p. 67.
17 *Essays of George Eliot*, pp. 437–48.
18 Kant, *Groundwork of the Metaphysic of Morals*, p. 110.
19 Beer, *Darwin's Plots*, p. 207.
20 Kant, *Groundwork of the Metaphysic of Morals*, p. 79.
21 Jean-Paul Sartre, *Existentialism and Humanism*, tr. Philip Mairet (London: Eyre Methuen, 1973) p. 55.
22 Jean-Paul Sartre, *Being and Nothingness*, tr. Hazel E. Barnes (New York: Philosophical Library, [1985]) p. 440. For a discussion of *Daniel Deronda* and

existentialism, see Jean Sudrann, '*Daniel Deronda* and the Landscape of Exile', *English Literary History*, xxxvii (1970) pp. 433–55.

23 Compare F. R. Leavis on the novel's 'fairly neatly separable masses' – *The Great Tradition* (Harmondsworth: Pelican, 1972) p. 97 – with Maurice Beebe, ' "Visions are Creators": The Unity of *Daniel Deronda*', *Boston University Studies in English*, i (1955) pp. 166–77, and David R. Carroll, 'The Unity of *Daniel Deronda*', *Essays in Criticism*, ix (1959) pp. 369–80.

24 In this connection see George Eliot's strictures upon 'silly novels by lady novelists' (*Essays of George Eliot*, pp. 300–24).

25 *GEL*, vi, p. 301.

26 John Bayley, 'The Pastoral of Intellect', in Hardy (ed.), *Critical Essays on George Eliot*, x.

27 Beer, *Darwin's Plots*, p. 195.

28 Eliot, *The Impressions of Theophrastus Such*, p. 270.

29 *GEL*, vi, p. 290.

30 Sartre, *Anti-Semite and Jew*, p. 34.

31 Ibid., p. 62.

32 Ibid., p. 57.

33 Ibid., ch. 3.

34 Ibid., p. 39.

35 The work of the Israeli semiotician Itamar Even-Zohar is of great interest here: see, for example, his article 'The Emergence of a Native Hebrew Culture in Palestine: 1882–1948' in *Studies in Zionism*, no. 4 (Oct 1981) pp. 167–84.

36 Louis Jacobs, *A Jewish Theology* (New York: Behrman House, 1973).

37 A standard reference work on Judaism is the *Encyclopedia Judaica*, 16 vols (Jerusalem, 1971–2).

38 See Baker, *George Eliot and Judaism*, pp. 170–80.

39 The more complete formulation is also in *GEL*, vi, p. 216.

40 Beer, *Darwin's Plots*, p. 215. On Judaic sources for Gwendolen, p. 199.

41 James in fact misquotes George Eliot. Her phrase is 'delicate vessels' (*Daniel Deronda*, ii.11, p. 109).

42 Heidegger, *Being and Time*, p. 174.

43 By metaphor I mean a rhetorical figure whereby a term denoting one thing, quality or action is substituted for another term with which it is not logically associated in experience. Metaphoric techniques of characterisation are in this view less inclusive and 'realistic' than metonymic ones. See Lodge, *The Modes of Modern Writing*, pt. ii, ch. 1, on the comparison of the two modes in fiction.

44 *GEL*, i, p. 242.

45 Feuerbach, *The Essence of Christianity*, p. 158.

46 G. H. Lewes, *Problems of Life and Mind. First Series: The Foundations of a Creed*, 2 vols (London: Trübner, 1874–5) i, pp. 144–5; cited in Shuttleworth, *George Eliot and Nineteenth-Century Science*, p. 20.

47 G. H. Lewes, *Problems of Life and Mind. Third Series*, 2 vols (London: Trübner, 1879) ii, p. 365; cited in Shuttleworth, *George Eliot and Nineteenth-Century Science*, p. 20.

48 G. H. Lewes, 'Spiritualism and Materialism', *Fortnightly Review*, n.s., xix

(1876) p. 716; cited in Shuttleworth, *George Eliot and Nineteenth-Century Science*, p. 20.

49 Sartre, *Being and Nothingness*, p. 572.
50 Sartre, *Existentialism and Humanism*, p. 48.
51 Ibid., p. 32.
52 Ibid., p. 53.
53 See Barbara Hardy's discussion of the 'didactic hero', in *The Novels of George Eliot*, p. 56.
54 Sartre, *Existentialism and Humanism*, p. 54.
55 See George Levine, 'Determinism and Responsibility', repr. Haight (ed.), *A Century of George Eliot Criticism*, pp. 349–60.
56 *GEL*, vi, p. 166.
57 Ibid., p. 98.
58 Ibid.
59 *GEL*, ii, p. 403.
60 William James, 'The Dilemma of Determinism', in *The Will to Believe and Other Essays in Popular Philosophy* (Cambridge, Mass.: Harvard University Press, 1979) p. 117.
61 S. L. Goldberg, 'Morality and Literature; with some Reflections on *Daniel Deronda*', in *Critical Review*, xxii (1980) pp. 3–20 (quotation from p. 5).
62 Ibid., p. 7.
63 MacIntyre, *After Virtue*, p. 57.
64 *GEL*, v, p. 314.
65 Newton, *George Eliot: Romantic Humanist*, p. 172.
66 The same attitude is obvious in the depiction of Godfrey Cass in *Silas Marner* and Lydgate in *Middlemarch*.
67 Sartre, *Being and Nothingness*, p. 33.
68 Of Byron's grand-niece George Eliot writes, 'It made me cry to see her young fresh face among the hags and brutally stupid men around her' (*GEL*, v, p. 314).
69 Beer, *Darwin's Plots*, p. 218.
70 Ibid., p. 230.
71 Ibid., p. 218.
72 See Sartre's definition of 'bad faith' in *Being and Nothingness*, p. 49.
73 See Robert Preyer's essay 'Beyond the Liberal Imagination: Vision and Unreality in *Daniel Deronda*', *Victorian Studies*, iv, no. 1 (Sep 1960) pp. 33–54.
74 Sartre, *Being and Nothingness*, p. 489.
75 See Dorrit Cohn, *Transparent Minds: Narrative Modes for Presenting Consciousness in Fiction* (Princeton, NJ: Princeton University Press, 1978) ch. 3.
76 Ernest Jones, *Sigmund Freud: Life and Work*, 3 vols (London: Hogarth Press, 1953–7) i, p. 191.
77 Sartre, *Existentialism and Humanism*, p. 26.
78 Lionel Trilling, *Sincerity and Authenticity* (London: Oxford University Press, 1972).
79 Beer, *Darwin's Plots*, p. 225.
80 Heidegger, *Being and Time*, p. 235.
81 Sartre, *Being and Nothingness*, p. 137.

82 Heidegger, *Being and Time*, p. 248.

83 Sartre, *Being and Nothingness*, p. 60.

84 See Lionel Trilling's discussion of *Little Dorrit* in *The Opposing Self* (London: Secker and Warburg, 1955) pp. 50–65.

85 Julius Guttmann, *Philosophies of Judaism*, tr. D. W. Silverman (New York: Schocken, 1973) pp. 143–4.

86 Harold Bloom, *Kabbalah and Criticism* (New York: Continuum, 1983) and *The Breaking of the Vessels*; Gershom Scholem, 'Kabbalah', in *Encyclopaedia Judaica*.

87 Cynthia Chase, 'The Decomposition of the Elephants: Double-Reading *Daniel Deronda*', in *PMLA*, xciii, no. 2 (Mar 1978) pp. 215–27.

88 Ibid., p. 219.

89 The relation between deconstruction and Kabbalah appears problematic: Bloom asserts a corrective logocentrism whilst also conceding that his intertextual view of poetic transmission displaces and decentres 'meaning' infinitely (*Kabbalah and Criticism*, p. 53).

90 Lionel Trilling, *Speaking of Literature and Society*, ed. Diana Trilling (Oxford: Oxford University Press, 1982) p. 75.

91 Edgar Rosenberg, *From Shylock to Svengali: Jewish Stereotypes in English Fiction* (Stanford, Calif.: Stanford University Press, 1960) p. 152.

92 MacIntyre, *After Virtue*, ch. 3.

93 See Robert C. Holub's recent account *Reception Theory: A Critical Introduction* (London: Methuen, 1984).

94 Wolfgang Iser, *The Act of Reading: A Theory of Aesthetic Response* (London: Routledge and Kegan Paul, 1978).

95 Ibid., p. 70.

96 Ibid., p. 53.

97 Ibid., p. 146.

98 Beer, *Darwin's Plots*, p. 155.

99 Leavis, *The Great Tradition*, p. 103.

100 See Buber's discussion of Feuerbach in *Between Man and Man*, tr. Ronald Gregor Smith (London: Fontana, 1961) esp. p. 46.

101 The philosophical references in Buber's in *I and Thou* are: Descartes, p. 73; Kant, pp. 143–4; existentialism, p. 133.

102 Ibid., p. 115.

103 Ibid., p. 67.

104 Ibid., p. 77.

105 Ibid., p. 129.

106 Ibid., p. 62.

107 Ibid., p. 78.

108 Ibid., p. 111.

109 Sartre, *Being and Nothingness*, p. 136.

110 Ibid.

111 Buber, *I and Thou*, p. 113.

112 Christian D. Ginsburg, *The Kabbalah: Its Doctrines, Development, and Literature* (London: George Routledge and Sons, 1925) p. 112.

113 Repr. in Haight (ed.), *A Century of George Eliot Criticism*, pp. 92–3.

114 *HJL*, ii, p. 30.

115 Since I shall be quoting something like forty times from an eighteen-page

article ('The Conversation' occupies pp. 65–93 of *Partial Portraits* and has been widely reprinted), it will be impracticable to itemise page references. The reader is advised to consult James's text.

116 James, *The House of Fiction*, p. 33.
117 Haight (ed.), *A Century of George Eliot Criticism*, p. 93.
118 Ibid., p. 92.
119 James, *Partial Portraits*, p. 52.
120 Ibid.
121 *HJL*, II, pp. 96–7.
122 See his famous essay 'Maule's Well, or Henry James and the Relation of Morals to Manners', in Yvor Winters, *In Defense of Reason* (Chicago: Swallow Press, 1937) pp. 300–43.
123 *HJL*, I, p. 363.
124 Here again I shall be quoting frequently from a brief and widely reprinted classic of James's criticism and will not list individual page references. Many editions of *The Portrait of a Lady* include the Preface; it occupies pp. 40–58 of *The Art of the Novel*.
125 See Bloom's discussion of intertextuality and influence in *A Map of Misreading*, ch. 1.
126 MacIntyre, *After Virtue*, pp. 176–7.
127 *Essays of George Eliot*, p. 451.
128 Haight (ed.), *A Century of George Eliot Criticism*, p. 57.
129 The title of Tony Tanner's well-known article, repr. in Tony Tanner (ed.), *Henry James: Modern Judgements* (London: Macmillan, 1968).
130 Umberto Eco, *A Theory of Semiotics* (Bloomington: Indiana University Press, 1979).
131 James, *The Art of the Novel*, p. 48.
132 Kant, *Groundwork of the Metaphysics of Morals*, p. 72.
133 T. S. Eliot, 'In Memory', *Little Review*, V, no. 4 (Aug 1918) p. 46.
134 MacIntyre, *After Virtue*, p. 23.
135 See Dorothea Krook, *The Ordeal of Consciousness in Henry James* (Cambridge: Cambridge University Press, 1962); Stephen Donadio, *Nietzsche, Henry James, and the Artistic Will* (New York: Oxford University Press, 1978); William Gass, *Fiction and the Figures of Life* (New York: Knopf, 1970); J. H. Raleigh, 'Henry James: The Poetics of Empiricism', in Tanner (ed.), *Henry James: Modern Judgements*; Armstrong, *The Phenomenology of Henry James*; and Richard A. Hocks, *Henry James and Pragmatic Thought: A Study in the Relationship between the Philosophy of William James and the Literature of Henry James* (Chapel Hill: University of North Carolina Press, 1974). Other influences on James's views were clearly the transcendentalists, the Puritans and their successors, and the French Naturalists.
136 *HJL*, IV, p. 383.
137 For a general introduction to William James's life and thought, see Ralph Barton Perry, *The Thought and Character of William James* (Cambridge, Mass.: Harvard University Press, 1935).
138 *HJL*, I, p. 125.
139 *HJL*, II, p. 424.
140 Ibid.

141 Henry James, *The Notebooks of Henry James*, ed. F. O. Matthiessen and Kenneth B. Murdock (New York: Oxford University Press, 1947) p. 15.
142 *HJL*, III, p. 146.
143 Leavis, *The Great Tradition*, p. 131.
144 James, *The Art of the Novel*, p. 57.
145 Ruth Bernard Yeazell, *Language and Knowledge in the Late Novels of Henry James* (Chicago: University of Chicago Press, 1976) ch. 2.
146 This account is indebted to Robert Liddell's *The Novels of George Eliot* (London: Duckworth, 1977).

CHAPTER 4. KNOWLEDGE: *MIDDLEMARCH* AND *THE GOLDEN BOWL*

1 *GEL*, I, p. 328.
2 *GEL*, III, p. 164.
3 Ibid., p. 376.
4 See, for example, Lacan, *Écrits*, ch. 5.
5 Ibid., ch. 1.
6 *Essays of George Eliot*, p. 413.
7 *GEL*, v, p. 380.
8 *GEL*, II, p. 156.
9 *GEL*, VI, p. 333–4.
10 George Levine, *The Realistic Imagination: English Fiction from Frankenstein to Lady Chatterley* (Chicago: University of Chicago Press, 1981).
11 Judith Wilt, *Ghosts of the Gothic: Austen, Eliot and Lawrence* (Princeton, NJ: Princeton University Press, 1980) p. 184.
12 See particularly Haight, *George Eliot: A Biography*; and Redinger, *George Eliot: The Emergent Self*.
13 Ibid., p. 314.
14 Herbert Spencer, *An Autobiography*, 2 vols (New York: Appleton, 1904) I, p. 459.
15 *GEL*, III, p. 119.
16 James, *The Art of the Novel*, p. 156.
17 James, *The House of Fiction*, p. 259.
18 Ibid., p. 264.
19 References to criticism in this paragraph are to Quentin Anderson, 'George Eliot in *Middlemarch*' in *The Penguin History of English Literature*, ed. Boris Ford, 7 vols (Harmondsworth: Pelican, 1954–1972) VI: *Dickens to Hardy* (1958); Raymond Williams, *The Country and the City* (London: Chatto and Windus, 1973); Eagleton, *Criticism and Ideology*; Rosemary Jackson, *Fantasy: The Literature of Subversion* (London: Methuen, 1981).
20 See Hardy, *The Novels of George Eliot*, esp. ch. 8.
21 James, *The House of Fiction*, p. 267.
22 *GEL*, v, p. 373.
23 *Essays of George Eliot*, pp. 287–8.

24 J. Hillis Miller, 'Ariadne's Thread: Repetition and the Narrative Line', *Critical Inquiry*, III (1976) p. 74.

25 Ibid.

26 J. Hillis Miller, 'Optic and Semiotic in *Middlemarch*', in *The Worlds of Victorian Fiction*, Harvard English Studies VI, ed. Jerome H. Buckley (Cambridge, Mass.: Harvard University Press, 1975) p. 144.

27 Ibid.

28 Ibid., p. 143.

29 Altieri, *Act and Quality*, p. 134. An interesting comparison here is K. M. Newton's discussion of 'signs', in *George Eliot: Romantic Humanist*, ch. 8.

30 Eliot, *The Impressions of Theophrastus Such*, pp. 254–5.

31 Beer, *Darwin's Plots*, p. 154.

32 Bayley, 'The Pastoral of Intellect', in Haight (ed.), *Critical Essays on George Eliot*, p. 207.

33 On the novel's evolution see Jerome Beaty, *'Middlemarch' from Notebook to Novel: A Study of George Eliot's Creative Method*, vol. XLVII of Illinois Studies in Language and Literature, ed. Harris F. Fletcher, John R. Frey and Joseph R. Smiley (Urbana: University of Illinois Press, 1960).

34 Beer, *Darwin's Plots*, p. 161.

35 Buber, *I and Thou*, p. 84.

36 Ibid.

37 See her discussion in Thomas Pinney, 'More Leaves from George Eliot's Notebook', *Huntington Library Quarterly*, XXIX (1965–6).

38 *Essays of George Eliot*, p. 287.

39 Sartre, *Being and Nothingness*, p. 229.

40 Hardy's essay 'Incompleteness and Implication: George Eliot's *Middlemarch*' originally appeared in *The Appropriate Form* and has recently been reprinted in *Particularities: Readings in George Eliot* (London: Peter Owen, 1982) pp. 15–36.

41 *GEL*, V, p. 376.

42 Robert Langbaum, *The Mysteries of Identity: A Theme in Modern Literature* (New York: Oxford University Press, 1977).

43 *GEL*, V, p. 441.

44 James, *The House of Fiction*, p. 267.

45 James, *The Art of the Novel*, p. 328.

46 James, *Essays in London and Elsewhere*, p. 131.

47 James, *Partial Portraits*, p. 133.

48 Ibid., p. 316. Sources for the references to Hawthorne, Balzac and Trollope that follow are given in initial citation in Chapter 2.

49 Henry James, *Letters to A. C. Benson and Auguste Monod*, ed. E. F. Benson (London: Elkin Mathews and Marrot; New York: Charles Scribner's Sons, 1930) p. 35.

50 Yeazell, *Language and Knowledge in the Late Novels of Henry James*, p. 3.

51 *HJL*, IV, p. 379. See also James's revealingly limited appraisals of Wells, Lawrence, Bennett and others in the late article 'The New Novel', repr. in *Notes on Novelists*, pp. 249–87.

52 James, *The Art of the Novel*, p. 330.

53 Ibid.

54 Ibid., p. 329.

55 J. A. Ward, *The Imagination of Disaster: Evil in the Fiction of Henry James* (Lincoln, Nebr.: University of Nebraska Press, 1961) p. 139.

56 Dorothea Krook (in *The Ordeal of Consciousness*) is one of many critics who interprets late James thus; however, R. B. J. Wilson disputes such a reading of *The Golden Bowl* in his penetrating and detailed commentary *Henry James's Ultimate Narrative: 'The Golden Bowl'* (St Lucia: University of Queensland Press, 1981). See his valuable survey on the novel's critical reception on this point (ch. 2).

57 On the ethics of love in James see Naomi Lebowitz, *The Imagination of Loving: Henry James's Legacy to the Novel* (Detroit: Wayne State University Press, 1965).

58 John Bayley argues in *The Characters of Love* (London: Constable, 1960) that through such a character as Maggie the novel implies that 'to be human is to be virtually unknown' (p. 238).

59 C. B. Cox, in *The Free Spirit: A Study of Liberal Humanism in the Novels of George Eliot, Henry James, E. M. Forster, Virginia Woolf, Angus Wilson* (London: Oxford University Press, 1963), sees George Eliot's humanism as expressing itself in the desire that 'characters should make new relationships with society' (p. 37), while James's is reflected in the fact that he 'ceaselessly investigates possible developments of the good life' (p. 38).

60 Krook, *The Ordeal of Consciousness*, p. 240. In *The Phenomenology of Henry James* Paul Armstrong argues that the novel is neither merely 'sordid' nor 'redemptive' (p. 139).

61 James, *The Art of the Novel*, p. 327.

62 Ibid., p. 328.

63 James, *The Question of our Speech [and] The Lesson of Balzac*, p. 10.

64 James, *The Art of the Novel*, pp. 328–9.

65 Ralf Norrman, *The Insecure World of Henry James's Fiction* (London: Macmillan, 1982).

66 Leo Bersani, 'The Narrator as Center in *The Wings of the Dove*', *Modern Fiction Studies*, VI (Summer 1960) p. 131. The theme is developed in Bersani's *A Future for Astyanax: Character and Desire in Literature* (Boston, Mass.: Little, Brown, 1969; London: Marion Boyars, 1978) ch. 5.

67 Peter K. Garrett, *Scene and Symbol from George Eliot to James Joyce* (New Haven, Conn.: Yale University Press, 1969) p. 103.

68 See Bakhtin's discussion of this and related features in *Problems of Dostoevsky's Poetics*.

69 In Tanner (ed.), *Henry James: Modern Judgements* (London: Macmillan, 1968) p. 292.

70 Armstrong, *The Phenomenology of Henry James*, p. 137.

71 Sartre, *Existentialism and Humanism*, p. 32.

72 Ibid., p. 33.

73 Ibid., p. 34.

74 James, *Notebooks*, p. 130.

75 Leavis, *The Great Tradition*, p. 185.

76 James, *The Art of the Novel*, p. 329.

77 James's less 'pastoral' use of flash-back techniques is apparent in comparing this description of Verver with the elaborate introduction to Lydgate in *Middlemarch*, ch. 15.

78 Yeazell, *Language and Knowledge in the Late Novels of Henry James*, ch. 2.
79 James, *The House of Fiction*, p. 260.
80 John Bayley aptly describes this as a 'complex antithetical pattern' between 'loving' and 'knowing' (*The Characters of Love*, p. 217).
81 Sartre, *Being and Nothingness*, p. 431.
82 Ibid., p. 375.
83 Ibid., pp. 408–9.
84 Ibid., p. 620.
85 See, for example, James's letter to Shaw about the theatre (*HJL*, iv, pp. 510–14).
86 Krook, *The Ordeal of Consciousness*, p. 320; Philip Weinstein, *Henry James and the Requirements of the Imagination* (Cambridge, Mass.: Harvard University Press, 1971) p. 193.
87 James, *The Art of the Novel*, p. 42.
88 Edith Wharton, *The Writing of Fiction* (New York: Octagon Books, 1966) p. 92. (First published 1924.)
89 Ora Segal, *The Lucid Reflector* (New Haven, Conn.: Yale University Press, 1969) p. 196.
90 Nicola Bradbury, *Henry James: The Later Novels* (Oxford: Clarendon Press, 1979) p. 150.

CHAPTER 5. MORALITY: *ROMOLA* AND *THE WINGS OF THE DOVE*

1 *GEL*, iv, p. 300; 'aesthetic teacher': *GEL*, vii, p. 44.
2 *Essays of George Eliot*, p. 213.
3 Ibid., p. 123.
4 *GEL*, iv, p. 103.
5 Ibid., p. 97.
6 *GEL*, vi, pp. 335–6.
7 *Essays of George Eliot*, p. 447.
8 *GEL*, iv, p. 97.
9 Niccolo Machiavelli, *The Prince*, tr. George Bull (Harmondsworth: Penguin, 1961) p. 97.
10 For a discussion of the Comtean background and other aspects of the novel see Avrom Fleishman, *The English Historical Novel: Walter Scott to Virginia Woolf* (Baltimore: Johns Hopkins University Press, 1971) ch. 6.
11 A more favourable view is given in Andrew Sanders, *The Victorian Historical Novel: 1840–1880* (London: Macmillan, 1978) ch. 8.
12 Baruch Hochman, *The Test of Character: From the Victorian Novel to the Modern* (Rutherford, NJ: Fairleigh Dickinson University Press, 1983).
13 Kant, *Groundwork of the Metaphysic of Morals*, p. 88.
14 Ibid., p. 67.
15 Shuttleworth, *George Eliot and Nineteenth-Century Science*, p. 106.
16 Many accounts of the novel centre on Romola rather than Tito. For instance, Carole Robinson in '*Romola*: A Reading of the Novel', *Victorian Studies*, vi

(Sep 1962), argues that 'the true conflicts of *Romola* occur within the heroine' (p. 30).

17 Hardy, *The Novels of George Eliot*, p. 77.
18 James, *French Poets and Novelists*, p. 18.
19 James, *The Art of the Novel*, p. 111.
20 James, *French Poets and Novelists*, p. 256.
21 James, *Partial Portraits*, p. 50.
22 Ibid., p. 49.
23 James, *French Poets and Novelists*, p. 114.
24 Haight (ed.), *A Century of George Eliot Criticism*, p. 42.
25 James, *Partial Portraits*, p. 55.
26 James, *Notes on Novelists*, p. 318.
27 Haight (ed.), *A Century of George Eliot Criticism*, p. 47.
28 Ibid., p. 39.
29 James, *Partial Portraits*, p. 55.
30 Ibid., p. 50.
31 Ibid., p. 51.
32 Ibid., p. 56.
33 Ibid., p. 54.
34 Haight (ed.), *A Century of George Eliot Criticism*, pp. 52–3.
35 James, *Partial Portraits*, p. 55.
36 Haight (ed.), *A Century of George Eliot Criticism*, p. 53.
37 Ibid., p. 48.
38 Ibid.
39 Booth, *The Rhetoric of Fiction*, p. 86. Booth's introduction to the Emerson translation of Bakhtin's *Problems of Dostoevsky's Poetics* constitutes a significant revision of the position outlined in *The Rhetoric of Fiction*. So, too, does his study *Critical Understanding: The Powers and Limits of Pluralism* (Chicago: University of Chicago Press, 1979).
40 Booth, *The Rhetoric of Fiction*, p. 112.
41 Ibid., p. 60.
42 Ibid., p. 28.
43 Ibid., pp. 272–3.
44 Against 'authorial silence': symbolism, p. 196; narrator as compelling as characters, p. 212; commentary limits indulgences, p. 83; commentary integrates fiction, p. 222; moral appraisal, pp. 174–5, 187, 189. (All references to *The Rhetoric of Fiction*.)
45 James, *Letters to Benson and Monod*, p. 35.
46 See John Goode's discussion of money and related matters in the novel: 'The Persuasive Mystery of Style: *The Wings of the Dove*', in John Goode (ed.), *The Air of Reality: New Essays on Henry James* (London: Methuen, 1972).
47 James, *The Art of the Novel*, p. 299.
48 The novel has aroused widespread critical disagreement. See, for example, Sallie Sears, *The Negative Imagination: Form and Perspective in the Novels of Henry James* (New York: Cornell University Press, 1968), where she argues that 'It is possible . . . to go through the novel and show the principal agents are not responsible for what happens; it is also possible to show that they are' (p. 85); and Quentin Anderson, *The American Henry James* (New Brunswick, NJ: Rutgers University Press, 1957), which contends that in the novel 'the

complexity lies simply in the notation of the shifting relations between things which are as definable as musical notes' (p. 244).

49 For one reading see George Sebouhian, 'The Transcendental Imagination of Merton Densher', *Modern Language Studies*, v (1975) pp 33–45.

50 Bradbury, *Henry James: The Later Novels*, p. 77.

51 Yeazell, *Language and Knowledge in the Late Novels of Henry James*, ch. 4.

52 Again, there is disagreement here. Jean Kimball, 'The Abyss and *The Wings of the Dove*', *Nineteenth-Century Fiction*, x (Mar 1956), believes that 'The real drama in *The Wings of the Dove* is the subjective drama, the entirely inward struggle for her own salvation which occupies Milly Theale during her time in London and Venice' (p. 296).

53 James, *The Art of the Novel*, p. 296.

54 Ibid., p. 299.

55 Ibid.

56 Ibid.

57 *Essays of George Eliot*, p. 270.

CONCLUSION

1 A point persuasively argued in Docherty's *Reading (Absent) Character*.

2 Sergio Perosa, *Henry James and the Experimental Novel* (New York: New York University Press, 1983); Patrick Swinden, *Unofficial Selves: Character in the Novel from Dickens to the Present Day* (London: Macmillan, 1973).

Bibliography

WORKS OF GEORGE ELIOT

The Works of George Eliot, Cabinet Edition, 24 vols (Edinburgh and London: William Blackwood, 1878–80).

Daniel Deronda, Clarendon Edition, ed. Graham Handley (Oxford: Clarendon Press, 1984).

Essays of George Eliot, ed. Thomas Pinney (London: Routledge and Kegan Paul, 1963).

Felix Holt the Radical, Clarendon Edition, ed. Fred C. Thomson (Oxford: Clarendon Press, 1980).

The George Eliot Letters, ed. Gordon S. Haight, 9 vols (New Haven, Conn.: Yale University Press, 1954–78).

The Mill on the Floss, Clarendon Edition, ed. Gordon S. Haight (Oxford: Clarendon Press, 1980).

Translation (under the name of Marian Evans) of Ludwig Feuerbach, *The Essence of Christianity* (London: Trübner, 1881).

WORKS OF HENRY JAMES

The Novels and Tales of Henry James, New York Edition, 24 vols (Charles Scribner's Sons, 1907–9; repr. 1961–5; reissued New York: Augustus M. Kelley, 1971).

The Art of the Novel: Critical Prefaces, ed. R. P. Blackmur (New York: Charles Scribner's Sons, 1934).

Autobiography [*A Small Boy and Others*; *Notes of a Son and Brother*; *The Middle Years*], ed. Frederick W. Dupee (Princeton, NJ: Princeton University Press, 1983).

The Bostonians, Bodley Head Edition, ed. Leon Edel (London: Bodley Head, 1967).

'Dallas Galbraith', *Nation*, VII (22 Oct 1868) pp. 330–1.

Essays in London and Elsewhere (London: Osgood, McIlvaine, 1893).

French Poets and Novelists (London: Macmillan, 1878).

Hawthorne, ed. Tony Tanner (London: Macmillan, 1967).

Henry James Letters, ed. Leon Edel, 4 vols (London: Macmillan, 1974–84).

The House of Fiction, ed. Leon Edel (London: Mercury Books, 1962).

The Letters of Henry James, ed. Percy Lubbock, 2 vols (London: Macmillan, 1920).

Letters to A. C. Benson and Auguste Monod, ed. E. F. Benson (London: Elkin Mathews and Marrot; New York: Charles Scribner's Sons, 1930).

Literary Reviews and Essays, ed. Albert Mordell (New York: Grove Press, 1979).

The Notebooks of Henry James, ed. F. O. Matthiessen and Kenneth B. Murdock (New York: Oxford University Press, 1947).

Notes and Reviews, ed. Pierre de Chaignon la Rose (Cambridge, Mass.: Dunster House, 1921).

Notes on Novelists, with Some Other Notes (London: Dent, 1914).

Partial Portraits (London: Macmillan, 1888) intro. Leon Edel (Ann Arbor: University of Michigan Press, 1970).

The Question of our Speech [and] The Lesson of Balzac (Boston, Mass., and New York: Houghton Mifflin, 1905).

The Sacred Fount, ed. Leon Edel (London: Rupert Hart-Davis, 1959).

WORKS ON GEORGE ELIOT

BOOKS

Baker, William, *George Eliot and Judaism* (Salzburg: Universität Salzburg, 1975).

Beaty, Jerome, *'Middlemarch' from Notebook to Novel: A Study of George Eliot's Creative Method*, vol. XLVII of Illinois Studies in Language and Literature, ed. Harris F. Fletcher, John R. Frey and Joseph R. Smiley (Urbana: University of Illinois Press, 1960).

Beer, Gillian, *Darwin's Plots: Evolutionary Narrative in Darwin, George Eliot and Nineteenth-Century Fiction* (London: Routledge and Kegan Paul, 1983).

Haight, Gordon S., *George Eliot: A Biography* (London: Oxford University Press, 1968).

——, (ed.), *A Century of George Eliot Criticism* (London: Methuen, 1966).

Hardy, Barbara, *The Novels of George Eliot: A Study in Form* (London: Athlone Press, 1963).

——, *Particularities: Readings in George Eliot* (London: Peter Owen, 1982).

——, (ed.), *Critical Essays on George Eliot* (London: Routledge and Kegan Paul, 1970).

Harvey, W. J., *The Art of George Eliot* (London: Chatto and Windus, 1961).

Knoepflmacher, U. C., *George Eliot's Early Novels: The Limits of Realism* (Berkeley, Calif., and Los Angeles: University of California Press, 1968).

Liddell, Robert, *The Novels of George Eliot* (London: Duckworth, 1977).

Newton, K. M., *George Eliot: Romantic Humanist. A Study of the Philosophical Structure of her Novels* (London: Macmillan, 1981).

Redinger, Ruby V., *George Eliot: The Emergent Self* (London: Bodley Head, 1976).

Shuttleworth, Sally, *George Eliot and Nineteenth-Century Science: The Make-Believe of a Beginning* (Cambridge: Cambridge University Press, 1984).

Wilt, Judith, *Ghosts of the Gothic: Austen, Eliot and Lawrence* (Princeton, NJ: Princeton University Press, 1980).

ARTICLES

Anderson, Quentin, 'George Eliot in *Middlemarch*', in *The Pelican Guide to English Literature*, ed. Boris Ford, 7 vols (London: Pelican, 1954–72) VI: *Dickens to Hardy* (1958) pp. 274–93.

Beebe, Maurice, ' "Visions are Creators": The Unity of *Daniel Deronda*', *Boston University Studies in English*, I (1955) pp. 166–77.

Carroll, David R., 'The Unity of *Daniel Deronda*', *Essays in Criticism*, IX (1959) pp. 369–80.

Chase, Cynthia, 'The Decomposition of the Elephants: Double-Reading *Daniel Deronda*', *PMLA*, cxiii, no. 2 (Mar 1978) pp. 215–27.

Goldberg, S. L., 'Morality and Literature; with some Reflections on *Daniel Deronda*', *Critical Review*, xxii (1980) pp. 3–20.

Miller, J. Hillis, 'Optic and Semiotic in *Middlemarch*', in *The Worlds of Victorian Fiction*, Harvard English Studies vi, ed. Jerome H. Buckley (Cambridge, Mass.: Harvard University Press, 1975) pp. 124–45.

Preyer, Robert, 'Beyond the Liberal Imagination: Vision and Unreality in *Daniel Deronda*', *Victorian Studies*, iv, no. 1 (Sep 1960) pp. 33–54.

Robinson, Carole, '*Romola*: A Reading of the Novel', *Victorian Studies*, vi (Sep 1962) pp. 29–42.

Sudrann, Jean, '*Daniel Deronda* and the Landscape of Exile', *ELH*, xxxvii (1970) pp. 433–55.

WORKS ON HENRY JAMES

BOOKS

Allen, Elizabeth, *A Woman's Place in the Novels of Henry James* (New York: St Martin's Press, 1984).

Anderson, Quentin, *The American Henry James* (New Brunswick, NJ: Rutgers University Press, 1957).

Armstrong, Paul B., *The Phenomenology of Henry James* (Chapel Hill: University of North Carolina Press, 1983).

Bradbury, Nicola, *Henry James: The Later Novels* (Oxford: Clarendon Press, 1979).

Daugherty, Sarah B., *The Literary Criticism of Henry James* (Columbus, Ohio: Ohio University Press, 1981).

Donadio, Stephen, *Nietzsche, Henry James, and the Artistic Will* (New York: Oxford University Press, 1978).

Edel, Leon, and Laurence, Dan H. (eds), *A Bibliography of Henry James* (London: Rupert Hart-Davis, 1957).

Gass, William H., *Fiction and the Figures of Life* (New York: Knopf, 1970).

Goode, John (ed.), *The Air of Reality: New Essays on Henry James* (London: Methuen, 1972).

Hocks, Richard A., *Henry James and Pragmatic Thought: A Study in the Relationship between the Philosophy of William James and the Literature of Henry James* (Chapel Hill: University of North Carolina Press, 1974).

Krook, Dorothea, *The Ordeal of Consciousness in Henry James* (Cambridge: Cambridge University Press, 1962).

Lebowitz, Naomi, *The Imagination of Loving: Henry James's Legacy to the Novel* (Detroit: Wayne State University Press, 1965).

Norrman, Ralf, *The Insecure World of Henry James's Fiction* (London: Macmillan, 1982).

Perosa, Sergio, *Henry James and the Experimental Novel* (New York: New York University Press, 1983).

Sears, Sally, *The Negative Imagination: Form and Perspective in the Novels of Henry James* (New York: Cornell University Press, 1968).

Segal, Ora, *The Lucid Reflector: The Observer in Henry James' Fiction* (New Haven, Conn.: Yale University Press, 1969).

Tanner, Tony (ed.), *Henry James: Modern Judgements* (London: Macmillan, 1968).
Ward, J. A., *The Imagination of Disaster: Evil in the Fiction of Henry James* (Lincoln, Nebr.: University of Nebraska Press, 1961).
Weinstein, Philip M., *Henry James and the Requirements of the Imagination* (Cambridge, Mass.: Harvard University Press, 1971).
Wilson, R. B. J., *Henry James's Ultimate Narrative: 'The Golden Bowl'* (St Lucia: University of Queensland Press, 1981).
Yeazell, Ruth Bernard, *Language and Knowledge in the Late Novels of Henry James* (Chicago: University of Chicago Press, 1976).

ARTICLES

Bersani, Leo., 'The Narrator as Center in *The Wings of the Dove*', *Modern Fiction Studies*, VI (Summer 1960) pp. 131–44.
Eliot, T. S., 'In Memory', *Little Review*, V (Aug 1918) pp. 44–7.
Goode, John, ' "Character" and Henry James', *New Left Review*, Nov–Dec 1966, pp. 55–75.
Sebouhian, George, 'The Transcendental Imagination of Merton Densher', *Modern Language Studies*, V (1975) pp. 35–45.

CRITICISM, CHARACTER AND THE NOVEL

Bayley, John, *The Characters of Love: A Study in the Literature of Personality* (London: Constable, 1960).
——, *Tolstoy and the Novel* (London: Chatto and Windus, 1966).
Bersani, Leo, *A Future for Astyanax: Character and Desire in Literature* (Boston, Mass.: Little, Brown, 1969; London: Marion Boyars, 1978).
Booth, Wayne C., *The Rhetoric of Fiction* (Chicago: University of Chicago Press, 1961).
Cohn, Dorrit, *Transparent Minds: Narrative Modes for Presenting Consciousness in Fiction* (Princeton, NJ: Princeton University Press, 1978).
Cox, C. B., *The Free Spirit: A Study of Liberal Humanism in the Novels of George Eliot, Henry James, E. M. Forster, Virginia Woolf, Angus Wilson* (London: Oxford University Press, 1963).
Bradbury, Malcolm (ed.), *The Novel Today* (London: Fontana, 1977).
Culler, Jonathan, *Structuralist Poetics: Structuralism, Linguistics and the Study of Literature* (London: Routledge and Kegan Paul, 1975).
Docherty, Thomas, *Reading (Absent) Character: Towards a Theory of Characterization in Fiction* (Oxford: Clarendon Press, 1983).
Fowler, Roger, *Linguistics and the Novel* (London: Methuen, 1977).
Garrett, Peter K., *Scene and Symbol from George Eliot to James Joyce: Studies in Changing Fictional Mode* (New Haven, Conn.: Yale University Press, 1969).
Graham, Kenneth, *English Criticism of the Novel, 1865–1900* (London: Oxford University Press, 1966).
Harvey, W. J., *Character and the Novel* (London: Chatto and Windus, 1965).
Langbaum, Robert, *The Mysteries of Identity: A Theme in Modern Literature* (New York: Oxford University Press, 1977).
Murdoch, Iris, *The Sovereignty of Good* (London: Routledge and Kegan Paul, 1970).

Price, Martin, *Forms of Life: Character and Moral Imagination in the Novel* (New Haven, Conn.: Yale University Press, 1983).

Stang, Richard, *The Theory of the Novel in England, 1850–1870* (London: Routledge and Kegan Paul, 1959).

Trilling, Lionel, *The Opposing Self* (London: Secker and Warburg, 1955).

——, *Sincerity and Authenticity* (London: Oxford University Press, 1972).

Uspensky, Boris, *A Poetics of Composition: The Structure of the Artistic Text and Typology of a Compositional Form*, tr. Valentina Zavarin and Susan Wittig (Berkeley, Calif., and Los Angeles: University of California Press, 1973).

Williams, Raymond, *Marxism and Literature* (London: Oxford University Press, 1977).

GENERAL CRITICISM

BOOKS

Altieri, Charles, *Act and Quality: A Theory of Literary Meaning and Humanistic Understanding* (Amherst: University of Massachusetts Press, 1981).

Bakhtin, Mikhail, *Problems of Dostoevsky's Poetics*, tr. Caryl Emerson (Minneapolis: University of Minnesota Press, 1984).

Barthes, Roland, *Writing Degree Zero*, tr. Annette Lavers and Colin Smith (New York: Hill and Wang, 1967).

——, *S/Z*, tr. Richard Miller (New York: Hill and Wang, 1975).

Bayley, John, *The Uses of Division: Unity and Disharmony in Literature* (London: Chatto and Windus, 1976).

Bloom, Harold, *The Anxiety of Influence: A Theory of Poetry* (New York: Oxford University Press, 1973).

——, *A Map of Misreading* (New York: Oxford University Press, 1975).

——, *Kabbalah and Criticism* (New York: Continuum, 1983). (First published 1975.)

——, *Poetry and Repression* (New Haven, Conn.: Yale University Press, 1976).

——, *The Breaking of the Vessels* (Chicago: University of Chicago Press, 1982).

Booth, Wayne C., *Critical Understanding: The Powers and Limits of Pluralism* (Chicago: University of Chicago Press, 1979).

Coleridge, Samuel Taylor, *Biographia Literaria, or Biographical Sketches of my Literary Life and Opinions*, ed. George Watson (London: Dent, 1975).

Culler, Jonathan, *On Deconstruction: Theory and Criticism after Structuralism* (London: Routledge and Kegan Paul, 1983).

Derrida, Jacques, *Of Grammatology*, tr. Gayatri Chakravorty Spivak (Baltimore: Johns Hopkins University Press, 1976).

Eagleton, Terry, *Criticism and Ideology: A Study in Marxist Literary Theory* (London: New Left Books, 1976).

——, *Marxism and Literary Criticism* (London: Methuen, 1976).

Eco, Umberto, *A Theory of Semiotics* (Bloomington: Indiana University Press, 1979).

Fleishman, Avrom, *The English Historical Novel: Walter Scott to Virginia Woolf* (Baltimore: Johns Hopkins University Press, 1971).

Gilbert, Sandra, and Gubar, Susan, *The Madwoman in the Attic* (New Haven, Conn.: Yale University Press, 1979).

Hardy, Barbara, *The Appropriate Form: An Essay on the Novel* (London: Athlone Press, 1971).

——, *Tellers and Listeners: The Narrative Imagination* (London: Athlone Press, 1975).

Hochman, Baruch, *The Test of Character: From the Victorian Novel to the Modern* (Rutherford, NJ: Fairleigh Dickinson University Press, 1983).

Holub, Robert C., *Reception Theory: A Critical Introduction* (London: Methuen, 1984).

Iser, Wolfgang, *The Act of Reading: A Theory of Aesthetic Response* (London: Routledge and Kegan Paul, 1978).

Jackson, Rosemary, *Fantasy: The Literature of Subversion* (London: Methuen, 1981).

Jameson, Fredric, *The Prison-House of Language: A Critical Account of Structuralism and Russian Formalism* (Princeton, NJ: Princeton University Press, 1972).

——, *The Political Unconscious: Narrative as a Socially Symbolic Act* (London: Methuen, 1981).

Jefferson, Anne, and Robey, David (eds), *Modern Literary Theory: A Comparative Introduction* (London: Batsford, 1982).

Leavis, F. R., *The Great Tradition* (Harmondsworth: Pelican, 1972). (First published 1948.)

Levine, George, *The Realistic Imagination: English Fiction from Frankenstein to Lady Chatterley* (Chicago: University of Chicago Press, 1981).

Lodge, David, *The Modes of Modern Writing: Metaphor, Metonymy, and the Typology of Modern Literature* (London: Edward Arnold, 1977).

Magliola, Robert R., *Phenomenology and Literature: An Introduction* (West Lafayette, Ind.: Purdue University Press, 1977).

Sanders, Andrew, *The Victorian Historical Novel: 1840–1880* (London: Macmillan, 1978).

Swinden, Patrick, *Unofficial Selves: Character in the Novel from Dickens to the Present Day* (London: Macmillan, 1973).

Trilling, Lionel, *Speaking of Literature and Society*, ed. Diana Trilling (Oxford: Oxford University Press, 1982).

Wellek, René, *A History of Modern Criticism, 1750–1950*, 4 vols (Cambridge: Cambridge University Press, 1955–65).

Wharton, Edith, *The Writing of Fiction* (New York: Octagon Books, 1966). (First published 1924.)

Williams, Raymond, *The Country and the City* (Frogmore, Herts.: Paladin, 1975).

Winters, Yvor, *In Defense of Reason* (Chicago: Swallow Press, 1937).

ARTICLE

Miller, J. Hillis, 'Ariadne's Thread: Repetition and the Narrative Line', *Critical Inquiry*, III (1976) pp. 57–77.

MISCELLANEOUS

Buber, Martin, *Between Man and Man*, tr. Ronald Gregor Smith (London: Fontana, 1961).

——, *I and Thou*, tr. Walter Kaufmann (Edinburgh: T. and T. Clark, 1970).

Carlebach, Julius, *Karl Marx and the Radical Critique of Judaism* (London: Routledge and Kegan Paul, 1978).

Encyclopaedia Judaica, 16 vols (Jerusalem, 1971–2).

Even-Zohar, Itamar, 'The Emergence of a Native Hebrew Culture in Palestine: 1882–1948', *Studies in Zionism*, no. 4 (Oct 1981) pp. 167–84.

Ginsburg, Christian D., *The Kabbalah: Its Doctrines, Development, and Literature* (London: George Routledge, 1925).

Guttmann, Julius, *Philosophies of Judaism*, tr. D. W. Silverman (New York: Schocken, 1973).

Heidegger, Martin, *Being and Time*, tr. John Macquarrie and Edward Robinson (Oxford: Basil Blackwell, 1962).

Jacobs, Louis, *A Jewish Theology* (New York: Behrman House, 1973).

James, William, *The Will to Believe and Other Essays in Popular Philosophy* (Cambridge, Mass.: Harvard University Press, 1979).

Jones, Ernest, *Sigmund Freud: Life and Work*, 3 vols (London: Hogarth Press, 1953–7).

Kant, Immanuel, *Groundwork of the Metaphysic of Morals*, tr. H. J. Paton (New York: Harper and Row, 1964).

Lacan, Jacques, *Écrits*, tr. Alan Sheridan (London: Tavistock, 1977).

——, *The Four Fundamental Concepts of Psycho-analysis*, tr. Alan Sheridan (Harmondsworth: Penguin, 1979).

MacIntyre, Alasdair, *After Virtue: A Study in Moral Theory* (London: Duckworth, 1981).

Macpherson, C. B., *The Political Theory of Possessive Individualism: Hobbes to Locke* (London: Oxford University Press, 1962).

——, *Democratic Theory: Essays in Retrieval* (Oxford: Clarendon Press, 1973).

——, *The Life and Times of Liberal Democracy* (London: Oxford University Press, 1977).

Meyer, Michael A., *The Origins of the Modern Jew: Jewish Identity and European Culture in Germany, 1749–1824* (Detroit: Wayne State University Press, 1967).

Murdoch, Iris, *Sartre: Romantic Rationalist* (London: Collins, 1967). (First published 1953.)

Rosenberg, Edgar, *From Shylock to Svengali: Jewish Stereotypes in English Fiction* (Stanford, Calif.: Stanford University Press, 1960).

Roth, Cecil, *A History of the Jews* (New York: Schocken, 1970).

Sartre, Jean-Paul, *Being and Nothingness*, tr. Hazel E. Barnes (New York: Philosophical Library, [1958]).

——, *Anti-Semite and Jew*, tr. George J. Becker (New York: Shocken, 1965).

——, *Existentialism and Humanism*, tr. Philip Mairet (London: Eyre Methuen, 1973).

Spencer, Herbert, *An Autobiography*, 2 vols (New York: Appleton, 1904).

Warnock, G. J., *The Object of Morality*, (London: Methuen, 1971).

Warnock, Mary, *Existentialism* (London: Oxford University Press, 1970).

Wittgenstein, Ludwig, *Philosophical Investigations*, tr. G. E. M. Anscombe (Oxford: Basil Blackwell, 1968).

Index